FOURTH EDITION

Daytrips

HOLLAND, BELGIUM
and LUXEMBOURG

D0878714

FOURTH EDITION

Daytrips

HOLLAND, BELGIUM
and LUXEMBOURG

40 *one day adventures*
by rail, bus or car

EARL STEINBICKER

HASTINGS HOUSE/DAYTRIPS
Publishers
Winter Park, Florida

ISBN: 0-8038-2062-3

Printed in the United States of America, Canada, Panama, United Kingdom, Netherlands, Spain, Poland, or Australia by Booksurge Global, using on-demand technology.

All photos by Earl Steinbicker

Peter Leers, Publisher

Comments? Ideas?

We'd love to hear from you. Ideas from our readers have resulted in many improvements in the past, and will continue to do so. And, if your suggestions are used, we'll gladly send you a complimentary copy of any book in the series. Please send your thoughts to Hastings House/Daytrips Publishers, P.O. Box 908, Winter Park FL 32790-0908, U.S.A., or fax us at (407) 339-5900, or e-mail to Hastings_Daytrips@Earthlink.net.

Contents

6

Introduction

Holland, Belgium, and Luxembourg together make up one of the most enchanting little corners of Europe, with more outstanding attractions per square mile than just about anywhere else on Earth. Known collectively by that awful acronym *Benelux* and historically as the Low Countries, they offer scores of pleasurable and all-too-little-known adventures for those willing to probe beyond the obvious delights of the capital cities. This book takes a careful look at 40 of the most intriguing destinations and tells you, in step-by-step detail, exactly how to go about exploring them on your own.

What is especially appealing about these compact lands is that virtually all of their most enjoyable sights can easily be savored on simple one-day excursions from either Amsterdam, Brussels, or Luxembourg City. Distances are remarkably short, the roads superb, and the modern trains run so frequently to just about everywhere that reference to timetables is hardly necessary.

Daytrips have many advantages over the usual point-to-point touring, particularly for short-term visitors. You can sample a far greater range of experiences in the same amount of time by seeing only those places that really interest you, instead of "doing" each country region by region. They also lead to a more varied diet of sights, such as spending one day in the most un-Dutch of cities, Maastricht, the next back in Amsterdam, and the third on a bucolic island off the northern coast.

There is no need to pre-plan every moment of your vacation since with daytrips you are always free to venture wherever you please. Feel like seeing Leiden this morning? Ah, but this is Monday, so you may be better off heading for Volendam instead, or taking a delightful cruise to the island of Texel. Is rain predicted for the entire day? You certainly don't want to be in Bokrijk in a shower, so why not try the wonderful museums in Liège? Is the day just too glorious to spend in Luxembourg City, regardless of its many charms? You can always take off for an outdoor adventure at Vianden and enjoy the sunshine. Then again, you might not want to go anywhere today.

7

Walking tours of the three base cities are included, as well as for the daytrip destinations. The operative word here is flexibility, the freedom of not being tied to a schedule or route.

All of the daytrips in this book may be taken by public transportation, and all by car as well. Full information for doing this is given in the "Getting There" section of each trip. A suggested do-it-yourself tour is outlined in both the text and on the local map provided. Time and weather considerations are included, along with price-keyed restaurant recommendations, background data, and sources of additional information.

The trips have been arranged in a geographic sequence following convenient transportation routes. In several cases it is possible to combine two trips in the same day. These opportunities are noted whenever they are practical.

Destinations were chosen to appeal to a wide variety of interests. In addition to the usual cathedrals, castles, and museums, there are also boat cruises, cheese markets, windmills, canals, caves, exquisite gardens, preserved medieval towns, bustling cities, great seaports, quaint fishing villages, outdoor folk museums, homes of famous artists, locations where history was made, places of natural beauty, plus an exciting railfan excursion, and much, much more.

It may come as a surprise to discover just how much these three small countries have to offer! As you read through this book you may very well decide to spend more than just a few days within their boundaries, or to even join the growing number of knowledgeable travelers who make the Low Countries the focus of an entire vacation.

Finally, a gentle disclaimer. Places have a way of changing without warning, and errors do creep into print. If your heart is absolutely set or a particular sight, you may want to check first to make sure that it isn't closed for renovation, or that the opening times are still valid. Relevant phone numbers and Internet sites are included for this purpose.

Happy Daytripping!

Section I

DAYTRIP STRATEGIES

The word "Daytrip" may not have made it into dictionaries yet, but for experienced independent travelers it represents the easiest, most natural, and often the least expensive approach to exploring a European country. This strategy, in which you base yourself in a central city and probe the surrounding country on a series of one-day excursions, is especially effective throughout Holland, Belgium, and Luxembourg.

ADVANTAGES:

While not the answer to every travel situation, daytrips offer significant advantages over point-to-point touring following a set plan. Here are a dozen good reasons for considering the daytrip approach:

1.   Freedom from the constraints of a fixed itinerary. You can go wherever you feel like going whenever the mood strikes you.

2.   Freedom from the burden of luggage. Your bags remain in your hotel while you run around with only a guidebook and camera.

3.   Freedom from the anxiety of reservation foul-ups. You don't have to worry each day about whether that night's lodging will actually materialize.

4.   The flexibility of making last-minute changes to allow for unexpected weather, serendipitous discoveries, changing interests, new-found passions, and so on.

5.   The flexibility to take breaks from sightseeing whenever you feel tired or bored, without upsetting a planned itinerary. Why not sleep late in your base city for a change?

6.   The opportunity to sample different travel experiences without committing more than a day to them.

7.   The opportunity to become a "temporary resident" of your base city. By staying there for a week or so you can get to know it in depth, becoming familiar with the local restaurants, shops, theaters, night life, and

other attractions—enjoying them as a native would.

8.   The convenience of not having to hunt for a hotel each day, along with the security of knowing that a familiar room is waiting back in your base city.

9.   The convenience of not having to pack and unpack your bags each day. Your clothes can hang in a closet where they belong, or even be sent out for cleaning.

10. The convenience (and security!) of having a fixed address in your base city, where friends, relatives, and business associates can reach you in an emergency. It is often difficult to contact anyone who changes hotels daily.

11. The economy of staying at one hotel on a discounted longer-term basis, especially with airline package plans. You can make reservations for your base city without sacrificing any flexibility at all.

12. The economy of getting the most value out of a railpass. Daytripping is ideally suited to rail travel since the best train service operates out of base-city hubs. This is especially true in the cases of Amsterdam and Brussels, and workable in the case of Luxembourg City.

Above all, daytrips ease the transition from tourist to accomplished traveler. Even if this is your first trip abroad, you can probably handle an uncomplicated one-day excursion such as the one to Haarlem or Bruges on your own. The confidence gained will help immensely when you tackle more complex destinations, freeing you from the limitations of guided tours and putting you in complete control of your own trip.

DISADVANTAGES:

For all of its attractions, the daytrip concept does have certain restrictions, such as staying at remote country inns. Should this deter you from making daytrips, you can still get the most from this guidebook by traveling directly between destinations without using bases. All of the walking tours and other information are still valid. You might also consider using daytrips part of the time and touring the rest.

CHOOSING A BASE CITY:

Nearly all of Benelux's best attractions can be experienced on one-day excursions from either Amsterdam, Brussels, or Luxembourg City—or from towns close to them. All three of these bases are natural transportation hubs, with a network of rail lines and highways radiating out in all directions. They are also convenient gateway cities for air travelers coming from overseas or other points in Europe. Additionally, one of them — Amsterdam —is a first-rate attraction in itself, while Brussels and Luxembourg City also offer a good range of worthwhile sights.

Amsterdam is the natural base for daytrips throughout nearly all of Holland, which is covered in Section II of this book. Section III deals with Belgium, for which Brussels makes the best base. The tiny Grand Duchy of Luxembourg, described in Section IV, is most conveniently explored by basing yourself in Luxembourg City.

ACCOMMODATIONS:

All three base cities tend to be tight on hotel space at certain times, such as during festivals, conventions, and major trade shows. For this reason it is always best to make advance reservations for at least the first few days of your stay. Doing this in connection with an airline package plan can also save you money.

Amsterdam—and to a lesser extent Brussels and Luxembourg City—offers the widest possible choice of accommodations, ranging from luxurious hotels to inexpensive inns, rooms in private houses, and an especially large selection of youth hostels. Another possibility, if you're staying in a base city for a week or more, is to rent a furnished apartment—a move that both cuts costs and allows you to feel more like a native. Arrangements for this should be made well in advance and secured with a deposit. Current information regarding this and other lodgings is available from overseas tourist offices of the countries concerned (see the Advance Planning Information entry for sections II, III, and IV), or you might want to check the classified ads in such publications as International Travel News.

It is not necessary to stay in the base city itself; you may prefer the suburbs or nearby towns, both of which are usually well served by commuter rail lines, and both of which are especially attractive if you're driving instead of traveling by rail. This option is usually less expensive and may actually be more enjoyable.

Should you arrive in a city without reservations, head directly to the nearest local tourist information office, which often has a branch at the airport or in or near the main train station. Their location, phone number, and website are given in the "Practicalities" section of each trip. Most of these offices can, for a small fee, find you a place to stay even at the last moment. They may even be able to get you bargain rates if the hotels happen to have a surplus of empty rooms at that time.

PRACTICAL MATTERS:

Practicalities particular to Holland are discussed at the beginning of Section II, to Belgium at the beginning of Section III, and to Luxembourg at the beginning of Section IV. Also check out the Appendix in Section V.

Section II

Daytrips in
HOLLAND

There is a lot more to Holland than just Amsterdam, wooden shoes, tulips, cheese, and windmills—delightful though these most certainly are. The 23 daytrips described in this section cover some of the very best sights in the nation, with a little something for every taste. That they can be comfortably enjoyed on easy daytrips from Amsterdam should make them all the more appealing.

THE COUNTRY

But first, there is that slight confusion over the name. Officially, the country is known as the Kingdom of the Netherlands. The term *Holland* refers only to the two western provinces, stretching roughly from Dordrecht in the south to Texel in the north, embracing Amsterdam, The Hague, and Rotterdam. In actual practice, however, just about everyone calls the whole country Holland—and so will this book.

That this fascinating land—whatever its name—should exist at all in its present form is nothing short of amazing. To paraphrase an old saying, God may have created the Earth, but it was the Dutch who made Holland. Over half of it lies below sea level at high tide and is kept dry only by an intricate system of dikes, drainage canals, and ceaseless pumping. Much of this land has been reclaimed from the sea, a process that is still going on; and the rest was once a soggy marshland. The thousands of windmills that dotted the landscape in years gone by were mostly put there to pump water. Although quite a few of these have been preserved, their former task is now performed by motors. The Dutch must continually guard the land from the encroaching sea, since any breakdown in the system could result in catastrophic floods—as happened as recently as 1953, when over 1,800 people drowned.

THE PEOPLE:

This long struggle against the elements has endowed the people with certain characteristics. They tend to be hardworking, methodical, and rather serious, and they have an intense regard for order and community despite their fierce individualism. Centuries of overseas trade have developed their sense of liberal toleration, a trait that is readily apparent in the streets of Amsterdam today, and that serves them well in the face of an extremely high population density. It has also made them exceptionally willing to accept foreign ideas, races, and languages. With rare exceptions, they are an unusually honest people whose words mean exactly what they say. And, oh yes, they can be a lot of fun when they let their hair down over a friendly beer.

A LITTLE BIT OF HISTORY:

Although the history of Holland goes back to prehistoric times and includes a long period of Roman domination, this once-inhospitable land did not achieve any real degree of importance until the Middle Ages. It was the rise of the merchant class in the developing towns that brought about an envious level of prosperity. During the 15th century, power came into the hands of the Burgundians and was later transferred to the Austrian Hapsburgs, and through them to the king of Spain.

The Reformation of the 16th century spread rapidly throughout the northern Netherlands. This was regarded as heresy by the bigoted Spanish king, Philip II, who took drastic measures to stamp it out with an army of 10,000 led by the duke of Alba. The rebellious Dutch, under their greatest hero, Prince William of Orange-Nassau (also known as "the Silent" for his diplomatic skills), eventually turned the tide, although the religious struggles continued until the mid-17th century.

With peace came the "Golden Age." Amsterdam flourished as Europe's great center for overseas trade. Dutch fleets sailed the world's oceans and established colonies in distant lands. A flood of refugees from all over Europe, taking advantage of the new religious freedom and soaring economy, brought with them a wide range of talents that further fueled the boom.

By the end of the century, however, decadence had set in. Wars with England and other European powers left Holland exhausted, and soon a new conservatism put a stop to the creative energies unleashed only decades earlier. The French Revolution led to the founding of the Batavian Republic and eventually to direct rule by Napoleon.

Dutch sovereignty was reestablished in 1814, but by 1830 the Catholic south rebelled and formed the new Kingdom of Belgium. With little in common, the two countries have remained apart ever since. Holland was neutral throughout World War I, falling victim to Nazi tyranny in 1940. Its major port of Rotterdam was almost totally destroyed, and its large Jewish population virtually annihilated. A brave Dutch Resistance helped to bring about final liberation by 1945. Although it soon lost its major colonies, Holland has regained its prosperity and is now among the most advanced nations in the world.

PRACTICALITIES

The 23 daytrips described in the next section assume that you are making Amsterdam your base of operations. This is the most logical and convenient choice, especially for those traveling by rail. There are, of course, other possibilities, including The Hague, Haarlem, Utrecht, or even smaller towns such as Hilversum. To use another city or town as your base, you will have to study a rail or highway map and adjust the travel directions accordingly. But first, take a look at the practical information that follows.

TRANSPORTATION:
Nearly all of the daytrips in Holland described in this book can be made by rail, all by car, and some by bus. Which of these you choose depends on purely personal factors, but you may want to consider the following information before deciding.

BY RAIL:
Probably no other country on Earth is as well suited to train travel as Holland. Its extremely high population density demands frequent departures, while its flat terrain and relatively short distances insure speedy travel time. All in all, trains are almost invariably the fastest way of getting around.

Serving more than 400 destinations with some 4,000 trains a day, the **Netherlands Railways** *(Nederlandse Spoorwegen* or *NS)* carries over a half-million passengers every working day in its clean and comfortable cars. Fares are quite reasonable and can be considerably reduced by purchasing one-day return tickets or by using one of the economical railpasses described later on.

There are very few places of tourist interest in Holland that cannot be reached by train, and even those secluded spots invariably have a connecting bus to the nearest rail line. Stations are usually located right in the heart of town, so close to the major attractions that most of the walking tours outlined in this book start right at the station.

Seasoned travelers often consider riding trains to be one of the very best ways of meeting the local people and making new friends. It is not at all unusual to strike up an engaging conversation that makes your trip all the more memorable. You will also get a marvelous view of the passing countryside from the large windows, especially enhanced by the fact that Dutch trains usually ride atop embankments designed to prevent floods. Then too, you are spared the worries of driving, especially after sampling the tasty Dutch beers.

All trains operated by the Netherlands Railways belong to one of the following categories, as indicated on schedules and departure platforms:

EC—*EuroCity.* International expresses with special comforts. Both first- and second-class seating is offered, and there is a supplementary fare, which is covered by the Eurail and Eurail SelectPasses, but not by national passes.

INT—International express trains with both first- and second-class seating. A supplementary fare is often charged on these, but not to holders of the Eurail or Eurail SelectPass.

IC—*Intercity.* These comfortable expresses are usually your best bet for travel within Holland. Most of them are made up of very modern cars and operate on frequently recurring schedules. There is no supplementary fare, and both classes are provided for.

Sneltrein—Semi-express trains used within Holland. Both classes are available.

Stoptrein—The name says it all. These locals connect very rural areas with cities and sometimes offer only second-class seating. A few are diesel operated.

High-speed service to Brussels and Paris is provided by **Thalys**, **W**: thalys.com. Connections can be made at Brussels for Thalys service to Cologne—and for **Eurostar** service to London via the Channel Tunnel, **W**: eurostar.com

Schedules are really not necessary as you will seldom, if ever, have more than a half-hour wait for a train going your way. Tables of departure are posted on yellow boards in each station, arranged by route and final destination and showing the platform number, while signs on the platform itself indicate the stops the train will make. Times are expressed using the 24-hour clock; thus a departure at 4:52 p.m. would be marked as 16.52.

A condensed schedule booklet listing most services of interest to tourists is available free at the information counters. Real rail fans will, of course, want to add the complete annual schedule book, called a *spoorboekje,* to their collection. There is a modest charge for this. Both **schedules and fares** can be obtained online at **W**: ns.nl

Reservations are neither necessary nor possible for travel within Holland, although you might want to consider them for long international journeys.

Most station platforms have both an "A" and a "B" end. Be sure you go to the correct one, as shown on the departure boards, since the same platform often handles two different trains simultaneously. A few trains split en route, making it essential that you get on the right set of cars. If in doubt, ask—just about everyone speaks English. Destinations are sometimes—but not always —marked on the cars themselves. First-class cars are indicated with the numeral "1" near the door, and occasionally with a yellow or blue stripe above the windows.

There is no regular food service on trains within Holland, although many have a roving mini-bar offering snacks, sandwiches, and beverages. The restaurants and cafeterias in the stations are usually quite good and offer excellent value for your money, especially in the smaller cities.

All but the most local of trains carry both first- and second-class accommodations. First class is, of course, a bit more comfortable and a whole lot less crowded during peak travel times, but most people will find second class to be perfectly adequate for the short journeys involved.

RAILPASSES can be a bargain if you intend to do a substantial amount of train travel. The Netherlands Railways (NS) accepts the following passes:

EURAILPASS—the best-known and most popular pass, allows unlimited first-class travel throughout 17 European countries, excluding Great Britain. It is available for periods of 15 or 21 consecutive days, or 1, 2, or 3 months. The Eurailpass includes a wide variety of fringe benefits, nearly all of which are in countries other than Holland. This is a good choice only if your travels will take you *beyond* Holland, Belgium, and Luxembourg.

EURAIL FLEXIPASS—Allows unlimited first-class travel on any 10 or 15 days within a 2-month period. It is valid in the same 17 countries and has the same benefits as the regular Eurailpass. This is an attractive deal only if you intend to spend much time exploring the base cities between making daytrips, and are also traveling in countries outside of Holland, Belgium, and Luxembourg.

EURAIL SAVERPASS—An economical version of the Eurailpass offering the same first-class benefits for groups of two or more people traveling together. This pass is available for the same periods as the regular Eurailpasses (above), and the travel must always be done as a group.

EURAIL YOUTHPASS—this low-cost version of the Eurailpass is available to anyone under the age of 26 and allows unlimited second-class travel in the same 17 countries for periods of 10 or 15 consecutive days, or 1, 2, or 3 months. There is also a Eurail Youth Flexipass valid for any 10 or15 days within a 2-month period.

EURAIL DRIVE PASS—A complex program that combines rail travel with car rentals at an attractive price, tailored to meet your specific needs.

EURAIL SELECTPASS—covers travel in any bordering 3, 4, or 5 countries in the Eurail network, for 5 to 15 days within a two-month period. NOTE that Holland, Belgium, and Luxembourg are considered to be one country (Benelux) as far as this pass is concerned. It is also available as a **Saverpass** and **Youthpass**.

EURAIL GERMANY 'N BENELUX PASS—Valid in Germany, Holland, Belgium, and Luxembourg for 5, 6, 8, or 10 days of travel. Also sold as a **Saverpass** or **Youthpass**.

BENELUX TOURRAIL PASS—This handy pass allows unlimited train travel on any 5 days within a 1-month period. Valid for travel throughout Holland, Belgium, and Luxembourg only, it is sold in both first- and second-class versions for adults and for juniors under 26.

HOLLAND RAIL PASS—A real bargain for trips within the Netherlands only, this pass is sold at train staions in the Netherlands as well as from sources before leaving home. It is available for either any 3 or any 5 days in a one-month period, in either 1st or 2nd class, with special discounts for two people traveling together. There is also a discounted senior version for those over 60, and a junior version (2nd-class only) for those under 26.

The passes described above are available through most travel agents, who also have current information and prices. Alternatively, you could contact **Rail Europe**, **T**: toll-free 1-800-438-7245 or **W**: raileurope.com.

Note that railpasses are not valid for travel on the Thalys or Eurostar high-speed trains, although discounts are given to their holders.

Remember that all railpasses must be used in accordance with the rules and instructions accompanying them, and that you must always be prepared to show your passport. When having passes validated, be certain that you agree with the dates *before* allowing the agent to write them in.

If you intend to take several of the daytrips in this book, and especially if one or two of them are to more distant places such as Maastricht or Middelburg, a railpass (especially the Holland Rail Pass) will probably wind up saving you some money. Even if the savings are less than that, a pass should still be considered for the convenience it affords in not having to line up for tickets, and for the freedom of just hopping aboard trains at whim. Possession of a railpass will also encourage you to become more adventurous in seeking out offbeat destinations. It allows you to take longer and more circuitous routes, which might be more interesting. Should you ever manage to get on the wrong train by mistake, your only cost will be your lost time. Railpasses can even be used to cut your dining expenses just by riding to a nearby small town for dinner, where restaurants are usually less expensive than in large cities. The same reasoning also holds true for hotels.

Those buying individual tickets should note that **one-day return fares** *(dagretour) are* available and will save you money over the regular one-way fares.

While virtually everyone in Holland speaks English, the signs in stations and on trains, as well as the words used on schedules, are in Dutch. The glossary in Section V should help you understand these. Travelers in the Flemish-speaking parts of Belgium will find it handy also.

Passengers flying in or out of Amsterdam's Schiphol Airport will be happy to know that there is a train station right at the terminal, connected by a moving sidewalk. From here, a train leaves every few minutes for Amsterdam's Centraal Station, while other frequent departures serve many cities in Holland and a few in Belgium and Germany.

BY BUS:

With such a wonderful rail service there would seem to be little need for buses outside the cities themselves, yet there are still some small towns and isolated areas to which the tracks do not lead. In nearly every such case you can simply take a train to the station nearest your destination, then transfer to a connecting bus. One trip, to Volendam, must be made entirely by bus, but that's only a 30-minute ride. Full details are given for each daytrip in this book.

BY CAR:

Holland has what is arguably the most intensive road network in Europe, and it's all free with the exception of a few tolls at major bridges and tunnels. Driving is exceptionally easy outside the big cities; the roads everywhere are smooth and well marked with signposts. You will, however, have problems parking in Amsterdam and in coping with that city's notorious traffic congestion.

All that's needed to drive in Holland is a valid driver's license and a registration for your car. The minimum age is 18 years. Members of the American AAA, British AA or RAC, as well as some other automobile clubs are entitled to the services of the **ANWB** (Royal Dutch Touring Club), whose yellow phones alongside major roads can be used to summon breakdown help. You will also find phone boxes marked *"Politie,"* which bring the police and should be used in case of an accident. Seat belts must be worn at all times. Unless otherwise marked, speed limits are 120 kph (75 mph) on motorways, 80 kph (50 mph) on other highways, 50 kph (30 mph) in built-up areas, and even less in residential areas.

Holland is filled with bicycles, which usually have their own lanes or separate paths as well as their own traffic lights. You must always be alert to their presence. Pedestrians have the right-of-way at marked crossings, as do passengers getting on or off trams.

WHEN TO GO:

Holland may be enjoyed at any time, but note that many of the attractions outside the big cities are closed between mid-autumn and early spring. Specific details are given for each daytrip. The best time to visit is undoubtedly between mid-spring and early autumn. June, with its longer days, offers the most sunshine. Whatever the season, be prepared for rapidly changing weather—and always carry a folding umbrella to insure that it won't rain. A light jacket or sweater will come in handy, even in August.

Amsterdam seems to be a popular summer destination for all of Europe's youth. This does not seriously affect the hotel situation, although confirmed reservations are still wise. The tourist hordes thin out considerably once you get beyond the downtown area.

HOLIDAYS:

Public holidays *(Feestdagen)* in Holland are more or less as follows:

New Year's Day *(Nieuwjaarsdag)*
Good Friday *(Goede Vridag)* (many places open)
Easter Sunday *(Eerste Paasdag)*
Easter Monday *(Tweede Paasdag)*
Queen's Day (April 30th) *(Koninginnedag)*
Liberation Day (May 5th) *(Bevrijdingsdag)* (most places open)

Ascension Day (6th Thursday after Easter) *(Hemelvaartsdag)*
Whit Sunday *(Eerste Pinksterdag)*
Whit Monday (7th Monday after Easter) *(Tweede Pinksterdag)*
Christmas *(Eerste Kerstdag)*
Second Christmas Day (December 26th) *(Tweede Kerstdag)*
Trains operate on holiday schedules on most but not all of these days.

LANGUAGE:

Dutch is related to German, with similar spellings but quite different pronunciations. No one will expect you to understand it, however, so don't worry. Virtually everyone in the country speaks fairly fluent English, and does so with pleasure.

MONEY:

Price ranges for attractions are shown in *euros* (€), the currency for both Holland and most of Western Europe. These are for full adult admissions; discounts are usually available for seniors, students, and children:

€	Up to 5 euros.
€€	6-10 euros.
€€€	11-20 euros.
€€€€	21 or more euros.

The value of the euro varies daily, but is usually in the range of US $1.20 to US $1.40. Banknotes are issued in values of 5, 10, 20, 50, 100, 200, and 500 euros; and coins in values of 1, 2, 5, 10, 20, and 50 cents as well as 1 and 2 euros. The design of banknotes is the same in all countries, but the coins vary by nationality — however all coins are valid in all Eurozone countries. Currently, besides Holland these include Austria, Belgium, Finland, France, Germany, Greece, Ireland, Italy, Luxembourg, Netherlands, Portugal, and Spain.

It is always advisable to do your money exchange transactions at a commercial bank, where you will get the best rate. The CWK offices in train stations, airports, and at border crossings, as well as some tourist information offices (VVVs), are handy places to change money when the banks are closed. Other money changers often charge outrageous commissions.

Traveler's Checks are the safest way to protect your money while abroad. They often, however, entail service charges both when you buy them and again when you convert them into euros in Holland.

Automated Teller Machines (ATMs) offer the best exchange rates to be found anywhere, and allow you to take money directly out of your home bank account as you need it. They are usually open 24 hours a day, are conveniently located all over Holland, and yield cash in euros. Check with your issuing bank before leaving home to make sure that your PIN code will work in Holland. Bear in mind that these machines don't always work, so always have a backup plan (or starve).

Credit cards are widely accepted at the more expensive establishments throughout Holland, but less often by budget hotels and restaurants. They may also be used to yield cash advances from ATM machines, provided you have a compatible PIN code. The most commonly accepted cards are Visa *(Carte Bleue)* and MasterCard *(EuroCard)*, with American Express a distant third.

MUSEUM CARD:

If you intend to visit six or more museums during your stay in Holland it will pay you to invest in the Museum Card *(Museum Jaarkaart)* giving you free admission to hundreds of museums around the country—including the best and most famous. Although it's good for an entire calendar year, the cost is so reasonable that it can pay for itself in just a few days. Available for adults or youths under 26, the card will encourage you to stop into many museums for just a short peek without having to justify the admission charge. It is sold at most museum entrances and local tourist offices throughout Holland, and requires a passport-size photo.

TELEPHONES:

Most **public telephones** use the convenient Telecard, a pre-paid debit card from which the cost of each call is subtracted until its face value is all used up. These cards are available in 5-, 10-, and 20-euro denominations at train stations, post offices, tourist offices, and many shops. Those issued by KPN are the most common, although there are other brands. Train stations usually have Telfort payphones, which require their own card. If you don't have this, there will certainly be a KPN phone nearby. Several tourist information offices are now using phone numbers prefixed with (0900); these are toll calls costing at least € 0.10 per minute, and possibly as much as € 0.70, so talk fast. Numbers beginning in (0800) are toll free.

You may wish to rent or purchase a **cell phone** (mobile phone) while in Holland, which is certainly a convenience if you're staying for a few weeks or longer. Most American cellular (mobile) phones will not work in Holland unless they are of the tri-band (900/1800/1900 MHz) variety on the GSM system with a compatible SIM card. Even then, you may be billed at very high rates by your American service provider. Check with them first. One source of rentals is **W**: cellularabroad.com. Purchases of **prepaid phones** can be made at specialty shops in Amsterdam and other Dutch cities, often for under € 100.

FOOD AND DRINK:

Several choice restaurants are listed for each destination in this section. Most of these are longtime favorites of experienced travelers and serve typically Dutch food unless otherwise noted. Nearly all are open for lunch, while many other Dutch restaurants are not. Their approximate price range, based on the least expensive complete meal offered, is indicated by the following symbols:

€   Inexpensive, but may have fancier dishes available.

€€   Reasonable. These establishments may also feature daily specials or "Tourist Menus."

€€€ Luxurious and expensive.

X: Days or periods closed.

Those who take dining very seriously should consult an up-to-date restaurant and hotel guide such as the classic red-cover *Michelin Benelux,* issued annually around the beginning of each year. It is always wise to check the posted menus before entering, paying particular attention to any daily set-meal specials.

Dutch breakfasts, often included in your hotel rate, tend to be enormous. After filling up on eggs, ham, cheese, cold cuts, bread, juice, and coffee, you may not have much room left for lunch. This is just as well, as you can then enjoy a light meal of *uitsmijter* (a fancy open egg-and-meat sandwich), *broodje* (a simple sandwich), *braadworst* (sausage), *pannekoeken* or *poffertjes* (pancakes), *patates* (French fries) or—Heaven forbid— *nieuwe haring* (a raw herring). The latter, with or without the chopped onions, is definitely an acquired taste and is a favorite with the Dutch people. All of these are quite inexpensive, quick to eat, and often sold from streetside stands or at outdoor cafés.

A busy afternoon's sightseeing should work up a healthy appetite for dinner, which the Dutch tend to eat rather early—usually between 6 and 8 p.m. No one ever goes away hungry from one of these repasts. Traditional Dutch cuisine is simple and quite substantial, relying on the quality of its ingredients rather than culinary tricks for its delicious taste. Some specialties are: *erwtensoep* (a thick pea soup with sausages, usually served in winter), *gerookte paling* (smoked eel), *hutspot* (beef stew), and *gebraden kip* (roast chicken). *Hollandse biefstuk* is an excellent beefsteak, while *Duitse biefstuk* is more like a Salisbury steak. Potatoes *(aardappelen)* and vegetables *(groente)* come with virtually every meal. Holland, of course, is famous for its fine cheeses *(kaas),* including Gouda, Edam, and Leidse— which seem to be tastier here than when exported.

Always a seafaring people, the Dutch have long embraced the exotic cooking of their overseas trading partners and former colonies. Foremost among these are the various Indonesian specialties such as *rijsttafel* (a miniature feast of many spicy dishes), *nasi goreng* (rice with meats, fish, vegetables, and more), and *bamigoreng* (the same, with noodles). In many neighborhood restaurants these tend to get mixed up with Chinese dishes, creating a uniquely Dutch "Oriental" style. You'll also come across a tremendous range of other restaurants, featuring just about every kind of international cooking there is, so your palate need never get bored.

A handy **Menu Translator** can be found in Section V of this book.

A good way to cut dining costs is to always check out the daily specials, identified by the word *dagschotel.* Your restaurant bill will almost invariably include a service charge and tax. It is customary to round out the amount to the next euro, leaving the small change and perhaps an additional tip if the service was exceptional.

Dutch **beers** are justly famous throughout the world, and if you're a beer drinker you are probably already familiar with them. They are usually referred to as *pils* on menus. It is always interesting to experiment with local brands other than the well-known export labels. Among distilled spirits, the most noted Dutch firewater is a type of gin known as *jenever*, which comes as *jonge* (young) or *oude* (old), and is always drunk neat. Beware.

SUGGESTED TOURS:

The do-it-yourself walking tours in this section are relatively short and easy to follow. On the assumption that most readers will be traveling by public transportation, they always begin at the local train station or bus stop. Those going by car can make a simple adjustment. Suggested routes are shown by heavy broken lines on the maps, while the circled numbers refer to attractions or points of reference along the way, with corresponding numbers in the text.

Trying to see everything in any given town could easily become an exhaust-ing marathon. You will certainly enjoy yourself more by being selective and passing up anything that doesn't catch your fancy in favor of a friendly café. Forgiveness will be granted if you fail to visit *every* museum.

Practical information, such as the opening times of various attractions, is as accurate as was possible at the time of writing. Everything is, of course, subject to change. You should always check with the local tourist office or the establish-ment itself if seeing a particular sight is crucially important to you.

As a way of estimating the time any segment of a walking tour will take, you can look at the scale on the map and figure that the average person covers about 100 yards/meters per minute. The maps, by the way, were drawn to best fit the page size. North does not necessarily point to the top, but is always indicated by an arrow.

* OUTSTANDING ATTRACTIONS:

An * asterisk before any attraction, be it an entire daytrip or just one exhibit in a museum, denotes a special treat that in the author's opinion should not be missed.

TOURIST INFORMATION:

Virtually every town of interest to tourists in Holland has its own informa-tion office, which can help you with specific questions or perhaps book local accommodations. These are always known by the letters **VVV** (often depicted as a blue-and-white triangle), which stand for words you couldn't possibly pro-nounce. The locations of these offices are shown on the town maps in this book by the word "info." or the symbol "**i**" and repeated along with the phone number

A Street Scene in Delft

and website under the "Practicalities " section for each trip. To phone ahead from another town in Holland you must first dial the area code, which always begins with 0 and is shown in parentheses, followed by the local number. Phone numbers are indicated by the symbol **T**. Pay phones use Telecards or coins and have operating instructions in English on them.

ADVANCE PLANNING INFORMATION:

The **Netherlands Board of Tourism (NBT)** has branches throughout the world that offer information services to travel agents and other travel professionals. They no longer distribute printed material. Individual tourists can obtain the same information from the **official website**, **W**: goholland.com or **W**: visitholland.com

Trip 1

*Amsterdam

Other European cities may be exciting, glamorous, sophisticated, or even unique. Amsterdam alone is *gezellig*. This untranslatable word, which more or less means cozy, also connotes intimacy, friendliness, and warmth. Perhaps that is why a city of only 740,000 souls should consistently capture fourth place among all of Europe's many tourist meccas, yielding in popularity only to London, Paris, and Rome.

Despite its delightfully human scale and old-fashioned charm, Amsterdam is a worldly place, filled with people of every imaginable origin. It is very different from the rest of Holland, of which it is the nominal capital—although the government actually resides at The Hague. Being the hub of an extremely efficient rail and highway network makes it the perfect base from which to explore the entire country on remarkably easy daytrips. This plan has the added attraction of returning you each evening to a city noted for its fine restaurants, cultural activities, and exciting night life, as well as for its wide selection of accommodations in every possible price range.

Amsterdam began as a tiny fishing village located near the point where the Amstel River flowed into the IJ and the Zuider Zee. In the late 13th century its inhabitants built a dam across the river to control flooding, thus the origin of the old name, *Amstelledamme,* recognized on a tax exemption agreement of 1275. The town received its charter in 1300 and was a rich trading port as early as the 15th century.

Both the Reformation and a period of Spanish rule temporarily halted its growth, but after 1578 its liberal attitudes attracted refugees fleeing the terrors of the Inquisition. It was their talents and hard work that culminated in the "Golden Age" of the 17th century, during which the city expanded with the addition of the concentric rings of canals that today lend so much color to Amsterdam. Trade declined during the French occupation of the late 18th and early 19th centuries, only to rebound after the opening of the North Sea Canal in 1876.

A wise series of zoning laws has since protected the inner city's essentially 17th-century appearance, preserving that wonderful coziness the

Dutch love so well. Their own long tradition of tolerance has led in rece.
decades to problems with drugs and counter-culture excesses, most o1
which will probably be solved in time.

There is far more in Amsterdam than can possibly be seen in one day.
The "get acquainted" walking tour described in this chapter will give you a
good sampling of the treats that await you after that, which can be enjoyed
between daytrips to the rest of Holland.

GETTING THERE:

Trains link Amsterdam's Centraal Station with just about every other town
in Holland, and operate at such frequent intervals that reference to schedules is
rarely necessary. Some typical running times are: Haarlem—15 minutes,
Utrecht—30 minutes, Alkmaar—35 minutes, The Hague—45 minutes, Delft—
55 minutes, Rotterdam—1 hour, and (about as far as you can possibly go)
Maastricht—2½ hours. There are also good international services to Belgium
(Brussels in well under 3 hours), Germany (Cologne in 3 hours), France (Paris in
just over 4 hours), and other European cities as well.

By Car, Amsterdam is only 24 km (15 miles) from Haarlem, 36 km (22
miles) from Utrecht, 40 km (25 miles) from Alkmaar, 55 km (34 miles) from The
Hague, 58 km (36 miles) from Delft, 75 km (47 miles) from Rotterdam, and the
tremendously long distance of 212 km (132 miles) from Maastricht—all by
superb modern highways. Recommended routes are shown in the chapters for
these and other towns.

By Air, Amsterdam is served with direct flights from every corner of
Europe and the world. Its magnificent Schiphol Airport is only 10 km (6 miles)
from the city center and has its own train station right at the terminal, with very
frequent departures for Amsterdam's Centraal Station (17 minutes away) as well
as to other cities in Holland, Belgium, and beyond.

GETTING AROUND:

Amsterdam has an amazingly good public transit system, easily one of the
best in Europe. Consisting of trams, buses, and subways *(Metro)*, it operates
between about 6 a.m. and midnight, with night buses *(nacht-bussen)* taking over
the main routes after that. Most of the routes begin or end right in front of
Centraal Station.

To make effective use of the system, you will need a pocket-size **transit
map**, which is available free at the **GVB** office in front of Centraal Station, on the
Leidseplein, and at other locations. This explains—in clear English —exactly how
to use public transportation in Amsterdam and describes the several ticketing and
pass options available to you, some of which can cut your costs considerably.
Buying a single ticket from the driver is convenient, but is always the most
expensive way to travel. Don't forget to stamp your ticket in the yellow stamping
machine upon boarding—there are occasional inspections, and failure to have a

time-stamped ticket will result in a fine.

The trams (streetcars) are a particularly enjoyable way of getting around and give you a wonderful view of the passing street scenes. Don't miss out on this urban treat.

PRACTICALITIES:

Some of Amsterdam's main attractions, especially the Rijksmuseum, can be very crowded during the peak summer season. Things are much calmer during late spring and early fall, when the weather is still fine.

A few of the major museums are closed on Mondays, and most do not open until 1 p.m. on Sundays and holidays.

Amsterdam's main **Tourist Office** *(VVV)*, **T**: (0900) 400-4040 (toll call), is located just outside Centraal Station. Besides answering your questions, it also provides an accommodations booking service, changes money, and sells maps and guidebooks. It is often very crowded during the peak tourist season, so you may want to use the branch office on Leidseplein instead. A useful Internet site to check is: **W**: visitamsterdam.nl.

FOOD AND DRINK:

You can satisfy virtually any appetite in Amsterdam, regardless of how exotic it may be. The wide choice of cuisines reflects the diverse ethnic mixture of the city's population, and offers the Dutch a welcome alternative to their tasty but sometimes monotonous diet.

The choice of restaurants listed below, all open for lunch, are along or near the suggested walking tour route. Other parts of the city are blessed with equally fine establishments—as you will quickly discover.

Oesterbar (Leidseplein 10) An upstairs/downstairs place specializing in seafood, open very late. Reserve. **T**: (020) 623-2988. €€€

Haesje Claes (Spuistraat 275, a block west of the Begijnhof) An old favorite for traditional fare in an Old Dutch ambiance; and a good value. **T**: (020) 624-9998. €€

Iguazu (Prinsengracht 703, 2 blocks northeast of Leidseplein) This South American steakhouse also offers chicken and seafood dishes. **T**: (020) 420-3910. €€

Café de Jaren (Nieuwe Doelenstraat 20, near the Muntplein) A grand café offering everything from a snack to a full meal, indoors or out on the terrace by the river. **T**: (020) 625-5771. €€

Bolhoed (Prinsengracht 60, near the Anne Frank House) Vegetarian cuisine raised to the gourmet level, in a stylish setting. **T**; (020) 626-1803. € and €€

Piccolino (Lange Leidsedwarstraat 63, a block northeast of Leidseplein) Pizza, calzones, and other Italian dishes. **T**: (020) 623-1495. € and €€

De Kueken van 1870 (Spuistraat 4, a block west of Dam Square) Dutch food at rock-bottom prices; interesting clientele but little atmosphere. **T**: (020) 620-4018. X: Sun. €

Green Planet (Spuistraat 122, a block west of Dam Square) Healthy vegetarian cuisine. **T**: (020) 625-8280. €

Dimitri's (Prinsenstraat 3, 2 blocks northeast of the Anne Frank House) Salads, burgers, and other light dishes in a French-style brasserie. **T**: (020) 627-9393. €

Pannekoekenhuis Upstairs (Grimburgwal 2, 3 blocks east of the Begijnhof) Pancakes stuffed with all sorts of tasty delights, The climb up the narrow staircase is an adventure in itself. **T**: (020) 626-5603. €

Hoi Tin (Zeedijk 122, just northwest of Nieuw Markt) A popular Chinese eatery with Cantonese fare and low prices. **T**: (020) 625-6451. €

Those in a hurry or still stuffed from an enormous Dutch breakfast will find a multitude of sandwich shops *(broodjeswinkels)* and pancake houses *(pannekoekhuysje)* for a small, inexpensive snack. The cafeterias in the major museums are also good time-and money-savers. Familiar fast-food outlets are quite common, particularly around Kalverstraat, Leidseplein, and Rembrandtsplein.

The venerable brown cafés *(bruine kroegen)* are an Amsterdam institution where you can get a friendly drink along with a maximum of Dutch atmosphere. They're located just about everywhere, and are so called because their walls are often stained brown after centuries of tobacco smoke. Each has its own peculiar ambiance, so you'll be sure to find one you like.

Many, if not most, so-called coffeeshops *(koffieshops)* are actually in the business of selling marijuana, although they may also serve coffee. This is more-or-less legal, within certain bounds. You can always tell these by the odor they emit.

SUGGESTED TOUR:

Circled numbers correspond to numbers on the map.

Begin your walk at **Centraal Station** ①, easily reached from anywhere in Amsterdam. Built in 1885 by the noted architect P.J.H. Cuypers, its ornate exterior is a fanciful mix of Gothic and Renaissance elements. It sits atop 8,687 piles on three artificial islands, an arrangement similar to that used by virtually all large buildings in this very water-logged city. Over 1,000 trains a day stop at its elevated platforms and radiate out to nearly all points in Holland. A classic among the railway stations of the world, it even served in 1900 as a model for Tokyo's central station.

The large open area in front of the station is called **Stationsplein**, the suffix *plein* meaning square. It may strike you as being more of a zoo during the summer, when it is often populated with as weird an assemblage of oddballs as you're likely to find anywhere. Among the crowds there are usually several performing street musicians, adding a joyful character to an already exuberant scene. Some of them are quite good and deserve a listening—and a tip. A multitude

AMSTERDAM 28

Amsterdam

500 Yards

N

Amsterdam's Centraal Station

of tram lines and many buses begin their routes here, as does the Metro. The main **Tourist Office** *(VVV)* is located in an historic old coffeehouse building on the water's edge. From this point all of Amsterdam lies spread out before you.

Continue straight ahead onto **Damrak**, a wide, if slightly seedy, shopping street bordering the inner harbor. Several companies along the jetties both here and elsewhere offer **canal cruises**, a wonderful way to spend an hour or so seeing Amsterdam from a unique angle. The evening cruises, often featuring wine and cheese along with the views, are the most enjoyable. Following the old course of the Amstel River, Damrak leads past the former **Stock Exchange** *(Beurs)*, an early example of modern architecture, which dates from 1903 and is noted for its decorative brickwork. Today it's used for special exhibitions and various other events.

Dam Square, usually just called *Dam,* is on the site of the original dam around which the town developed in the late 13th century. Still the heart of the city, this large open area is frequently crowded with a fascinating assortment of people. The National Monument, near its center, commemorates the Dutch role in World War II, while standing nearby is the world-famous 19th-century Hotel Krasnapolsky as well as several large department stores.

The massive **Royal Palace** *(Koninklijk Paleis)* ② dominates the entire west side of Dam. Once regarded as the eighth wonder of the world, it was built in the mid-17th-century as a town hall and was adopted as a royal residence in 1808 by Louis Bonaparte, appointed King of the Netherlands by his brother, Napoleon. He left behind a magnificent collection of Empire furniture, which is still there along with all of the wonderful art. It may seem surprising that such a regal structure has no formal entrance, but this was deliberately done to keep rioting mobs from breaking in. Today, the palace is only occasionally used by the queen, and is open to the public at some other times. **T**: *(020) 620-4060,* **W***: koninklijkhuis.nl. Usually open July–Aug., daily 12:30–5; Closed Sept. 2005 until Sept. 2007 for renovations. Guided tours at 2 p.m. €.*

Next to this is the **New Church** *(Nieuwe Kerk)* ③, which actually dates from the early 15th century and which has been heavily altered many times since. Traditionally used for royal investitures, its principal function today is as a venue for concerts and exhibitions. The interior is noted for its baroque wood-carving, 16th- and 17th-century organs, and stained-glass windows. There are also tombs of several of Holland's national heroes. **T**: *(020) 638-6909. Open daily 10–6, until 10 on Thurs. Museum card accepted. €.*

Across the square is **Madame Tussaud's Amsterdam** ④, the Dutch answer to the British original. Ever-changing exhibitions here depict famous people and events from both the past and the present, all modeled in wax and enhanced with the latest in special effects technology. Although this is a commercial enterprise, it is thoroughly enjoyable and gives you a chance to view history from a popular Dutch perspective. **T**: *(020) 622-1010. Open daily 10–6:30, closes at 4:30 on major holidays. €€€€.*

At this point you may want to make a little side trip to one of Holland's most interesting—and poignant—attractions. The route on the map crosses three major canals: the **Singel**, once the town's outer defensive moat; the aristocratic **Herengracht**, where the richest merchants had their homes; and the **Keizersgracht**, where the slightly less wealthy lived in elegance. The 17th-century houses along these waterways are remarkably well preserved today, and many are used as offices, museums, and the like, as well as for highly desirable residences.

In former times, the merely prosperous had to make do with the **Prinsengracht**, along which you will find the:

*ANNE FRANK HOUSE ⑤, **T**: (020) 556-7105. *Open April–Aug., daily 9 a.m.–9 p.m.; rest of year, daily 9–7. Closed Yom Kippur. €€.*

Much has been written about the heart-rending tragedy that occurred here, but words can never convey the touching experience of an actual visit. The Frank family were Jews who had fled Nazi Germany in 1933 and set up a business in Amsterdam. Holland was occupied by Hitler's forces in 1940, and by 1942 the situation had become so grim that the Franks went into hiding in secret, hidden quarters at the rear of the shop. They were discovered in 1944 and sent to concentration camps, where all except Mr. Frank perished. Left behind was the diary of their teenage daughter, Anne, which was returned to the father after the war and later published. Translated into a multitude of languages and made into plays and movies, *The Diary of Anne Frank* is an eloquent testimony to the spirit of mankind. The tiny quarters in which the family lived have been preserved, and the rest of the house now serves as a center for the study of racism and fascism.

Continue on to the nearby **Westerkerk** ⑥, a beautiful early-17th-century church with the highest tower in town. You may climb all 279 feet of it for an astonishing *view across the city. The properly Spartan interior contains a fine organ from 1687 as well as Rembrandt's tomb, although it is not known whether the artist is actually buried here. A carillon in the tower plays lovely tunes every half-hour, day and night. **T**: *(020) 624-7766. Church open July–Aug., Mon.–Sat. 11–3; April–June and Sept., Mon.–Fri. 11–3. Free. Tower open Mon.–Sat. 10–5:30. €.*

Another interesting attraction, just cater-corner across the Prinsengracht, is the **Houseboat Museum "Hendrika Maria"** opposite number 296. Visitors can explore the interior of this 1914 canal boat, once used for cargo and later converted to living. **T**: (020) 427-0750. Open Tues.–Sun. 11–5. €. From here, a short stroll down Raadhuis Straat returns you to the Royal Palace ② and Dam Square.

Busy, narrow, and completely pedestrianized, **Kalverstraat** is Amsterdam's most popular shopping street. Despite its crowds, it leads to one of the quietest and most unusual attractions in town. Turn right into a tiny alleyway at number 92 to reach the **Amsterdam Historical Museum** ⑦, located in the rambling rooms and corridors of the former municipal orphanage. Parts of this fascinating complex date from as far back as the 16th century. The number of interesting displays here is immense, as befits one of the world's major trading cities. To see even a decent sampling of them will require several hours, so you may want to return on another day. Holders of the economical Museum Card can, of course, just wander through for a quick look without having to invest in an admission charge. A floor plan in English, showing a suggested route, is available. **T**: *(020) 523-1822*, **W**: *ahm.nl. Open Mon.–Fri. 10–5, Sat.–Sun. 11–5. Closed major holidays. €€. Museum Card accepted.*

The south exit from the museum opens into the utterly delightful *Begijnhof ⑧, an anachronism in this busy metropolis. Founded in 1346 as a quiet residential courtyard for members of a lay sisterhood who cared for the poor and sick, but were not bound by religious vows, it is still lined with ancient houses, one of which (number 34) dates from 1470. The rest are from the 16th through the 18th centuries, and are occupied by elderly women who pay nominal rents. The church at the south end was turned over to the Scottish Presbyterian Church in 1607 and was used by the Pilgrim Fathers before leaving for the New World. It remains with that faith today. Opposite it is a small Catholic chapel where the *Begijns* continued to worship in secret after the Reformation. Don't miss exploring this little oasis of serenity in the middle of a bustling city. *Open daily in the mornings. Free.*

A tiny passageway leads onto Spui. Turn right and walk past the Singel Canal to the Herengracht, the loveliest of Amsterdam's canals. Many of the 17th-century houses here feature elaborate gables and, of course, the ubiquitous hoisting beams still used to haul furniture to the upper floors. Cross the water and turn

In the Begijnhof

left to the **Bijbels Museum** ⑨, located in a fine old house from 1662. This non-denominational museum is devoted to Judeo-Christian exhibitions of Biblical subjects and of ancient life in the Holy Land. **T**: *(020) 624-2436. Open Mon.–Sat. 10–5, Sun. 1–5. €. Museum Card accepted.*

Continue along the canal and turn right on Leidsestraat. This busy shopping street leads to the **Leidseplein**, a highly popular square lined with cafés, restaurants, and entertainments. You may want to return there in the evening, but for now make a left turn after crossing the Keizersgracht Canal and amble down to Nieuwe Spiegelstraat. A right turn on this attractive street will take you past a wonderful assortment of quality antique shops. Directly ahead of you lies the world-famous:

*RIJKSMUSEUM ⑩, **T**: (020) 674-7047, **W**: rijksmuseum.com. Open *daily 10–6. €€. Museum Cards accepted. Gift shop. Cafeteria. Most of the building is closed for renovation until sometime in 2008, until then only the great masterpieces are displayed in the now-completed new wing.*

This is surely one of the greatest art galleries in Europe. Now, there are many *Rijksmuseums* (the word simply means "national museum") throughout Holland, but this is *the* Rijksmuseum. Its strong resemblance to the Centraal Station is more than coincidental; they were both built by the same architect in the 1880s. Hordes of visitors come here each day to see Rembrandt's masterpiece, the **Night Watch*, whose name is a misnomer, as the large canvas actually depicts a daylight scene, long obscured by so much grime that it was thought to be at night. Located in its own gallery, the painting is very easy to find—just follow the crowds.

While there, you will of course want to see works by some of the other **Dutch Masters**, such as Frans Hals, Vermeer, Jan Steen, and many more. The collection of Rembrandts is particularly rich, as would be expected. Non-Dutch artists represented include Bruegel, Rubens, Fra' Angelico, Tintoretto, Botticelli, El Greco, Goya, and Velázquez. With over 250 rooms, the museum displays more art and related objects than you could possibly digest in one visit, so you may want to plan on coming back at another time. This makes a good argument for purchasing the economical Museum Card *(Jaarkaart),* available at the entrance and elsewhere.

There are two other outstanding art museums in the immediate neighborhood, beautifully transformed into a park-like pedestrian zone. The first of these is the:

*VAN GOGH MUSEUM ①, **T**: (020) 570-5200, **W**: vangoghmuseum.nl. *Open daily 10–6, until 10 on Fri. €€. Museum Cards accepted. Audiotour device rental €.*

Devoted primarily to the life and works of the renowned Dutch-born painter Vincent van Gogh (1853–90), the museum also features pieces by some of his contemporaries, as well as his own private collection of Oriental art. In all, there are some 200 paintings and 500 drawings by van Gogh alone. All of this is housed in a strikingly modern structure.

Next door to this is the **Stedelijk Museum** ②, Amsterdam's municipal museum of modern art. Founded in the 1890s to display contemporary works for which there was no room in the already-overflowing Rijksmuseum, it is especially noted for its excellent temporary exhibitions. The permanent collection includes works by the Dutch artists van Gogh, Mondriaan, Karel Appel, and de Kooning. Among the foreigners represented are Chagall, Picasso, Cezanne, Dubuffet, Manet, Monet, Matisse, and Vlaminck; as well as present-day Americans such as Warhol and Lichtenstein. The outdoor sculpture garden is embellished with works by Rodin, Moore, and others. **T**: *(020) 573-2911. Temporarily relocated at Oosterdokskade 5 during renovations, scheduled to reopen in 2008. Ask the tourist office for directions. Open daily 10–6, until 9 on Thurs., closing at 4 on some holidays. €€. Museum Cards accepted. There may be an extra charge for special exhibitions.*

Now follow the map along the Singelgracht Canal (not to be confused with the Singel), passing many of the houseboats on which thousands of Amsterdammers live, either by choice or because they can't find apartments on dry land. The route will also take you past the former Heineken Brewery, now the **Heineken Experience**, which has extremely popular tasting tours daily from Tuesdays through Saturdays (see "Additional Sights" below).

Make a left into Frederiksplein and continue along Sarphatistraat across the Amstel River, then turn left past the locks to the rather quaint **Magere Brug** ⑬, a hand-operated wooden drawbridge originally built in 1671 and faithfully reconstructed several times since. Stroll across this and turn right along the water's edge. From here you might want to take a little side trip to the **Museum Willet-Holthuysen** ⑭, a fully-restored 17th-century canal house at 605 Herengracht. Several of the rooms are set in different centuries, so visitors get a sense of local life through the centuries. **T**: *(020) 523-1822. Open Mon.– Fri. 10–5, Sat.–Sun. 11–5. Museum Cards accepted.* €.

Continue along the Amstel River to the **Blauw Brug**, an ornate bridge obviously inspired by the Pont Alexandre III in Paris. Despite its name, it's not blue. From here, Amstelstraat leads into **Rembrandtsplein** ⑮, a large square with many attractive cafés and restaurants, an excellent place for a well-deserved rest stop. Along with the Leidseplein, this is a very popular spot for nightlife. The difference between the two is that the Rembrandtsplein appeals to a somewhat more sedate crowd than the young people who dominate the Leidseplein.

Muntplein ⑯ is just a block away. Named for the 15th-century Munttoren, an elegant tower that once housed the mint and is now an Amsterdam landmark, this large square is actually a bridge over the junction of two canals. The 17th-century steeple atop the tower has a carillon that chimes out old Dutch tunes every hour. Right behind it, on the Singel Canal, is the colorful floating **flower market**, where you can buy flowers right off the barges on Mondays through Saturdays.

Cross the little extension of the Amstel River and turn left on Oude Turfmarkt past the Allard Pierson Museum, which houses the University of Amsterdam's archaeological collections. The route now threads its way through an old part of town, going through one of the university's buildings in a delightful passageway called the Oudemanhuispoort, sheltering a variety of second-hand bookstalls. Crossing another drawbridge, it follows Staalstraat and turns left just before the modern City Hall *(Stadhuis)* and Opera House. Continue on to the:

REMBRANDT HUIS ⑰, **T**: (020) 520-0400. *Open Mon.-Sat. 10–5, Sun. 11–5, opening at 1 on some holidays. Museum Card accepted.* €€.

Located at 4 Jodenbreestraat, this was for about 20 years the home of the renowned artist, whose full name is Rembrandt Harmenszoom van Rijn. Born in Leiden in 1606, he bought this rather comfortable house in 1639, after he was already famous and commanded lucrative commissions. Rembrandt lived luxuriously in those days, and after his popularity declined—due partly to his refusal to compromise his art by flattering patrons—his expensive tastes got him into financial trouble. He was declared bankrupt in 1656, and the house was sold to help pay the debts, although he continued to live in it until 1660. Despite these crushing burdens and the deaths of both his wife and son, Rembrandt's art became increasingly rich in spiritual values right up until his death in 1669. Purchased by the city in 1906, the interior of the house has been restored as nearly as possible to its original condition, with some of his personal possessions on display. It contains a fabulous collection of some 250 etchings by the master.

From here you might want to make a little side trip into the old Jewish quarter, just a few blocks to the southeast. Continue down Jodenbreestraat to Mr. Visserplein, near which is the famous **Mozes en Aaron Kerk**. An impressive neoclassical Catholic church built in 1840 whose name reflects the Jewish character of this area, it serves today primarily as a youth center. Close by, on Jonas Daniel Meijerplein, stands the beautiful **Portugees—Israelitische Synagogue** ⑱, built in the baroque style in 1675 by the local Sephardic community. These were descendants of refugees from Portugal and Spain, one of the many religious groups who have always found acceptance among the tolerant Dutch. Visitors are welcome to view the fine interior, said to be modeled after the Temple of Solomon. **T**: *(020) 624-5351. Open Sun.–Fri. 10–4.* €.

Crossing the adjacent square, you will pass the **Dock Worker Statue**, a memorial to the brave Amsterdammers who went on a 24-hour strike in February, 1941, in protest against Nazi deportation of Jews. Near this is the **Joods Historisch Museum** ⑲, located in four adjoining former synagogues. Its exhibits are mostly concerned with the history of Jewish life in Holland. **T**: *(020) 626-9945. Open daily 11–5, closed on Yom Kippur. Museum Cards accepted.* €€.

Return on Jodenbreestraat and turn left on Nieuwe Hoogstraat. At this corner stands the Zuiderkerk, the first church to be built in Amsterdam after the Reformation. It served as a subject for some of Rembrandt's paintings, as well as an inspiration for Sir Christopher Wren in his designs for London church steeples. A right turn at the canal takes you past the 17th-century **Trippenhuis**, a magnificent mansion built by two wealthy munitions manufacturers. Note the gun-barrel motifs on the chimneys and on the pediment. From 1815 until 1885 this was the home of the Rijksmuseum. Opposite, at number 26, is the **Little Trip House**, built for one of the servants and reputed to be the narrowest house in the world.

Just a few more steps and you are in the Nieuw Markt, a large open square noted for its imposing **Waag**, or weighhouse. Originally a 15th-century gate in the old town walls, it has seen many other uses over the years. During the 17th century, the surgeon's guild held their weekly anatomy lessons here, as is commemorated by Rembrandt's two renowned paintings on the subject. You are now entering the notorious *Walletjes,* Amsterdam's infamous **Red Light District**. It is perfectly safe for tourists to walk around here, but be sure to hang onto your wallet and be careful about taking pictures. True to its name, there actually are red lights illuminating the shop windows, behind which sit the available girls. Prostitution is legal here, and soft drugs (marijuana) are sold in some of the so-called "coffee houses." Zeedijk, actually a rather elegant old street, is lined with sleazy porno shops and cheap bars, as are many of the surrounding streets and alleyways.

Ironically, right in the middle of all this "sin" stands the venerable **Oude Kerk** ⑳, Amsterdam's oldest church. Built around 1306 and enlarged over the next few centuries, it is also the biggest church in town. Much of its pre-Reformation splendor has survived the Calvinist desecrations, making it among the most interesting churches in Holland to visit. Of particular interest are the three 16th-century stained-glass windows in the north aisle, opposite the choir, and the elaborately carved wooden choir stalls. **T**: *(020) 625-8284. Open Mon.–Sat. 11–5, Sun. 1–5. €.*

Now follow the canal to the last attraction on this walking tour. The **Museum Amstelkring** ㉑, otherwise known as *"Ons Lieve Heer op Solder"* ("Our Dear Lord in the Attic"), is a perfectly preserved example of the clandestine Catholic churches that thrived in Amsterdam during the Calvinist era. Actually, they were tolerated as long as they remained "invisible." As the name suggests, this one was in the attic of three adjoining houses. The rest of the building, which you pass through, is furnished as it was in the 17th and 18th centuries. Still used for occasional services, such as weddings, the secret church is open for visits. **T**: *(020) 624-6604. Open Mon.–Sat. 10–5, Sun. 1–5. Museum Cards accepted. €€.* From here it's a short stroll back to Centraal Station.

ADDITIONAL SIGHTS:

Amsterdam has a great many other attractions, which could not be covered on this walking tour, but which you might want to visit between daytrips to other parts of Holland. Among the most interesting are:

The **Nederlands Historisch Schcepvaartsmuseum**, or Netherlands Maritime Museum, is located on Kattenburgerplein at the east end of Prins Hendrikkade, about a mile southeast of Centraal Station (bus number 22 or 28). A real treat for ship enthusiasts, this 17th-century arsenal has fabulous displays of Holland's maritime history, as well as a few actual vessels moored outside. **T**: *(020) 523-2222. Open Tues.–Sun. 10–5, closed some major holidays. Museum Cards accepted. €€.*

The **Heineken Experience** at Stadhouderskade 78, a short stroll east of the Rijksmuseum (trams 16, 24, or 25 from Centraal Station) offers three free beers or soft drinks during this exploration of the art of brewing, all set in their historic brewery. **T**: *(020) 523-9436,* **W**: *heinekenexperience.com. Open Tues.–Sat., 10–6. Visitors under drinking age must be accompanied by an adult. €€.*

The **Tropenmuseum** (Tropical Museum) is at the edge of the Oosterpark, about two miles southeast of Centraal Station. You can get there via tram numbers 9 or 14, or bus number 22. Formerly concerned with colonial affairs, it is now mostly devoted to life in Third World countries. **T**: *(020) 568-8233. Open Mon.–Fri. 10–5, Sat.–Sun. noon–5. Museum Cards accepted. €€.*

The Muntplein

The **NEMO—NewMetropolis Science & Technology Center** is at 2 Ooster-dijk, a mile east of Centraal Station, at the IJ Tunnel; take bus 22 to Kadijksplein. This hands-on museum explores the frontiers of science and its applications, and provides virtual visits into complex techno experiences. **T**: *(020) 531-3233. Open Tues.–Sun. 10–5. €€€.*

Volendam, Marken, and Edam

Volendam is almost certainly the number one daytrip destination for tourists staying in Amsterdam. Most of its many visitors come on highly promoted guided tours, but you can have much more fun by doing it yourself. Not only will you see more worthwhile sights, but you'll travel at your own pace—and save money, too. This easy little excursion includes a boat trip to nearby Marken, and winds up in the delightful cheese town of Edam before returning to Amsterdam.

Sophisticated travelers may dismiss Volendam—and to some extent Marken—as tourist traps, which of course they are, but they're good ones if taken in the right spirit. Cute, quaint, and ever so commercialized, these two small towns can nevertheless be very enjoyable places to visit. Much less touristed, Edam offers genuine Old Dutch charm along with a refreshing interlude away from the hordes.

When the former Zuider Zee was cut off from the North Sea by the completion of the Afsluitdijk in 1932, it became the IJsselmeer, which is gradually being reclaimed by the creation of *polders,* areas of dry land lying below sea level and protected by dikes. Until then, both Volendam and Marken were fishing villages whose prosperity depended on access to the open sea. Now, surrounded by fresh water and under the threat of eventually becoming nearly landlocked, they have found a new source of employment in the tourist trade. Much of their charming, old-fashioned character has been preserved, even if some of it is more than a little commercialized. Despite this, and despite the pictures in travel brochures, exceedingly few of the local people continue to wear the traditional costumes they were once famous for. Edam, on the other hand, is the real thing. Lying slightly inland, its well-preserved atmosphere has made it a choice residential community for some of Amsterdam's commuters.

GETTING THERE:

This compact trio of small towns, just outside Amsterdam, is in one of The few areas of Holland that is not served by rail.

Buses depart central Amsterdam frequently for the 30-minute ride to Volendam. You can board one of these from the platforms to the left as you leave Centraal Station—just across the water beyond the tourist office *(VVV)*. Routes number 110 and 112 go direct to Volendam; take number 111 if you prefer to start with Marken. Be careful not to confuse these with the NZH *"Marken Express"* bus, which is for package tours.

By Car, take the Ij Tunnel from central Amsterdam and continue on the N-I0 and N-247 highways to Volendam, a distance of 21 km (13 miles). It is possible to drive to Marken by way of Monnickendam, but the boat is more fun.

By Bicycle: Travelers with strong legs can easily pedal their way to all three towns. The route is level all the way, and bike paths avoid the car traffic. The total round-trip distance is a bit over 50 km (30 miles). Ask at any bike rental shop about the best route.

PRACTICALITIES:

This trip can be made on any fine day between early April and the end of October. Good weather is essential. A few sights are closed on Sunday mornings. The tourist office *(VVV)* for Volendam, **T**: (0299) 363-747 or **W**: vvv-volendam.nl, is at 37 Zeestraat, by the bus stop. In Edam, the local VVV is in the Town Hall on Damplein, **T**: (0299) 315-125 or **W**: vvv-edam.nl.

FOOD AND DRINK:

Some choice restaurants are:

IN VOLENDAM:

Spaander (Haven 15, just north of the harbor) A hotel with a dining room and outdoor café. **T**: (0299) 363-595. €€ and €€€

Van Den Hogen (106 Haven, on the harbor) A good value for quality food. **T**: (0299) 363-775. €€ and €€€

Cathrien Brasserie (35 Haven, at the north end of the harbor) A popular restaurant by the waterfront, with Old Dutch atmosphere and outdoor tables. **T**: (0299) 363-705. € and €€

IN MARKEN:

DeTaanderij (1 Havenbuurt, on the harbor) Snacks, light lunches, and full meals—with plenty of local atmosphere. **T**: (0299) 602-206. € and €€

IN EDAM:

De Fortuna (3 Spuistraat, near the Speeltoren) Mostly for dinner as this is a wonderful place to end the day. A light lunch is also served. **T**: (0299) 271-671. Light lunch €€, dinner €€€

SUGGESTED TOUR:

Circled numbers correspond to numbers on the map.

Begin your walk in Volendam at the **bus stop** ① on Zeestraat. Those coming by car will find several parking lots in the immediate area. Next to this is the local tourist office and the **Volendams Museum**—a good place to get acquainted with the local lifestyle, especially as it was in times past. Here life-size interiors have been

Volendam

300 Yards

Edam

300 Yards

The Harbor at Volendam

re-created, along with a general store, a boat builder's workshop, and a fishermen's hangout. There are plenty of authentic local costumes and—a most unusual treat—an entire interior decorated with millions and millions of cigar bands. **T**: *(0299) 369-258 or* **W**: *volendamsmuseum.nl. Open daily 10–5.* €.

Continue straight ahead to the harbor and turn left. The town is full of interesting little sights, best seen by just ambling around aimlessly. The shops, cafes, and restaurants along Haven are completely tourist oriented—at some of them you can even have your picture taken wearing the old traditional costumes. There is, of course, no shortage of wooden shoes for sale, should you actually want a pair. Be sure to get off the main street and stroll among the small houses to the north and west.

Return to the **harbor** ② and board a **Marken Express boat** to Marken, first buying a round-trip *(retour)* ticket and making sure that the boat is going direct to Marken. These leave about every half-hour, from 10 a.m. until 5:30 p.m. daily, between March 1st and October 31st. There are outdoor seats on the top deck and a bar down below. **T**: *(0299) 363-331 or* **W**: *markenexpress.nl.*

Marken was an island, isolated from the rest of Holland until 1957, when a causeway was built connecting it to nearby Monnickendam. This is eventually to become a part of the proposed Markerwaard polder, whose development has been held up (hopefully forever) by environmental considerations. Being Calvinist for many centuries, its traditions are quite different from those of Catholic Volendam. You will actually see older people here wearing the rather severe local costumes, and perhaps even wooden shoes. Although the island is often overrun with tourists, the natives pay little attention to them other than extracting a few euros in the shops near the harbor.

In the Marker Museum

The boat arrives at Marken's compact ***harbor** ③, which is lined with picturesque little wooden houses. One or two of these can even be visited for a small fee. The same style of building continues throughout the entire village, which is remarkably free of traffic, as only the local residents are allowed to drive there. Visitors must park in the huge lot at the end of the causeway. A walk through the village will reveal many interesting details, and should include a visit to the main church, from whose ceiling hang ship models and fishing nets. Close to this is the **Marker Museum** ④, located in four small adjoining smokehouses on the Kerkbuurt. Reconstructed room settings here tell the story of local life in former times, a treat not to be missed. **T**: *(0299) 601-904. Open April-Oct., Mon.-Sat. 10-5, Sun. noon-4. Museum Card accepted. €.*

Just beyond the village, particularly to the north, are small market gardens, where you might see older farmers working the land in their traditional costumes, including wooden shoes. Return to the harbor and board the boat back to Volendam. Ask to make certain that it is not going somewhere else, as some of them do.

From the Volendam harbor ②, stroll back to the bus stop ① and get on the next bus to Edam (routes 110 or 112), a trip of only 3 km (2 miles). Edam began in the 12th century as a little settlement on the Ee River, and received its charter as early as 1357. It was an important shipbuilding center until the 17th century, when flood control measures cut it off from the Zuider Zee. The surrounding land, formerly underwater, made excellent pasturage, thus paving the way for its world-famous cheese industry. Alas, precious little Edam cheese is still made in Edam itself, although the town continues to function as an aging and distribution center. You are probably familiar with Edam cheese in its export version, with the red skin; what is sold locally has a yellow skin and seems to have a stronger flavor. Try some!

From the **Edam bus stop** ⑤ it is only a short stroll into the heart of this lovely old town. Follow the map to the **Speeltoren** ⑥, a 15th-century tower to a church that was torn down in 1883. It has one of the oldest carillons in Holland, built in 1561, and it leans a bit to one side.

*Damplein, the picturesque main square of the town, is actually a broad humped bridge, from which there are delightful views in all directions. Next to it, in an unusually attractive 16th-century house, is the **Edams Museum** ⑦. Step inside to see the wonderful old furnishings, and don't miss the paintings of some of the local celebrities, including the 445-pound innkeeper from the 16th century and the 16th-century man with the 10-foot beard. The most unusual attraction in the museum is its floating cellar, made of brick and tiles, which still goes up and down as the groundwater level changes. *Open April–Oct., Tues.-Sat. 10-4:30, Sun. 1:30-4:30. Closed Nov.–March, Mon. €.*

Across the square from this is the 18th-century **Town Hall** *(Stadhuis)* ⑧ with its elegant façade and interesting council chamber decorated with biblical scenes. This is also the home of the local tourist office. Now follow the map past the 15th-century **Houtenhuis**, the oldest wooden house in town, at the corner of Breestraat and Eilandsgracht. Grote Kerkstraat leads to the **Grote Kerk of St. Nicholaas** ⑨, an enormous Gothic church from the 15th century. It is famous for its early-17th-century stained-glass windows, 18th-century organ, and Gothic pews. *Open April–Oct., 2–4:30.*

Return on Matthijs Tinxgracht to the 16th-century **Kaaswaag** ⑩, where cheese was once weighed before being sold. During the summer months demonstration cheese markets are held here, and local Edam cheese may be purchased. *Markets in July–Aug., Wed., 10:30–12:30.* Now return to the bus stop ⑤, from which bus numbers 110 or112 will take you back to Amsterdam in only half an hour.

*Haarlem

One of the oldest cities in Holland, Haarlem is also among the least changed. Its quiet streets exude an aura of refinement that makes it quite different from lively Amsterdam. During the 17th century it was a major art center, with many outstanding talents revolving around the singular genius of Frans Hals. Much of this era can still be felt today amid the narrow lanes and delightful old buildings of the town's historic center.

Haarlem's roots go back as far as the 10th century, when a feudal castle offered protection against marauding West Frisians. The counts of Holland soon established their seat in this strategic location and the town grew rapidly, receiving its charter in 1245. It bravely fought the Spaniards in 1573, surrendering only after a cutoff of the food supply had brought it to the brink of starvation. The reprisals were brutal, with many of Haarlem's citizens massacred and the town largely destroyed. Recaptured by the Dutch under William of Orange, it entered a period of prosperity that has lasted ever since.

Haarlem is most famous as the flower capital of Holland. Its horticultural industry had long been established, and grew to enormous size after the introduction of the tulip from Turkey to the ideal sandy soil just south of the city. Chance mutations there resulted in wild color variations, providing the base for a lucrative business in the export of bulbs. Short excursions to the growing fields by bus or car, described at the end of the chapter, can easily be added to this daytrip.

GETTING THERE:

Trains depart Amsterdam's Centraal Station at very frequent intervals for the 15-minute run to Haarlem. Return service operates until late evening.

By Car, take the N-5/A-5 highway *(Haarlemmerweg)* from central Amsterdam due west to Haarlem, a distance of 24 km (15 miles). The most convenient parking there is between the Grote Markt and the Spaarne River.

PRACTICALITIES:

Haarlem may be visited at any time, but note that the Grote Kerk is not open to tourists on weekend mornings, and that the major museums are closed on Mondays and some holidays. Short excursions to the flower growing area can be made, in the case of Keukenhof, daily between the end of March and the end of May; and in the case of Aalsmeer, Mondays through Fridays all year round, but before 11 a.m. only.

The local **tourist office** *(VVV)*, **T**: (0900) 616-1600 (toll call) or **W**: vvvzk.nl, is located just outside the train station. You might want to ask them about the various **hofjes** (almshouses) for which the town is noted. Most of these are not on this walking route, but may be interesting places to visit.

FOOD AND DRINK:

There are a great many restaurants along most of the walking route. Some good choices are:

Peter Cuyper (70 Klein Houtstraat, between the Crote Kerk and the Frans Hals Museum) French and Dutch cooking in a quaint atmosphere, outdoor terrace in summer. Reservations suggested. **T**: (023) 532-0885. X: Sat. lunch, Sun., Mon. €€ and €€€

Napoli (1 Houtplein, 2 blocks southwest of the Frans Hals Museum, across the canal) Italian cuisine in a classy setting. **T**: (023) 532-4419. €€ and €€€

Café Applause (Grote Markt 3) Light lunches and elegant dinners, served in style. **T**: (023) 531-1425. €€ and €€€

Carillon (27 Grote Markt, facing the Grote Kerk) Both a tavern and a restaurant, with outdoor tables in summer. **T**: (023) 531-0591. € and €€

Eko Eetkafé (Zijlstraat 19, 4 blocks northwest of Grote Markt) Healthy organic vegetarian dishes, as well as seafood. **T**: (023) 532-6566. € and €€

SUGGESTED TOUR:

Circled numbers correspond to numbers on the map.

Haarlem was the terminus of the first Dutch rail line, which was opened in 1839 and which ran to Amsterdam. The present **station** ①, built in the Art Nouveau style in 1908, is a fitting introduction to this historical city. From here it is a half-mile walk down Kruisweg, Kruisstraat, and the pedestrianized Barteljoris-straat to the **Grote Markt**, one of the more impressive town squares in Europe. The statue near its center honors Laurens Coster, born in Haarlem in 1370, who is locally believed to have invented printing from movable type, despite evidence that Germany's Gutenberg was first with the discovery. A colorful outdoor flower market is held in the square on Saturdays from 9 a.m. to 4 p.m.

The west side of the market square is bordered by the **Stadhuis** (Town Hall) ②, built on the site of the 13th-century hunting lodge of the counts of Holland. The oldest part of the present structure dates from the mid-I4th century, while the rest of the building has been enlarged and altered many times since. Visitors are allowed to see the Great Hall *(Gravenzaal)* and possibly other parts of the elegant interior, but only by advance appointment, and only on weekdays.

Continuing around the square will bring you to the magnificent **Vleeshal** ③, a Renaissance meat market from 1603 that is now used as an extension of the Frans Hals Museum for temporary art exhibitions. Close to it and attached to the church is the **Vishal**, a fish market built in 1768. It is also used by the museum for temporary exhibitions. Nearby, also on the square, stands the **Verweghal**, a new

Haarlem

400 Yards

N

Kennemer Plein

Station

info.

Rozenstraat

Kenaustraat

Bus

Lange Herenstr.

Parklaan

Prinsen Bolwerk

TO AMSTERDAM

Jansweg

Nieuwe Gracht

Parklaan

Hooimarkt

SPAARNE

Kindehuis Singel

Kinderhuisvest

Witte Herenstr.

Nassaustraat

Nassaulaan

Nassaulaan

Kruisweg

Ridderstraat

Zakstraat

Harmenians Weg

Papentoren Vest

Koudenhorn

Kruisstraat

Bartelkjorisstr.

Smedestr.

Jansstraat

Bakenesser Gracht

Zijl Straat

Raaks

Jacobstr.

Zuiderstr.

Gasthuisstr.

Gedempte

Jacobijnestr.

Koningstraat

Grote
Markt

Anegang

Donkere Spaarne

Hout markt

Botermarkt

Oude

Frankestraat

Schagchelstr.

Warmoestr.

Kleine Houtstr.

Spaarne

Lange Heren Vest

Amstr.

K. Amstr.

Gierstraat

Grote Hout Straat

Heiligland

Groot — Heiligland

Gracht

Kleine Houtstr.

Turfmarkt

Buro Wal

Klein

Gasthuis Vest

Kampervest

Kamper Singel

Zomer Vaart

Raam Vest

Raam Singel

Gasthuis Singel

Houtplein

Kleine Houtweg

K. Poellaan

Linschotenstr.

Barendsestr.

In the Grote Kerk

museum of modern and contemporary art; especially the creations of Dutch artists. *Open Mon.–Sat. 11–5, Sun. and holidays noon–5. €€. Museum Cards accepted.* Just across the square is the **Hoofdwacht**, the former guardhouse of the police, whose facade dates from 1650.

Despite these interesting buildings, the market square is almost totally dominated by the huge ***Grote Kerk** ④, also known as the **Church of St. Bavo**. Begun around 1400 and largely completed by 1550, it was originally a Catholic cathedral and has fortunately retained some of its pre-Reformation decorations, although it now belongs to the Dutch Reformed Church. The entrance for visitors is around the corner, through the verger's house at Oude Groenmarkt 23. Inside, the most impressive feature is the splendid **Müller organ** of 1738, one of the largest and most famous in the world. Its 5,000 pipes have responded to the touch of such outstanding musicians as Mozart (then ten years of age), Handel, and Schweitzer. With luck, you might get here in time to enjoy one of the frequent recitals and hear what it must have sounded like to them. The artist Frans Hals is buried in the choir, under slab number 56. There is a plaque dedicated to Laurens Coster, the printing innovator, near the crossing, and he is buried somewhere in this church, but no one knows where. A pamphlet in English explaining many of the other features is available at the entrance. **T**: *(023) 532-4399. Open to tourists April–Sept., Tues.–Fri. 10–4, Sat., Sun. & Mon. 1–4. €.*

Now follow the map through some interesting streets to the world-renowned:

In the Frans Hals Museum

*FRANS HALS MUSEUM ⑤, **T**: (023) 511-5778 or **W**: franshalsmuseum.com. *Open Tues.–Sat. 11–5, Sun. noon–5. Museum Card accepted. Gift shop. Café. €€.*

This splendid museum is located in the former *Oudemannenhuis,* an alms-house for men, built in 1608. Even if you have little interest in art, a visit here will give you a chance to see the exceptionally well-preserved interior of an outstanding building. Frans Hals was probably born in Antwerp in 1580, but moved to Haarlem while still a child. He spent the rest of his long life in that city, and achieved great fame with his amazingly lively portraits. Several of his most famous works, particularly the eight group portraits, form the nucleus of the museum's collection, which includes quite a few other artists as well. Of special interest are the many Dutch genre paintings depicting everyday life during the "Golden Age," sometimes quite a life of debauchery. There are also period room settings, furniture, and the applied arts.

The route now follows a canal and the Spaarne River to the **Cravenstenen-brug** ⑥, a picturesque lift bridge of traditional Dutch design. A variety of **boat trips** leave from the canal side here, some as short as 75 minutes. From here you might want to make a little side trip to Haarlem's only remaining town gate, the **Amsterdamse Poort** ⑦. Looking terribly medieval, this fortification dates from the late 14th century. To get there, just follow the map down Wijde Steeg and Spaarnwouderstraat.

Return and cross the bridge to the:

*TEYLERS MUSEUM ⑧, **T**: (023) 531-9010 or **W**: teylersmuseum.nl. *Open Tues.–Sat. 10–5, Sun. & holidays noon–5. Museum Card accepted. €€. Audioguide rental €. Gift shop. Café.*

Founded in 1778, this is the oldest museum in Holland—and it sure looks its age. Nothing ever seems to have changed here. The incredibly old-fashioned displays encompass a wide range of interests, from sketches by Rembrandt, Raphael, and Michelangelo, to ancient fossils, bones, and rocks. Perhaps the most interesting are the weird electrical apparatuses from the late 18th century, such as the enormous electrostatic generator that looks like something out of a Frankenstein movie. You will never forget this place.

Stroll along the river to Damstraat, at the corner of which is the **Waag,** a stone structure built in 1598 for the purpose of weighing goods arriving by ship. From here, the route returns you to the station via the 14th-century **Waalse Kerk** ⑨, the oldest church in Haarlem. It is surrounded by an especially attractive *Begijnhof,* formerly a convent. Farther along you will come to the **Hofje van Staats** ⑩, one of the many *hofjes* that grace the city. This particular almshouse dates from 1730. Step in for a quick look, then continue on to the nearby station.

NEARBY SIGHTS:

If you happen to be in Haarlem between the end of March and the middle of May, you may want to visit the world-famous **Keukenhof Gardens**. During that time the bulbs are in bloom, millions and millions of them, all spread out over a 70-acre site of astonishing beauty. **T**: *(0252) 465-555 or* **W**: *keukenhof.com. Open late March to mid-May, daily 8 a.m.–7:30 p.m. €€€. Buses, marked for Lisse, leave frequently from the front of Haarlem Station.* Flower lovers may also want to visit the year-round international flower auction at **Aalsmeer**, near Schiphol Airport. **T**: *(0297) 392-185 or* **W**: *vba-aalsmeer.nl. Open Mon.–Fri., 7:30–11 a.m. €. Be sure to get there early, and see the town later. Again, there is a bus from Haarlem Station, and others direct from Amsterdam.*

Hoorn and the Historic Triangle

H ere is an easy and thoroughly enjoyable daytrip that is just filled with sun and fun. You can travel by train or car to the historic port of Hoorn, then ride an ancient steam train through the lovely North Holland landscape to Medemblik, where you board an excursion boat to Enkhuizen. From there it's a short train ride back to Hoorn, a most delightful place to explore on foot.

Known as the "Historic Triangle," *(Historische Driehoek),* this rich agricultural area is loaded with memories of the former Zuider Zee, the arm of the North Sea that became the land-locked IJsselmeer. Many of its traditions may be probed at the Westfries Museum in Hoorn, while the magnificent and truly fascinating outdoor museum at Enkhuizen — described in the next chapter—brings the rural past to life. This latter attraction could be included on this trip instead, by cutting both walking tours short and eliminating the museum in Hoorn.

First settled in the early 14th century, Hoorn was a major port for international trade until the late 17th century. It gave its name to Cape Horn, the southernmost tip of South America, which was discovered in 1616 by the locally-born navigator, Willem Schouten. This was an important center of the Dutch East Indies Company, which brought about the prosperity so clearly seen in the town's many beautiful old buildings. Alas, as trade increased, so did the draught of the ships needed to carry the goods. The local waters are relatively shallow and subject to silting, and so the maritime trade gradually moved to deeper ports. One of the most attractive towns in Holland, Hoorn thrives today as a regional shopping and yachting center.

GETTING THERE:

Trains, marked for Enkhuizen, depart Amsterdam's Centraal Station at half-hour intervals for the 36-minute run to Hoorn. Return service operates until late evening.

By Car, the most attractive route to follow from central Amsterdam is through the Ij Tunnel, then the N-10 and N-247 roads north by way of Edam to Hoorn. It may be slightly faster to take the A-7/E-22 motorway instead. In either case, the distance is about 40 km (25 miles).

PRACTICALITIES:

This trip may be taken on any day during July and August; on Tuesdays through Sundays during April–June and September–October, or on weekends during January–March and November–December. The "Historic Triangle" steam train and boat combination does not operate at other times. To avoid disappointment you should check first with the information office in Amsterdam's Centraal Station, or with the museum in Hoorn. Good weather is essential, as is an early start—around 8 a.m. at the latest.

The **Tourist Office** *(VVV)* in Hoorn, **T**: (072) 511-4284 (toll call) or **W**: vvvhoorn.nl, is at Veemarkt 4, three blocks south of the train station. Current schedules for the "Historic Triangle" combination can be had at **T**: (0229) 214-862 or **W**: museumstoomtram.nl

FOOD AND DRINK:

Snacks and drinks are available on both the steam train and the boat. Restaurant choices for Enkhuizen are noted in the next chapter. Some good restaurants in Hoorn are:

Brasserie Bontekoe (Nieuwendam 1, near the Binnenhaven) Tavern cuisine in a 17th-century warehouse. **T**: (0229) 217-324. X: Sun., Mon., Tues. €€

De Waag (Rode Steen 8, near the Westfries Museum) Light lunches, plus full French and seafood specialties in the evenings. **T**: (0229) 215-195. € and €€

Azië (49 Veemarkt, a block south of the train station) Superb Chinese cuisine, with a good-value lunch. **T**: (0229) 218-555. € and €€

SUGGESTED TOUR:

Circled numbers correspond to numbers on the maps.

Begin your tour at the **Hoorn Train Station** ①, where you cross a pedestrian bridge over the tracks to the:

MUSEUM STOOMTRAM HOORN–MEDEMBLIK (Museum Steam Train)

②, **T**: (0229) 214-862 or **W**: museumstoomtram.nl. *Operates daily July–Aug., Tues.–Sun. in April–June and Sept.–Oct., and on weekends in Jan.–March and Nov.–Dec. Closed on some holidays. Combination steam train and boat fare €€€€.*

There is a great deal of intriguing activity here, as locomotives and open-ended cars, some nearly a century old, are shunted about. Buy a combination ticket for the ***steam train and boat** *(combi stoomtram + boot)* and study the printed schedule (in English) carefully. These rides are privately operated and are not covered by any railpass.

You will probably have time before departure to enjoy visiting the yards and special steam exhibitions. No one seems to mind your walking around on the tracks or even in the train sheds and machine shops. This is a very popular outing with Dutch families, so expect to run into hordes of little children.

Historic Triangle Area

N

MEDEMBLIK
See detail map below

See map of Enkhuizen trip for detail
ENKHUIZEN

Steam Train Line

A-7 / E-22

Main Rail Line

TO ALKMAAR

HOORN
See map of Hoorn for detail

TO AMSTERDAM

IJSSELMEER

5 Miles

Route Through Medemblik

TO HOORN

Station   info.

Oude Haven

Oostersteeg

Breedstraat

Nieuwstraat

Torenstraat

Oosterhaven

Gedempt Achterom

Westerhaven

In the Steam Train Station at Hoorn

Now board the ancient train and take delight in the passing countryside. The ride to Medemblik takes about one hour, and there is a primitive bar car to help you pass the time. Upon arrival at **Medemblik Station** ③, walk straight ahead down the main street to the **harbor** ④, where you will find the large excursion boat (probably the *M.S. Friesland)* that will take you to Enkhuizen. This delightful cruise on the IJsselmeer takes about 75 minutes. Again, snacks and drinks are available.

From the **Enkhuizen Pier** ⑤ it is only a few steps to the train station, where there are frequent trains back to Hoorn. While here, however, you might want to explore one or more of the outstanding attractions this town is famous for. You will find a full description of these, along with a map, in the next chapter. Remember that a stop here will most likely eliminate the possibility of a visit to the Westfries Museum in Hoorn.

Return to Hoorn by train and begin your walking tour of the old port town by following the map to the **Town Hall** *(Stadhuis)* ⑥, a lovely twin-gabled building from 1613. Continue down Nieuwstraat past the enormous **Grote Kerk**, a 19th-century church that has been strangely converted into shops. Kerkstraat leads to Rode Steen, the town's main square. Named after the red stone that was once a place of public execution, this large open square is surrounded by exqui-site old buildings.

One of these structures, the highly-ornate 17th-century Staten College (State Council) is now the home of the **Westfries Museum** ⑦. Step inside to witness

Hoorn

IJSSELMEER

300 Yards

The Rode Steen in Hoorn

the wealth this town once possessed. Sumptuous furniture, paintings, weapons, ship models, and anything else associated with the history of the region—they're all there, all displayed in elegant surroundings. **T**: *(0229) 280-028. Open Mon.– Fri. 11–5, Sat.–Sun. 2–5. Museum Cards accepted.* €.

On the opposite side of the square is the **Waag**, an especially nice weigh-house from 1609. Stroll down Grote Oost past the Oosterkerk, a Gothic church founded in 1450. Its stained-glass window from 1620 depicts a famous naval battle. Turn right at Slapershaven and amble along the picturesque harbor, busy with pleasure boats. The early-16th-century **Hoofdtoren** ⑧ was a part of the old fortifications, and sports a delicate belfry from 1651. From here you may want to just wander around and soak up the delicious atmosphere before returning to the train station and Amsterdam.

ADDITIONAL ATTRACTION:

Hoorn has another nearby museum that might interest you. The **Museum van de Twintigste Eeuw** (Museum of the Twentieth Century) celebrates a hundred years of local life at Bierkade 4. **T**: *(0229) 214-001 or* **W**: *museumhoorn.nl. Open Tues.–Fri. 10–5, Sat.–Sun. noon–5.* €.

Enkhuizen

T he way of life in northern Holland was dramatically changed in 1932 when the former Zuider Zee was sealed off from the sea to become the freshwater IJsselmeer. No longer were fishing and shipping of great importance; new industries appeared and brought with them a different kind of prosperity. As the old traditions began to die away, there was a very real danger that they would be forgotten forever. Fortunately, the Dutch government recognized this peril to the nation's heritage and began to gather artifacts to form the first Zuider Zee museum, established in the lovely old port of Enkhuizen in 1950.

In the meantime, old houses, churches, and other structures were saved and moved to a site just outside the town, where they were reassembled into villages. After decades of work, this was finally opened in 1983 as the Zuider Zee Outdoor Museum, one of the best and most enjoyable open-air museums in the world. Not only have the buildings been preserved, but also the crafts, trades, lifestyles, and traditions that went with them. This is surely one of the most fascinating attractions in all of Holland, something that really is not to be missed.

Enkhuizen itself is an unusually attractive old port. Founded in the 14th century, its economy peaked in the 17th, when many of its most impressive buildings were erected. After that it more or less went to sleep, only to be reawakened by tourists in search of a well-preserved past.

GETTING THERE:

Trains depart Amsterdam's Centraal Station at half-hour intervals for the one-hour ride to Enkhuizen. Return service operates until late evening.

By Car, the most enjoyable route from central Amsterdam is to take the IJ Tunnel, followed by the N-10 and N-247 highways past Edam to Hoorn. You might get there faster via the A-7/E-22 motorway instead. From Hoorn take the local road to Enkhuizen and park in the Zuider Zee Museum lot, at the beginning of the dike road to Lelystad. The total distance from Amsterdam is 62 km (38 miles).

PRACTICALITIES:

The Zuider Zee Outdoor Museum is open daily in July–August; on Tuesdays through Sundays from late March through June and September–October, but closed the rest of the year. Its companion indoor museum remains open all year round except on Mondays in January through June and September–December. Good weather is essential for enjoyment of this trip.

The local **Tourist Office** *(VVV),* **T**: (0228) 313-164 or **W**: enkhuizen.nl, is on the harbor just east of the train station.

FOOD AND DRINK:

You will find a restaurant and several inexpensive cafeterias and cafés within the outdoor museum area, and one in the indoor museum as well. Some choice restaurants in Enkhuizen itself are:

Die Drie Haringhe (Dijk 28, 4 blocks northeast of the station) Upstairs in a 17th-century warehouse; indoor or outdoor tables. **T**: (0228) 318-610. X:Tues. €€ and €€€

De Kapel (Westerstraat 128a, near the Westerkerk) Traditional Dutch cuisine along with more exotic dishes, all served in an ancient chapel **T**: (0228) 323-272. X: Sun., Mon. €€

SUGGESTED TOUR:

Circled numbers correspond to numbers on the map.

Leave the **train station** ① and follow the map a short distance to the tourist office, where you can purchase a ticket to the:

*ZUIDER ZEE MUSEUMS, T: (0228) 351-111 or **W**: zuiderzeemuseum.nl. *Outdoor museum open late March–June and Sept.–Oct., Tues.–Sun. 10–5; July–Aug. daily 10–5. Indoor museum open all year round except on Mon. in Jan.–June and Sept.–Dec., 11–5. Closed Christmas and New Year's Day. Museum Card accepted. Combined ticket €€. Indoor museum only at a reduced price in winter.*

Continue on to the **Zuider Zee Museum pier** ②, boarding a ferry to the **main parking lot** ③. Those coming by car should begin their tour here. The boat then takes you to the Outdoor Museum. Be sure to allow a minimum of at least two hours to see it, and don't forget to pick up a map and a guide pamphlet in English.

You'll have a lovely panoramic view of Enkhuizen as you approach the ***Outdoor Museum** *(Buitenmuseum)* ④. Once there, you can wander around some 130 buildings grouped into several villages. Quite a few of these are open for inspection, and many are staffed with people performing the old crafts and trades. Various events and activities are staged throughout the day. Everything is very well explained with signs, exhibitions, and even a video show. You won't

ZUIDER ZEE
OUTDOOR
MUSEUM

N

Groene Wierdijk

Noordergracht

Noorderweg

Handvastwater

Leger

Visserdijk

Spaans

Wegjes

Vijzelstraat

Waagstraat

Kaasmarkt

Nieuwstr.

Zwaanstr.

Westerstraat

Zuider Havendijk

Breedstraat

Oosterhavenstr.

Kade

Wierdijk

Venedie

St. Janstr.

Dijk

Paktuinen

Parklaan

Flevolaan

TO AMSTERDAM

Station

info.

IJSSELMEER

N-302

TO LELYSTAD

500 Yards

Enkhuizen

In the Zuider Zee Outdoor Museum

go hungry or thirsty either, as there are several places to eat or drink along with an attractive crafts shop.

To continue into Enkhuizen, take the land exit marked for *Stad en Binnenmuseum.* Just beyond this is the **Zuider Zee Indoor Museum** *(Binnenmuseum)* ⑤, occupying several old warehouses of the Dutch East Indies Company. Opened in 1950, the museum displays a remarkably thorough collection of fishing boats, house furnishings, utensils, and just about everything else that pertains to life in this region prior to 1932. The most popular exhibits here are probably those of local costumes in period room settings

Continue across an old lift bridge to the **Town Hall** *(Stadhuis)* ⑥, a rather imposing structure from 1688. Behind it is the former jail *(Oude Gevangenis)* of 1612. In about another block or so you will come to the **Waag** *(Weighhouse)* ⑦, an early Renaissance building from 1559. It is now used as the town museum, and has some interesting displays of early medical instruments along with the expected curiosities.

Stroll down the pedestrians-only Westerstraat, passing the 15th-century **Westerkerk** ⑧. You might want to step inside to see one of the nicest choir screens in the country, dating from 1542, as well as the 16th-century pulpit. Now follow the map to the picturesque **Old Harbor**. At the far end of this is the dramatically sited **Drommedaris Tower** ⑨ of 1540, a massive fortification with dungeons and one of the best carillons in Holland.. From here it's only a short stroll back to the train station, or the ferry back to the parking lot.

ENKHUIZEN 60

Zaanse Schans

Y ou don't have to go far from Amsterdam to see working windmills
in a setting of preserved quaintness. The Zaanse Schans is an extremely popular destination for visitors in search of a bit of *Oud Holland,* all neatly packaged and ready to be enjoyed. At first, this may seem like
the ultimate Dutch tourist trap, but it can also be a lot of fun and should not
be missed.

As the Zaan region, just northwest of Amsterdam, developed indus-
trially, its traditional buildings were in danger of being lost forever. Fortunately, some of Holland's precious heritage was saved in the 1950s by the
Zaanse Schans Foundation, which moved an assortment of old windmills,
houses, and other interesting structures to a 20-acre site on the banks of the
Zaan River. Restored to their 18th-century appearance, the houses are not just
an outdoor museum—indeed, most of them are actually lived in today,
bringing real life to what would otherwise be only another tourist attraction.
Some of the working windmills as well as all of the craft shops and small
museums may be visited.

This trip can easily be combined in the same day with one to Alkmaar,
described in the next chapter. They are both on the same rail line.

GETTING THERE:

Trains, bound for Alkmaar, depart Amsterdam's Centraal Station at frequent intervals for the 16-minute ride to Koog-Zaandijk, which is just a
short walk from the site. Be sure to get on a local train *(stoptrein).* Return
service operates until late evening.

By Car, leave Amsterdam via the Coen Tunnel and take the A-8 and A-7
motorways past Zaandam in the direction of Purmerend, then follow signs to
Zaanse Schans. The total distance from central Amsterdam is 16 km (10
miles). Parking at the site is free for the first 30 minutes, then € for the next
hour and €€ thereafter.

PRACTICALITIES:

The Zaanse Schans site is always open, and admission to it is free. Most of
the attractions there are open on Tuesdays through Sundays, with some also
open on Mondays. The hours from March through October are 10 a.m. to 5

Windmills at Zaanse Schans

p.m. During the winter most sights are open only on weekends. If you combine this daytrip with Alkmaar, you may prefer to go on a Friday, in which case you should see Alkmaar first.

For further information contact the site's Visitor Center, **T**: (075) 616-8218. The official website is **W**: diza.nl/schans/eng/, but more practical information is available at **W**: zaanseschans.nl. Windmill fanciers might check out **W**: zaansemolen.nl

FOOD AND DRINK:

Two good places to eat within the Zaanse Schans site are:

De Hoop Op d'Swarte Walvis (along Kalverringdijk, the main street) Superb French dining in an 18th-century house. Reservations preferred, **T**: (075) 616-5629. X: Sat. lunch, Sun. lunch. €€€ and €€€+

De Kraai (at the east end of the site) All sorts of pancakes, some with meat or cheese, along with sandwiches and drinks. Self-service in a colorful old warehouse, outdoor tables available. **T**: (075) 615-6403. X: winter. €

SUGGESTED TOUR:

Circled numbers correspond to numbers on the map.

Begin at the **Koog-Zaandijk Station** ① and follow the signs to Zaanse Schans, a walk of about ten minutes. Those coming by car should park at the eastern end of the site itself and adjust the walk accordingly.

Kalverringdijk is the main street of the village. On the left as you enter, there is an attractive French-style garden with a small tea pavilion, now a **Pewter Shop** in which visitors can watch pewter objects being handcrafted. The house next to it was originally a workshop from the 17th century, and now houses a fascinating

N

Kalver Polder

Parking

info.

10

Zeilenmakerspad

De Kwakels

TO AMSTERDAM

Parking

Zonnewijzerspad

9

8

6

7

Kalverringdijk

5

4

3

2

ZAAN

Zaanse Schans

300 Yards

1

Koog-Zaandijk Station
TO AMSTERDAM ➔

ZAANSE SCHANS 63

Clock Museum ②, where you can examine antique timepieces from around the world and particularly from this part of Holland. **T**: *(075) 617-9769. €, Museum Card holders free.*

Adjacent to this is a 19th-century **Grocery Store** ③, operated as a small museum. Step inside to see (and smell!) how food was sold in the days before supermarkets. Continue on past several other old houses and the noted restaurant "De Hoop Op d'Swarte Walvis," an 18th-century structure once used as an orphanage. Near the end of the row is **Het Noorderhuis** ④, a merchant's house built in 1670. Its interior is filled with antique room-settings complete with figures in period costumes, and may be visited. **T**: *(075) 617-3237. €, Museum Card holders free.*

Boat trips on the Zaan River, going past a nice variety of windmills and lasting about 50 minutes, may be taken from the **pier** ⑤. **T**: *(075) 614-6762. Operates March through Oct., Tues.–Sun. €.* Close to this is an 18th-century windmill, **De Huisman**, first built to grind snuff and later used for making mustard. A shop inside sells the mustard in an assortment of lovely containers.

From here, a row of windmills stretches along the river. The first of these, **De Poelenburg**, was built in 1869 to saw wood. *€.* A much older one, called ***De Kat** ⑥ and originally built elsewhere in the region in 1696, still grinds pigments for paints. You are welcome to climb all over its interior and watch the process at work. **T**: *(075) 621-0477. €.* Beyond it is a mill used to extract oil from grains. Known as **De Zoeker** ⑦, it is also open to visitors. **T**: *(075) 628-7942. €.* Another mill that can be visited is **De Bonte Hen**, just to the north. The mills extending beyond this are in various states of reconstruction.

Return to the village and turn left on Zeilenmakerspad (Sailmaker's path). Passing the oldest house at Zaanse Schans, built for a Zaandam merchant in 1623 and now home to an antique shop, you will soon come to the **Bakery** ⑧. Beginning as *a* private house in 1658, it was converted to make bread in 1753 and is now restored as a small museum. Note the outdoor toilet over a ditch at its rear—those canal waters were not always so clean! **T**: *(075) 617-3522. €, Museum Card holders free.*

On your left is the **Cheese Farm** ⑨, where they sell good homemade cheese. Yes, you can taste some. Continue on past the small drainage windmill, which still functions, and cross a tiny lift bridge. You are now at the eastern end of the site, where a café and self-service restaurant occupies a complex of old structures, along with gift shops. The **Wooden Shoe Workshop** ⑩ is sure to have a pair of clogs in your size, should you feel so inclined.

Beyond this, across the parking lot, stands the striking new **Zaans Museum**. Here the whole saga of Europe's oldest industrial area comes to life through artifacts, reconstructions, videos, and other modern presentations. **T**: *(075) 616-2862. Open Tues.–Sat. 10–5, Sun. noon–5. €. Museum Cards accepted. Café.*

Return via a path called De Kwakels, along which is an old shipyard. It is now only a short walk back to the station or the parking lot.

Alkmaar

The world-famous Cheese Market at Alkmaar is a tradition going back to the early 17th century. Although more efficient distribution methods have been developed over the years, this colorful weekly wholesale auction is still held, partly as a tourist attraction and partly to preserve a worthwhile link with the past.

But there is much more to this lovely old town than cheese. The historic center, surrounded by moats and canals, still maintains its Old World character, with many fine buildings from the 15th through the 18th centuries remaining in use today.

Alkmaar was first mentioned in the 10th century and received its charter in 1254. It played a pivotal role in the Dutch struggle for independence when the town defeated the Spaniards in 1573 by opening the sluices, thus flooding the surrounding area. This marked the beginning of the end of Spanish domination in the Low Countries, and led eventually to self-rule.

You may prefer to combine this daytrip with one to Zaanse Schans, described in the previous chapter. If you do so on a Friday in season, be sure to visit Alkmaar first.

GETTING THERE:

Trains leave Amsterdam's Centraal Station frequently for the 30- to-45-minute ride to Alkmaar, with return service until late evening.

By Car, the fastest route is the N-5/A-5 highway west in the direction of Haarlem, then the A-9 north to Alkmaar. The total distance from central Amsterdam is 40 km (25 miles). You might want to drive back by way of Zaandam, stopping at Zaanse Schans en route.

PRACTICALITIES:

Tourists by the thousands flock to Alkmaar on Friday mornings between mid-April and mid-September to see the famous Cheese Market in action. If this spectacle does not excite you, consider coming on another day. The Municipal and Beer museums are closed on Mondays, while the Cheese Museum closes on Sundays and also on Saturdays from November through March.

The local **Tourist Office** *(VVV)*, **T**: (072) 511-4284 or **W**: vvvalkmaar.nl, is in the historic weighhouse at Waagplein 2.

FOOD AND DRINK:

Being a favorite tourist attraction, Alkmaar has a wide variety of restaurants and cafés in all price ranges. Some good choices for lunch are:

Hof van Alkmaar (1 Hof van Sonoy, 2 blocks northwest of the Waag) Luxury dining in an old almshouse just off Nieuwesloot. **T**: (072) 512-1222. X: Mon. €€€

Bios (54a Nieuwesloot, 2 blocks southeast of the Stedelijk Museum) A modern brasserie with a good restaurant upstairs. **T**: (072) 512-4422. X: Mon. €€

Henry's Grand Café (34 Houtil, a block northwest of the Waag) Both light and full lunches and dinners. **T**: (072) 511-3283. € and €€

De Kajuit (at the Fries Bridge 3 blocks east of the Beer Museum) All kinds of pancakes. **T**: (072) 512-5850. X: Mon. €

Stationsrestauratie (in the train station) Good food at low prices. €

SUGGESTED TOUR:

Circled numbers correspond to numbers on the map.

Leave the **train station** ① and follow the map into the historic center. On your left is the Noord Hollands Kanaal, opened in 1825 to link Amsterdam directly with the North Sea. Much too shallow for large ships, it was later superseded by the larger North Sea Canal. A right turn on Paternosterstraat leads to the **Stedelijk Museum** (Municipal Museum) ② on the Canadaplein. Its exhibits, including a great deal of good art, artifacts, and historic objects, relate mainly to the town and surrounding areas; with a particular emphasis on the famous siege of 1573. Often overlooked by visitors, this museum can be a real find. If you come on a Friday morning in season you might want to return here after seeing the Cheese Market, which is all over by noon. **T**: *(072) 577-0737 or* **W**: *stedelijkmuseumalkmaar.nl. Open Tues.–Fri. 10–5, Sat.–Sun. 1–5.* €. *Museum Cards accepted.*

Turn left on Nieuwesloot and follow it to Waagplein, where the famous ***Cheese Market** is held on Fridays from 10 a.m. to noon, between mid-April and mid-September. A delightful anachronism in an age of efficient distribution, this staged event carries on traditions begun in the early 17th century, primarily for the benefit of the thousands of tourists who come to witness the spectacle. The cheeses, sold by auction to wholesale dealers, are mostly of the Goudse or Edam varieties, although usually without the red export covering that you are probably familiar with. Brought to the large open square by truck, they are tested by prospective buyers, who accompany their bids with brisk clapping of hands. Deals are consummated by handshakes, after which the real ceremony begins.

Cheese porters, wearing immaculate white uniforms and belonging to an ancient guild, carry heavy loads of the cheeses on traditional litters to the weigh-house *(Waag)*, where the totals are tallied, then to the purchasers' trucks. Working in pairs, they jog along with a peculiar gait to prevent spills. There are four

Alkmaar

300 Yards

N

Station

Scharloo

Geesterweg

Geestersingel

Helderseweg

Stationsplein

Stationstraat

Lindenlaan

Nassaulaan

Kennemer Singel

Geest

Gasthuisstraat

Paternosterstr.

NOORD HOLLANDS KANAAL

Heul

Koorstraat

Schoutenstr.

Hoogstr.

Doelenstraat

Konings Weg

Kanaal Kade

Noorder Kade

Nieuwesloot

Nieuwlandersingel

Oude Gracht

Laat

Breed Straat

Lange Straat

Zilverstr.

Ridderstr.

Payglop

Achterstr.

Pieterstr.

Kwakelkade

Boterstr.

Houttil

Waag Plein

Baangracht

Hofstr.

Info.

Voordam

Dijk

Mient

Ridtsevoort

Verdronkenoord

Laat

Fnidsen

Kooltuin

Achterweg

Wageweg

Frieseweg

Baan Singel

St. Annastr.

Randersdijk

←TO AMSTERDAM

Korte Vondelstr.

Bierkade

Kanaal Dijk

① ② ③ ④ ⑤ ⑥ ⑦ ⑧ ⑨

companies of porters, each with its own hat color, and each consisting of six porters, a weigher, and a foreman.

A good place to watch all of this activity is from the windows of the **Kaas Museum** (Cheese Museum), located upstairs in the weighhouse, or Waag ③. Originally built as a church in 1341, this magnificent structure was converted to its present use as early as 1582. The lovely Renaissance façade and ornate tower were added soon after that. A carillon plays between 11 a.m. and noon on market days, and jousting figures on horseback appear as a trumpeter blows a clarion call. Exhibits in the museum are concerned with both past and present methods of cheese production, with delicious samples on sale. **T**: *(072) 511-4284 or* **W**: *kaasmuseum.nl. Open April–Oct., Mon.–Sat. 10–4, opening at 9 on Fridays; and on Mon.–Fri. in winter. Museum Card accepted. €.*

Having tasted the cheese, you may be ready for the **National Beer Museum** *(Nationaal Biermuseum)* ④, just a few steps beyond the Waagplein. Housed in the former "De Boom" brewery, it traces the history of beer making throughout the ages. You can enjoy some of the liquid refreshment in the bar or at the adjoining canal-side café. **T**: *(072) 511-3801. Open April–Oct., Tues.–Fri. 10-4, Sat.–Sun. 1:30–4; Nov.–March, Tues.–Sat. 1–4. Museum Card accepted. €, beer extra.*

Cross a bridge to Voordam and stroll along the canal, possibly stopping at the unusual **Dutch Stove Museum** *(Nederlands Kachelmuseum)* ⑤. Yes, this exhibition is completely devoted to those wonderfully old-fashioned Dutch stoves. **T**: *(072) 515-9418. Open April–Oct., Fri. and Sun. noon–4; rest of year Sun. noon–4. €. Museum Cards accepted.*

Now follow the map through some of the most colorful streets in town. Along the way you will pass the 16th-century **Vismarkt** (Fish Market) ⑥, noted for its sculpted roof figures and old pump from 1785. Around the corner from this, at number 23 Mient, is a house whose gable displays Alkmaar's coat of arms— with the lions facing the wrong way as an insult to the town fathers.

Continue down Lange Straat, the main shopping street, to the **Stadhuis** (Town Hall) ⑦, a late Gothic structure begun in 1509.

Just a few more steps and you are at the **Grote Kerk** ⑧, a splendid Dutch Reform church dedicated to St. Laurens. Built between 1470 and 1516 in the Gothic style, it has a very impressive interior. The large organ in the nave dates from 1643, while the small one in the north ambulatory— from 1511—is the oldest still in use in Holland. Recitals are frequently held on Cheese Market days.

The route now wanders down to the old waterside ramparts, along which is the 18th-century **Molen van Piet** ⑨. Still grinding flour as it has for centuries, this ancient windmill may be visited. **T**: *(072) 511-2574. Open May–Sept., Fri. 10–5, also on Sat. in June–July.* A stroll through the park and a left turn over the bridge onto Geesterweg will return you to the station.

Texel

Lying just two miles off the shores of North Holland, the delightfully peaceful island of Texel is a rather unusual but highly enjoyable destination for a daytrip from Amsterdam. Much of it is devoted to nature reserves, especially for birds, and to raising the famous Texel sheep. There are, however, a few villages, of which the most interesting is Den Burg. You won't be alone there since its cafés and shops are popular with Dutch, German, and British vacationers, who mostly stay at the seaside resort of De Koog.

This is an especially nice place to explore by rented bicycle or by a combination of buses and walking. One day of its rural tranquillity makes a perfect breather in the middle of a hectic sightseeing schedule. There are absolutely no mandatory cultural sights, although the attractions do include a preserved old-time dwelling, a collection of antique farm implements, a maritime and beachcombers' museum, and a nature preserve.

Texel is the largest and southernmost of the West Frisian (or *Wadden)* islands, which stretch across the north coast of Holland all the way to Germany. Most of it is polder land, whose reclamation from the sea began as early as the 11th century. Visits to the wildlife sanctuaries must be arranged in advance. Information about this is available from the Texel tourist office in Den Burg. The name, incidentally, is pronounced as *Tessel.*

GETTING THERE:

Trains to Den Helder depart Amsterdam's Centraal Station at half-hour intervals, with the ride taking 75 minutes. From the station at Den Helder take an NZH bus number 33 to the ferry terminal and board the boat for the 20-minute ride to Texel. Return trains run until late evening, but note that the last boat is usually around 9 p.m.

By Car, the best route from Amsterdam is via the A-7 (E-22) motorway past Hoorn. Take the exit for Den Oever/Den Helder, following this to the ferry terminal *(veerhaven)* at Den Helder, about 80 km (50 miles) north of Amsterdam. Your car can be taken on the boat without delay, although you might prefer to park here and use buses or rental bicycles on the island.

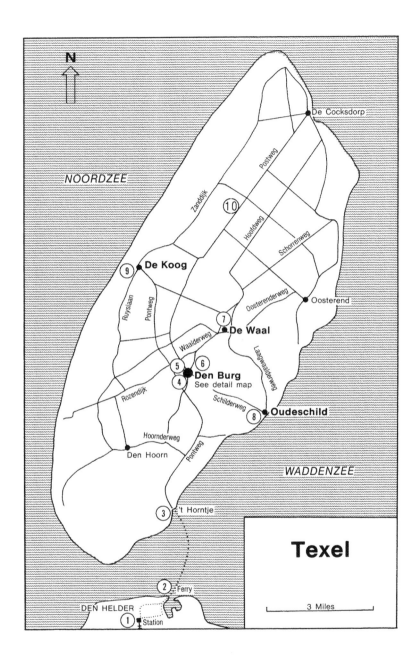

N

NOORDZEE

De Cocksdorp

Postweg

Zanddijk

⑩

Hoofdweg

Schorrenweg

⑨ **De Koog**

Ruyslaan

Pontweg

Oosterenderweg

Oosterend

⑦

Waalderweg

De Waal

Laagwaalderweg

⑤ ⑥

④ **Den Burg**

See detail map

Rozendijk

Schilderweg

⑧ **Oudeschild**

Hoornderweg

Den Hoorn

Pontweg

WADDENZEE

③ 't Horntje

Texel

② Ferry

3 Miles

DEN HELDER

① Station

TEXEL   70

PRACTICALITIES:

Fine weather is essential for this trip, which should be made between mid-May and mid-September. Most of the attractions are closed on Sundays, one on Saturdays, and one on Mondays.

The **Texel Ticket** is a one-day pass valid for all scheduled buses on the island. It is sold at bus stations, tourist offices, and by the drivers. €.

The **Texel Tourist Office** *(VVV),* **T**: (0222) 314-741 or **W**: vvv-texel.nl, is at Emmalaan 66, 3 blocks south of the bus stop in Den Burg. Ask about the **Texel Museum Combi-Card**, valid for all five museums on the island.

FOOD AND DRINK:

Snacks and drinks are available on the ferryboat. Besides several outdoor cafés, some places to eat are:

Bij Jef (34 Herenstraat in Den Hoorn) Gourmet-level dining on inspired cuisine, served in a stylish restaurant. Reserve. **T**: (0222) 319-623. €€€ and €€€+

Café De Smulpot (5 Binnenburg, in the center Den Burg) Specializes in Texel dishes, meat, and fish. **T**: (0222) 312-756. €€

De Lindeboom (14 Croeneplaats, 2 blocks north of the bus stop in Den Burg) A small hotel with a restaurant. **T**: (0222) 312-041. €€

De Twaalf Balcken (20 Weverstraat, 2 blocks southeast of the Oudheidskamer in Den Burg) A pub serving local specialties, grills, and vegetarian dishes. **T**: (0222) 312-681. X: Sun. € and €€

Vispaleis-Rokerij De Ster (13 Heemskerckstraat in Oudeschild) Fresh fish sandwiches, soups and the like, to eat on the spot or take out. **T**: (0222) 312-441. €

SUGGESTED TOUR:

Circled numbers correspond to numbers on the maps.

Arriving at the **Den Helder Train Station** ①, immediately board bus number 33, which is marked for "Texelse Boot." This will take you to the **ferry terminal** ②. Buy a round-trip ticket and board the ferry for the 20-minute ride to the Texel pier at **'t Horntje** ③. From there you can either board a bus marked for Den Burg or rent a bicycle and pedal your way, a level distance of four miles. Bikes are also available in Den Burg and elsewhere on the island. A **Texel Ticket** one-day bus pass, bought from the driver, will save you money.

*Den Burg is the main village on Texel and has neatly accommodated itself to the summer tourists with shops and outdoor cafés. On Mondays it is busy with a colorful open-air market. From its **bus stop** ④ it is only a short stroll south to the **Tourist Office** *(VVV)* ⑤, where you might want to ask about visiting a wildlife sanctuary or some of the other attractions not described here. Otherwise, continue on to the **Oudheidskamer** ⑥, an old 17th-century village house filled with folkloric antiquities—and one well worth a quick visit. **T**: *(0222) 314-956. Open April–Oct, Mon.–Fri. 10–12:30 and 1:30–3:30. €.*

TEXEL 72

An interesting walk or bicycle ride of less than a mile and a half can be made through the countryside to the farming hamlet of **De Waal** ⑦. Here, in a converted barn, you will find the **Agrarisch en Wagenmuseum** (Farm and Wagon Museum). All sorts of farm implements and wagons, from as far back as 1700, are displayed along with a rustic show narrating more than you ever wanted to know about Texel agriculture; truly a bucolic delight for some. **T**: *(0222) 312-951 or* **W**: *wagenmuseum.nl. Open Easter to mid-Oct, Mon. 1:30–5, Tues.–Fri. 10–5, Sat. 10–4, Sun. 2–4. Museum Card accepted.* €.

You may want to explore more of the island, especially if you've rented a bicycle or brought a car. Some nice destinations are:

Oudeschild ⑧, reached by bus from Den Burg, is a picturesque old fishing harbor. Be sure to visit its **Maritiem & Jutters Museum** (Maritime and Beachcomber Museum), a fascinating collection of junk washed up on the beach or salvaged from nearby wrecks, all set in a restored harbor scene with historic structures along with demonstrations of the old skills. **T**: *(0222) 314-956 or* **W**: *texelmaritem.nl. Open Tues.–Sun. 10–5, also on Mon. in July–Aug.* €.

De Koog ⑨ is Texel's seaside resort, where you'll find the usual amenities. It can be reached by bus from Den Burg or the ferry port, or by bike or car. Just south of this is **EcoMare**, a nature recreation center with live seals and displays of Texel's natural history, next to a pretty area for dune walks. There is also an interesting aquarium. **T**: *(0222) 317-741 or* **W**: *ecomare.nl. Open daily 9-5; last admission at 4:30.* €€.

Be sure to begin your return journey before the last ferryboat departs, usually around 9 p.m.

ADDITIONAL ATTRACTIONS:

The nearby **Texel Airport** ⑩ offers two more attractions, the first of which is the **Luchtvaart Museum Texel 1940–1945**. Airborne activities during World War II are remembered in this display of vintage aircraft and other artifacts. **T**: (0222) 311-689. Open Tues.–Sun. 11–5. €. Those interested in seeing the island from the air should contact **Texel Air** at **T**: (0222) 311-436 or **W**: paracentrumtexel.nl for a flight—or to try your hand at paragliding.

Leiden

Holland's first university was established at Leiden in 1575 and is still going strong. Especially renowned for its faculties of medicine and law, it remains the nation's most prestigious center of higher learning. With such a scholarly background, it is perhaps not surprising that the city possesses an exceptionally broad range of museums. These are, in fact, its major attraction to tourists. If you enjoy visiting museums, you will love Leiden.

Although thought by some to have Roman origins, Leiden was probably founded in the 12th century. Its prosperity dates from the 14th-century immigration of Flemish weavers who fled north to escape the plague. Another form of pestilence came in the form of the Spanish army, which besieged the city in 1574. Refusing to surrender, the population suffered terribly from hunger and disease before finally being rescued by William the Silent's naval forces sailing over a landscape flooded by cutting the dikes. The Spaniards retreated in such a hurry that, according to legend, they left behind an uneaten pot of beef stew. Quickly consumed by the starving citizens, this became the basis for the traditional Dutch dish of *hutspot.* The day of their salvation, October 3rd, is still celebrated with city-wide festivities. As a reward for their steadfast courage, William allegedly offered them a choice of tax relief or a university. Tax rates probably being lower in those days, they opted for the school.

Leiden is also noted as the birthplace of Rembrandt, Jan Steen, and several other famous painters. The Pilgrim Fathers, having fled England for Amsterdam, moved to the university town in 1609, where they lived until departing for the New World in 1620.

Holders of the economical Museum Card will be delighted to know that it is accepted at virtually all of Leiden's many great museums. This trip could easily be combined in the same day with one to Delft, described in a later chapter. There is direct train service between the two towns.

GETTING THERE:

Trains leave Amsterdam's Centraal Station very frequently for the 35-minute ride to Leiden. Return service operates until late evening, after which hourly trains run all night long.

By Car, take the A-4 highway past Schiphol Airport. Leiden is 40 km (25 miles) southwest of central Amsterdam.

PRACTICALITIES:

Avoid coming to Leiden on a Monday, when practically everything is closed. Most museums are open on Sundays and holidays after noon. October 3rd is the local festival day—expect all attractions to be closed.

The local **Tourist Office** *(VVV),* **T**: (0900) 222-2333 (toll call) or **W**: leiden.nl, is at 2d Stationsweg, a block south of the station. Ask them about boat trips on the canals, which depart from several points and last about an hour. Some other websites to check out are: **W**: leidenpromotie.nl for general tourist information, **W**: museumgroep.nl for local museums, and **W**: leiden.edu for the university.

FOOD AND DRINK:

Some good restaurant choices in the old part of town are:

Stadscafé Van der Werff (2 Steenstraat, 2 blocks south of the station) A grand old café and restaurant with excellent French-inspired food. **T**: (071) 513-0335. €€

Café Einstein (19 Nieuwe Rijn, below the Burcht) Light meals and drinks right on the canal. **T**: (071) 512-5370. €

Annie's Verjaardag (1a Hoogstraat, near the Burcht) Light lunches, salads, and sandwiches in a cellar down by the canal. **T**: (071) 512-5737. €

Soup Factory (Steenstraat, 3 blocks southeast of the station, near the Ethnology and Lakenhal museums) Thick, nourishing homemade soups. €

SUGGESTED TOUR:

Circled numbers correspond to numbers on the map.

From the **Train Station** ① walk straight ahead on Stationsweg until you get to a canal. On the right stands the first of Leiden's many museums. At this point you'll have to decide which of these interest you most, since you can't possibly see them all in one day without suffering a terminal case of cultural burnout. The **Rijksmuseum voorVolkenkunde** (Ethnology Museum) ② presents a sweeping survey of civilizations from outside the European world. Of particular interest here are the marvelous Buddhas from Japan; religious artifacts from Indonesia, Tibet, China, and elsewhere; houses and boats from the South Pacific; and displays on Native American, Mexican, and South American cultures. The main focus is, naturally, on the former Dutch colonies. **T**: *(077) 512-8437 or* **W***: rmv.nl. Open Tues.–Sun. 10–5. Museum Card accepted.* €€.

Continue down Steenstraat and follow the map across the canalized waters of the Rijn *(Rhine)* river, whose main flow is now to the south through Rotterdam. The lovely Rapenburg canal leads to what is perhaps Leiden's most outstanding museum, the:

*RIJKSMUSEUM VAN OUDHEDEN *(National Museum of Antiquities)* ③, **T**: (071) 516-3163 or **W**: rmo.nl/engels. *Open Tues.–Fri. 10–5, Sat.–Sun. and holidays noon–5. Museum Card Accepted. €€.*

Housing one of the major archaeological collections in Europe, the Oudheden gets off to an impressive start right in the entry hall with the entire Temple of Taffeh, donated in 1969 in recognition of Holland's role in the rescue of Nubian treasures threatened by the construction of the Aswan dam. Originally built in the 1st century AD, it was converted during the 4th century for the worship of Isis and later used as a Christian church. Other displays here are of equal caliber, covering Egyptian, Creek, Roman, and other eras of classical antiquity. The top floor is devoted to archaeology in the Netherlands, from prehistoric times through the Middle Ages.

Now cross the canal and wander down to the **Academie** ④, the main building of the university since 1581. Originally built as a church, it has a fine bell turret and now houses, among other things, the small **Academisch Historisch Museum**. Displays here all relate to the long history of the university. **T**: *(071) 527-7242. Open Wed., Thurs., and Fri., 1–5. Free.* Behind the building is one of the oldest botanical gardens in Europe, the **Hortus Botanicus.** A perfect place to relax, it was laid out in 1590 and features an extraordinary assemblage of plants and trees from all over the world, both outdoors and in greenhouses. Don't miss the historic Clusiusgarden, a re-creation of the original 16th-century garden. You can enter the gates at Rapenburg 73. **T**: *(071) 527-5144 or* **W***: hortus.leidenuniv.nl. Open daily in summer 10–6; Sun.–Fri. in winter 10–4. Museum Cards accepted. €.*

Now follow the map to the **Pieterskerk** ⑤, a large 15th-century church with a fine interior. Next to it is the **Jan Pesijnshofje**, a 17th-century almshouse built on the site of the home of John Robinson, the leader of the Pilgrims. A plaque in English explains all.

The route continues past the **Stadhuis**, or Town Hall, with an impressive restored façade of 1600 in the Dutch Renaissance style. Behind this, along the Nieuwe Rijn canal, a lively **outdoor market** is held on Wednesdays and Saturdays. Cross the unusual bridge and wander through some narrow streets to the **Burcht** ⑥, a 12th-century fortress atop a mound of Saxon or possibly Roman origin. It once guarded the confluence of the Old and New Rhine *(Rijn)* rivers, both of which have long since been turned into canals with most of the water diverted to the south. You can climb to the top of the citadel for a superb view of Leiden.

Return to Nieuwstraat and take a look at the **Hooglandse Kerk**, an imposing church from the 15th century. It contains the tomb of the heroic Mayor Van der Werff, who led the citizens during the terrible siege of 1574. According to legend, at one point the starvation became so bad that many wanted to surrender, but the mayor set an example by offering his own body as food. This was rejected, and relief came soon after.

Very close to this, at 9 Beschuitsteeg, is the small **Leiden American Pilgrim**

Leiden

N

400 Yards

TO AMSTERDAM
Station
Schuttersveld
Stationsplein
Stations Weg
Rijnsburger Singel
Mors Singel
Windmill
Lammer Markt
Lange Gracht
Binnenvestgracht
Steenstraat
Narmstr.
Morsstraat
Turfmarkt
Oude Singel
Oude Vest
Lange Mare
Caecilia Straat
Claren Steeg
Voldersgracht
Kort Galge
Gaige Water
Haarlemmer Straat
Apothekers Dijk
Van Der Werf Straat
Noordeinde
Boom Markt
Stille Rijn
Aal Markt
Oude Rijn
Groenhaven Gracht
Lange Brug
Bree Straat
Hooglandse Kerkgracht
Doelen Gracht
Rapenburg
Maarsmanstr.
Vismarkt
Witte Singel
Houtstr.
Rapenburg
Nieuwe Rijn
Botermarkt
Nieuwstr.
Hooi Gracht
Paterstraatje
Nieuwsteeg
Bree Straat
Kaiserstraat
Vliet str.
Doeza Straat
Rapenburg
Steenschuur
Lange Brug
Garen Markt
Korevaarstraat
Witte Singel
Boisotkade
Raam Steeg
Jan Van Hout Kade
Zoeterwoudse

1 2 3 4 5 6 7 8 9 10

Museum ⑦, which celebrates life among the Pilgrims in Leiden before they left for America in 1620. **T**: *(071) 512-2413. Open Wed.–Fri. 1–5, Sat. 10–5.–Sat. 1-5. €.*

Continue on through the old town, following the map to the **Boerhaave Museum** ⑧. Specializing in the history of science from a Dutch point of view, it displays a formidable collection of antique instruments and medical devices. Among the treasures are some wonderful skeletons in the Anatomical Theatre, scary electrostatic generators, and ancient microscopes. **T**: *(071) 521-4224 or* **W**:, *museumboerhaave.nl/english. Open Tues.–Sat. 10–5, Sun. and holidays noon–5. Museum Card Accepted. €€.*

Cross another canal and stroll over to Leiden's superb art gallery, the:

*STEDELIJK MUSEUM "DE LAKENHAL" ⑨, **T**: (071) 516-5360 or **W**: lakenhal.nl/en/. *Open Tues.–Fri. 10–5, Sat.–Sun. and holidays noon–5. Museum Card accepted. €. Additional charge for some shows. Gift shop. Café.*

Erected in 1640, this former cloth weavers' guildhall now exhibits 16th- and 17th-century paintings by such local artists as Jan Steen and Lucas van Leyden. Native-son Rembrandt is represented by an early work. There are also period room settings, sculptures, decorative art works, armor, tiles, and historical artifacts on display.

On the way back to the station you'll pass a windmill used as the **Molenmuseum "De Valk"** ⑩. Built in the mid-18th century, it has been restored to its condition of about 1900, and may be visited. **T**: *(071) 576-5353 or* **W**: molenmuseum.myweb.nl. Open *Tues.–Sat. 10–5, Sun. and holidays 1–5. Museum Card accepted. €.*

ADDITIONAL ATTRACTION:

If you're not yet tired of museums, you might want to try this one, located off the map just two blocks southwest of the train station:

NATURALIS (National Museum of Natural History) ⑪, 2 Darwinweg. **T**: (071) 568-7600 or **W**: naturalis.nl. *Open Tues.–Sun. 10–6, daily in July–Aug. Museum Card Accepted. €€.*

Thoroughly modern, this intriguing museum uses the latest techniques to show off its vast collection of flora and fauna, the creation of Earth and its inhabitants, and many treasures from around the world—including the million-year-old Java Man.

The Hague

(Den Haag or 's-Gravenhage)

Amsterdam is officially the capital of the Netherlands, but the government and all that goes with it sits at The Hague, making this in fact the real capital. With more than 60 foreign embassies, three royal palaces, and the parliament, The Hague has an air of international sophistication that sets it apart from every other Dutch city. Actually, "Europe's largest village" did not become a city at all until as late as the 19th century, when King Louis Bonaparte granted it a charter. Don't look for canals here—there are precious few—or typical Dutch charm, for this is first and foremost a place of stately elegance.

The Hague began as a hunting preserve for the counts of Holland. During the mid-13th century a proper castle was built, around which the town developed. Since then it has always been a favored venue for diplomatic negotiations, and as such, naturally developed a sense of luxurious living and recreation. This character remains with it today and is enhanced by a multitude of excellent museums, cultural institutions, exclusive shops, and fine restaurants.

By limiting the number of museums and other attractions you visit, it is quite easy to combine this trip in the same day with one to Scheveningen. This is actually a part of The Hague although it lies a few miles to the northwest. Described in the next chapter, the Scheveningen trip includes a famous seaside resort, several superb museums, and the ever-popular Madurodam "Holland in a Nutshell."

GETTING THERE:

Trains depart Amsterdam's Centraal Station very frequently for the 45-minute ride to Den Haag HS *(Hollands Spoor Station)*, the mainline station for The Hague. Here you transfer to another frequently running train for Den Haag Centraal *(CS)* Station, a quick 2-minute ride. There is also local train service direct from Amsterdam Centraal to Den Haag Centraal. Return service operates until late evening, after which hourly trains run all night long.

By Car, take the A-4 highway past Schiphol Airport and Leiden. The Hague (Den Haag or 's-Gravenhage) is 55 km (34 miles) southwest of Amsterdam.

GETTING AROUND:

You may want to use the trams or buses for part of this trip, especially if you combine it with the trip to Scheveningen in the next chapter. Public transit maps, information, and passes are available at the HTM office (**T**: (070) 384-8666 or **W**: htm.net) at Den Haag Centraal Station, or at the tourist office.

PRACTICALITIES:

Some of the best sights in The Hague are closed on Mondays. Check the descriptions of the attractions you'd like to visit to determine which day of the week to come on. Good weather is important if you intend to combine this trip with the one to Scheveningen.

The local **Tourist Office** *(VVV)* is next to Den Haag Centraal Station, **T**: (0900) 340-3505 (toll call), **W**: vvv.denhaag.nl

FOOD AND DRINK:

The Hague is well endowed with restaurants and cafés, especially in the expensive category. Some outstanding choices are:

PUCK (33 Prinsestraat, a block north of the Grote Kerk) Incredibly inventive fusion dishes; a treat for the adventurous. **T**: (070) 427-7649. X: Sun., Mon. €€€

Le Bistroquet (98 Lange Voorhout, 4 blocks west of Centraal Station) A small and very popular French restaurant with indoor or outdoor tables. **T**: (070) 360-1170. X: Sat. lunch, Sun., holidays. €€€

Restaurant Le Haricot Vert (9a Molenstraat, near the Royal Palace) Classic French cuisine in a 17th-century house. **T**: (070) 365-2278. X: Mon. €€ and €€€

't Goude Hooft (13 Groenmarkt, 3 blocks west of the Binnenhof) Noted for its Old World atmosphere and traditional Dutch cuisine. **T**: (070) 346-9713. €€

Babbelen (1b Kettingstraat, 2 blocks east of the Grote Kerk) High quality creative cuisine in a friendly setting. **T**: (070) 362-2431. €€

See You at Noon (14 Korte Houtstraat, 2 blocks southeast of the Mauritshuis) A huge variety of tasty sandwiches. X: Sun. €

Prins Taveerne (165 Noordeinde, between Paleis Noordeinde and Panorama Mesdag) Light lunches, salads, and sandwiches in a classic café. **T**: (070) 364-3875. €

SUGGESTED TOUR:

Circled numbers correspond to numbers on the map.

Begin at The Hague's modern **Centraal Station** ① and follow the map a short distance to the 17th-century:

THE HAGUE 80

The Ridderzaal in the Binnenhof

*MAURITSHUIS ②, **T**: (070) 302-3435 or **W**: mauritshuis.nl. *Open April–Aug., Mon.–Sat. 10–5, Sun. 11–5; Sept.–March, Tues.–Sat. 10–5, Sun. 11–5. Museum Card accepted. €€. Possible surcharge for special exhibitions.*

The Mauritshuis is a Dutch Renaissance mansion that today houses one of the best small art museums in the world. Officially known as the Royal Picture Gallery *(Koninklijk Kabinet van Schilderijen)*, its collection includes quite a few of Rembrandt's most notable works such as the*Anatomy Lesson of Dr. Tulp,* along with world-famous masterpieces by Frans Hals, Jan Steen, Vermeer, Van Dyck, Hans Memling, both Cranachs, and many others. Be on the lookout for the unusual *Adam and Eve in Paradise,* a joint collaboration of the talents of both Rubens and Bruegel.

From here it is only a few steps into the **Binnenhof** ③, the courtyard of the former castle and now the seat of the Dutch parliament. Long the center of political life in the Netherlands, it may be seen on guided tours that begin in the basement of the 13th-century Ridderzaal (Knights' Hall), a stunning medieval structure with conical towers, in the center of the courtyard. The tour, given in English and other languages, begins with an audiovisual show and a visit to the Ridderzaal upstairs, where joint sessions of the parliament are held, and where its

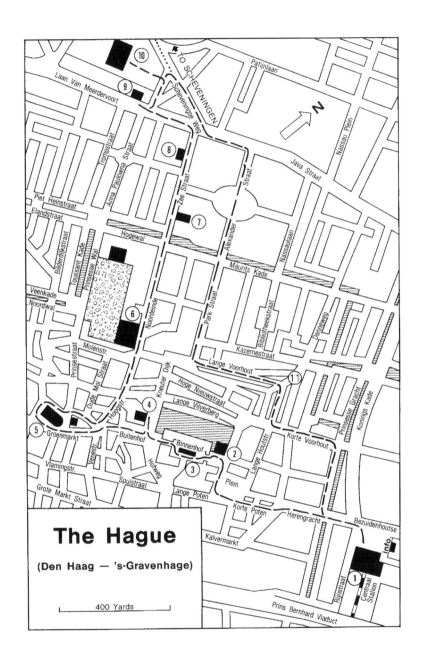

The Hague

(Den Haag — 's-Gravenhage)

400 Yards

members are addressed by the Queen. It then moves on to one of the two chambers of the States General, as the parliament is called, as the workings of Dutch democracy are explained as you. **T**: *(070) 364-6144. Open Mon.–Sat. 10–4, last tour at 3:45. Closed public holidays and when special meetings take place. Tours: €. Advance bookings are recommended to avoid a wait. The Exhibition Hall is free and open the same times.*

Exit from the west end of the Binnenhof and turn right to the 14th-century **Gevangenpoort** (Prison Gate) ④, which once guarded the entrance to the counts' castle. Used as a prison until the 19th century, it now houses an interesting museum of hideous torture instruments. You can visit its dark cells on conducted tours that depart frequently from the small entrance to the left. **T**: *(070) 346-0861 or* **W**: *gevangenpoort.nl. Open Tues.–Fri. 10–5, Sat.–Sun. noon–5. Museum Cards accepted. €.*

Stroll through the Buitenhof, originally the outer courtyard of the castle and now a lovely square. A few steps beyond this is the **Grote Kerk** ⑤, also known as Sint Jacobskerk. Dating from the 14th century, and later modified, this is the most interesting church in The Hague. Its 320-foot tower was first built in 1423 and has long been a major landmark. Step inside to see the remarkable stained-glass windows, the pre-Reformation pulpit, and the coat-of-arms of the Knights of the Golden Fleece.

The route now leads up the pedestrians-only Noordeinde to an equestrian statue of William the Silent. Opposite this is the **Paleis Noordeinde** ⑥, an old royal palace erected in 1553 as a private mansion. Recently renovated, it is presently used as Queen Beatrix's office and so cannot be visited. You can, however, enjoy the garden behind it and take a look at the royal stables, which remain in use.

Continue up Noordeinde, here lined with expensive shops, and cross a section of the old town moat, now used as a canal. Zeestraat leads to the **Panorama Mesdag** ⑦. Billed as the world's largest panoramic painting, this huge circular canvas is among the few survivors of a once-popular genre. It was created in 1881 by the local artist H. W. Mesdag and depicts the nearby seaside town of Scheveningen (see next chapter) as it looked at that time. The illusion of reality is so startling that it makes you feel you have stepped back in time to another era. **T**: *(070) 310-6665 or* **W**: *panorama-mesdag.nl. Open Mon.–Sat. 10–5, Sun. and holidays noon–5. €.*

Just up the street is the **Museum for Communication** *(Museum voor Communicatie)* ⑧, where you can explore the history of communications in the Netherlands. It is also noted for its large collection of stamps from all over the world, and for its special exhibitions. **T**: *(070) 330-7500 or* **W**: *muscom.nl. Open Mon.–Fri. 10–5, Sat.–Sun. and holidays noon–5. Museum Cards accepted. €€.*

The same artist who created the Panorama Mesdag, a man of independent means, lived in a mansion just around the corner. This is now the **Rijksmuseum H. W. Mesdag** ⑨, which specializes in works of The Hague School and the French

Barbizon School of the 19th century. Although the museum is a bit strange and the manner of display terribly old fashioned, the art itself is superb and offers an unusual opportunity to see minor works by such famous artists as Delacroix, Corot, Millet, Courbet, Rousseau, and Daubigny. There are, of course, quite a few paintings by Mesdag himself. **T**: *(070) 362-1434. Open Tues.–Sun. noon–5. Museum Cards accepted. €.*

The enormous **Peace Palace** *(Vredespaleis)* ⑩ is only a few steps away. Built as a headquarters for international agencies that promote world peace, it was financed by a donation from Andrew Carnegie. Ironically, its completion date of 1913 nearly coincides with the outbreak of World War I. Since the 1920s it has been occupied by the International Court of justice (a UN agency) and the Academy of International Law, as well as by the Permanent Court of Arbitration. Its pompous interior is heavily decorated with gifts from nations all over the world, and is worth seeing for the rich diversity it offers. **T**: *(070) 302-4242 or* **W***: vredespaleis.nl. Generally open Mon.–Fri. 10–4, closing at 3 from Oct.–May. Tours at 10, 11, 2, 3, and 4. They last about 50 minutes, with museum about 90 minutes. Advance reservations are needed,* **T**: *(070) 302-4137 or E-mail: guidedtours@planet.nl. Check with the tourist office for current information as there are no tours when the court is in session. €.*

From here you may want to continue with the **Scheveningen** daytrip described in the next chapter, as you are practically there. To do this, just board northbound tram number 7 or 8 at the stop opposite the Peace Palace. Otherwise, you can return to the center of The Hague by following the route on the map, or by taking southbound tram number 7 to Den Haag Centraal Station or tram number 8 direct to Den Haag HS Station.

On the way back, you might want to stop at one more attraction. If you have ever been intrigued by the impossible creations of the 20th-century Dutch artist M.C. Escher, whose bizarre world may have you questioning reality itself, be sure to visit the ***Escher in het Paleis** exhibition. Located in the former **Royal Palace** ⑪ on Lange Voorhout, it features not only those original works that have been reproduced so widely for the last half-century or so, but also computer animations and virtual reality installations that will further twist your mind. **T**: *(070) 338-1120 or* **W***: escherinhetpaleis.nl. Open Tues.–Sun. 11–5. €€.*

Scheveningen

The popular seaside resort of Scheveningen is actually a part of The Hague, but is located a few miles from the city center and has enough sights of its own to keep you busy for an entire day. Its name is so difficult to pronounce correctly that during World War II it was used as a test to separate the genuine Dutch from German infiltrators.

Scheveningen began as a small fishing village in the 14th century, although only a little of that atmosphere survives today. It became popular as a resort in the early 1800s and by the end of the century was a favored meeting place for European society. Today, its restored ambiance, and its casino and pier, are once again attracting crowds of vacationers. To round things out, this trip includes several attractions in the northern part of The Hague as well as the world-famous Madurodam, a miniature slice of Holland that delights young and old alike.

This trip can easily be combined in the same day with one to The Hague, described in the last chapter. Doing this will cut down the amount of time that can be spent seeing the sights, but will still be very enjoyable.

GETTING THERE:

Trains leave Amsterdam's Centraal Station very frequently for the 45-minute ride to Den Haag HS *(Hollands Spoor Station),* the mainline station for The Hague. From the front of the station take tram number 9 in the direction of Scheveningen. Return service operates until late evening. If you combine this trip with one to The Hague you should follow the directions at the end of the previous chapter.

By Car, follow the directions to The Hague in the previous chapter and park near Centraal Station, from which you can take tram number 1, 7, or 9 to Scheveningen.

GETTING AROUND:

Unless you drive to each attraction, you will need to use the trams for parts of this trip. Information, maps, and passes are available from the HTM offices at the train stations or at the tourist office. You can, of course, just ask the conductor and pay as you board.

PRACTICALITIES:

This trip should really be made in the summer, and only on a fine warm day at that. Some of the museums are closed on Mondays, while Madurodam is open daily all year round. The casino is open daily and requires that you be "smartly dressed," whatever that means.

The **Tourist Office** *(VVV)* in Scheveningen is located at 1134 Gevers Deynootweg, near the casino, or you can inquire at the office next to Den Haag Centraal Station. **T**: (0900) 340-3505 (toll call) or **W**: scheveningen.nl/gb/

FOOD AND DRINK:

Some choice restaurants are:

Radèn Mas (125 Gevers Deynootplein, near the casino) Indonesian specialties. **T**: (070) 354-5432. €€ and €€€

Golden Duck (29 Dr. Lelykade, on the inner harbor) Chinese cuisine. **T**: (070) 354-1095. X: Tues. €€

La Galleria (105 Gevers Deynootplein, near the casino) A full range of Italian dishes, indoors or out. **T**: (070) 352-1156. €€

In addition, there are plenty of inexpensive snack bars and fast-food outlets along the waterfront and near the casino.

SUGGESTED TOUR:

Circled numbers correspond to numbers on the map.

Begin your tour by boarding tram number 9 from the front of **Den Haag HS** *(Hollands Spoor)* **Station**, the mainline station for The Hague, in the direction of Scheveningen. If you are starting from downtown The Hague you should board tram number 7 from Centraal Station instead, and if you are continuing from the Peace Palace at the end of the last trip you can take number 7 from the stop opposite the palace.

Get off the tram at the Congresgebouw stop at the intersection of Johan de Wittlaan. From here it's a short walk to the museum complex on Stadhouderslaan:

*HAAGS GEMEENTEMUSEUM ①, **T**: (070) 338-1111 or **W**: gemeente museum.nl. *Open Tues.–Sun. 11–5. Museum Card accepted. €€. Possible surcharge for special exhibits.*

The Haags Gemeentemuseum is the city's municipal museum and specializes in modern art, the applied arts, musical instruments, and costumes. It has the world's largest collection of works by Piet Mondriaan (including his famous *Victory Boogie Woogie*) as well as paintings by such 19th- and 20th-century luminaries as Monet, Jongkind, Millet, Sisley, Courbet, Van Gogh, Picasso, and Leger. The musical instruments are from all over the world and date from as far back as the 15th century. Among the applied arts exhibits are period room settings

NORTH SEA

Strandweg

Gevers Deynootweg

Dr. Lelykade

West Duin Weg

Doornstr.

Franken Slag

F. Hendrik Laan

Staten Laan

Tram #10

Johan De Witt Laan

Prof. B.M. Telders Weg

Scheveningse Weg

Juliaan Kokstr.

Kerkstr.

Tram

Badhuiskade

Stevin Straat

Zwolsestraat

Nieuwe Parklaan

Haringkade

Badhuisweg

Doorniksestr.

Pompstations Weg

Tram #1, #9

Nieuwe Parklaan

Tram #7, #8

L. Scheveningse Weg

MADURODAM

Jacob Cats Laan

Kerkhof Laan

Waalsdorper Weg

Peace Palace

Laan Van Meerdervoort

Stadhouders Laan

Tram

Zeestraat

Javastraat

Tram #9

Raam Weg

THE HAGUE

Noordeinde

Konings Kade

Tram

info.

TO DEN HAAG HS STATION

Centraal Station

info.

Scheveningen

See detail map
of The Hague

500 Yards

N

and objects from every corner of the planet, from the prehistoric to the present. Allow plenty of time for a visit.

Adjacent to this, and sharing a common entrance, is the:

MUSEON ②, **T**: (070) 338-1338 or **W**: museon.nl. Open *Tues.–Sun. 11–5.Fri. 10-5, Sat.-Sun. and holidays noon-5. Museum Card accepted. €€. Reduced combo ticket with Omniversum, below, available.*

This thoroughly contemporary science museum uses the latest techniques to cover no less a subject than man's life on Earth and beyond. Its dazzling displays and audiovisual shows are great fun to experience, especially for children, but they can also exhaust you.

Just around the corner is the spectacular **Omniversum** ③, a "space theater" in which the audience sits under a dome, almost completely surrounded by multiple film projections. The shows vary, but their theme is always one of science and discovery. This is a very popular attraction and fills up quickly, so it is best to make reservations by phone or by stopping in before visiting the previous two museums. **T**: *(0900) 666-4837 (toll call) or* **W**: *omniversum.nl. Open Mon. 9:30–3, Tues.–Wed. 9:30–5, Thurs.–Fri. 9:30 a.m.–10 p.m., Sat.–Sun. 10 a.m.–10 p.m.€€.*

From the front of the municipal museum you can board tram number 10 to the **Scheveningen Harbor** *(Haven)* ④, the end of the line. This is where the original fishing village began in the 14th century. Although the harbor is still busy with fishing and shipping activities, very little of its old-time atmosphere survives today. The waterfront along Dr. Lelykade is noted for its fine seafood restaurants. You might want to visit the **Marine Biological Museum** *(Zeemuseum)* ⑤, with its specimens of marine life from all the seven seas. **T**: *(070) 350-2528. Open Mon. 10–4, Tues.–Sat. 10–5, Sun. 1–5. Museum Card accepted. €.*

Now follow the map to the Strandweg, a promenade along the edge of the beach, and continue towards the pier. Along the way there are many snack bars and other seaside diversions, including the **Scheveningen Sea Life Centre** where you can walk through a transparent tunnel under a huge aquarium filled with exotic creatures. **T**: *(070) 355-8781 or* **W**: *sealife.nl. Open daily 10–7, remaining open until 8 in July–Aug. €€.*

The **Casino** ⑥ is housed in a strikingly modern structure opposite the historic Kurhaus, an enormous heap of fanciful architecture dating from 1885. If you'd like to try your luck at roulette, blackjack, punto banco, slots or other games, are 18 or older, have your passport in hand, and are "smartly dressed," this is the place. There's also food, beverages, and various entertainments. **T**: *(070) 306-7777 or* **W**: *hollandcasino.nl. Open daily 1:30 p.m. to 3 a.m. Closed May 4 and Dec. 31. Admission €€.*

The **Pier** ⑦ juts out into the North Sea just beyond this. Equipped with the usual fun and games as well as an observation tower and a bungy jump for the fearless, it is open daily with a small admission charge. Heading back inland, you might want to visit the **Scheveningen Museum** ⑧ at Neptunusstraat 92. Life in the old fishing village is re-created here with room sets, costumes, model ships, and fishing artifacts. **T**: *(070) 350-0830. Open Tues.–Sat. 10–5, Sun. 1–5. Museum Card accepted. €.*

From the front of the casino at Gevers Deynootplein you can take tram number 1 or 9 to what is undoubtedly one of Holland's greatest tourist attractions. Whatever you do, don't miss a visit to the magical:

*__*MADURODAM__ ⑨, **T**: (070) 416-2400 or **W**: madurodam.nl. *Open daily April–June 9–8; July–Aug. 9 a.m.–10 p.m.; Sept.–March 9–6. Last admission one hour before closing. €€€, includes guidebook. All profits go to charity. Gift shop. Restaurants.*

About 150 of Holland's most outstanding buildings have been reproduced as 1/25th-scale models and laid out as a miniature city over a five-acre site. Not only are they amazingly well detailed, but many of them provide action as well. Trains run along two miles of track, tiny cars speed down highways, boats move through the harbor, airliners taxi on the tarmac, and windmills turn in the breeze. There are sound effects, too, with music coming from within the churches, the barrel organs, and the street fairs. At night it becomes a different world when over 50,000 lights come on. Now, you may think that this is just for kids, but in fact most of the people who come to Madurodam are adults—and even the most skeptical of them love it!

From here you can take tram number 9 back to either Den Haag Centraal or Den Haag HS (mainline) station.

A Small Corner of Madurodam

Trip 12

Delft

L ong famous for its distinctive blue porcelain, historic Delft is among the best preserved and most picturesque places in Holland. Its lovely old buildings and tree-shaded canals make it everything a Dutch town should be, a scene right out of a painting by Vermeer. That renowned 17th-century artist was in fact born in Delft, and lived and died there. Another celebrated resident was William the Silent, in some ways the father of modern Holland, who was murdered there in 1584.

Settled since at least the 11th century, Delft received its charter in 1246. Trade grew with the development of a harbor on the Maas River, a short distance away in what is now Rotterdam. A great fire in 1536 almost totally destroyed the town, but it was soon rebuilt. The manufacture of porcelain brought about a great prosperity that lasted until the late 18th century. Later revived, this industry today plays only a minor role in the town's economy.

As you will quickly discover, Delft is very popular with tourists. Fortunately, most of them never get beyond the pottery shops in the market place, leaving the tranquil streets and narrow canals there for you to enjoy in peace. This trip could be combined in the same day with one to Leiden, described in an earlier chapter. There is direct train service between the two towns.

GETTING THERE:

Trains depart Amsterdam's Centraal Station frequently for the 55-minute ride to Delft Centraal. A local *(stoptrein)* runs at half-hour intervals and goes directly there, while the express (IC) trains require a change at Den Haag HS Station. Return service operates until late evening.

By Car, take the A-4 highway southeast to Den Haag, followed by the A-13 into Delft. The total distance from Amsterdam is 58 km (36 miles).

PRACTICALITIES:

Most of the museums are closed on Mondays, and the main churches are not open to tourists on Sundays. A colorful outdoor market is held on the Markt every Thursday from 9 a.m. until 5 p.m., and there is a fascinating flea market along the canals on Saturdays from mid-April through September.

The local **Tourist Information Point** *(TIP)*, **T**: (0900) 515-1555 (toll call) or **W**: delft.nl, is at 4 Hippolytusbuurt, 2 blocks northwest of the Markt.

FOOD AND DRINK:

Delft has an unusually broad range of restaurants and cafés, mostly geared to the tourist trade. Among the better choices are:

Prinsenkelder (11 Schoolstraat, by the Prinsenhof Museum) Elegant French-inspired dining, indoors or out. Reservations preferred, **T**: (015) 212-1860. X: Sat. lunch, Sun. €€€

Le Vieux Jean (3 Heilige Geest Kerkhof, by the Oude Kerk) Classic cuisine in a small, intimate restaurant. **T**: (015) 213-0433. X: Sun., Mon. €€€

Stadscafé de Waag (11 Markt, in the Waag) An atmospheric place for light lunches, *broodjes,* cheeses and even full meals. **T**: (015) 213-0393. X: Sun., Mon. € and €€

Kleyweg's Stads-Koffyhuis (133 Oude Delft, near the Oude Kerk) A popular spot for light lunches, pancakes, sandwiches, snacks and the like. Dine indoors or out, or on the moored terrace boat. **T**: (015) 212-4625. X: Sun. €

Stads Pannekoeckhuys (113 Oude Delft, near the Oude Kerk) 90 different varieties of pancakes, indoors or out by the canal. **T**: (015) 213-0193. X: Mon. €

Locus Publicus (67 Brabantse Turfmarkt, 3 blocks south of Nieuwe Kerk) All kinds of sandwiches and beers, in a pub with outdoor tables in summer. **T**: (015) 213-4632. €

Stationsrestauratie (in the station) Convenient and inexpensive dining. **T**: (015) 212-5334. €

SUGGESTED TOUR:

Circled numbers correspond to numbers on the map.

It is an easy and rather pretty walk from the **Train Station** ① to the market square *(Markt),* a busy place lined with outdoor cafés and shops. Just follow the map. At its west end stands the imposing **Town Hall** *(Stadhuis)* ②, a Renaissance structure built in 1618. The tower dates from the 14th century and was part of the original building that was destroyed in the great fire of 1536. It may be possible to step inside to view the richly decorated council chamber and wedding hall. **Horse carriage rides** depart from the outside of the building for a short trot around the town. **T**: *(015) 256-7828 or* **W**: *delftsepaardentram.nl. Operates daily May–Oct. Rides €.*

The east end of the square is dominated by the:

*NIEUWE KERK *(New Church)* ③, **T**: (015) 212-3025 or **W**: nieuwekerk-delft.nl. *Open April–Oct, Mon.–Sat. 9–6; rest of year, Mon.–Sat. 11–4. Tower same times and prices, but closes an hour earlier. €, includes Oude Kerk, below.*

This Gothic church, despite its name, is not all that new, having been built between 1384 and 1496. Its tower — all 365 feet of it — may be climbed for a fine

Delft

300 Yards

DELFT 92

view, and contains a noted 17th-century carillon that serenades the square below. Step inside to see the magnificent mausoleum of Holland's greatest hero, William the Silent, who was assassinated in Delft in 1584. In the vaults below (not open to the public) lie the remains of more than 40 other members of the royal House of Orange, including Queen Wilhelmina, who died in 1962. Other features of the church include some fine stained-glass windows and an exhibition on royal funerals.

The walk now leads around the rear of the church, passing a small canal, a remarkably picturesque little bridge, and some gorgeous houses. Turn left on Voldersgracht, a narrow lane alongside an equally narrow canal. On Saturdays in summer a **flea market** is held here, where you can have fun bargaining for all kinds of junk and perhaps a few treasures. Some of the 17th-century façades along the street are interesting, notably that at number 6, as is the former meat market *(Vleeshal),* decorated with animal heads, at the west end. The **Waag** ④, a former weigh house built in 1770, was once the guildhall of the gold and silversmiths, and today serves as a small theater.

Continue on, following the map, to the:

*OUDE KERK *(Old Church)* ⑤, **T**: (015) 212-3015 or **W**: oudekerk-delft.nl/eng/. *Open April–Oct., Mon.–Sat. 9–6; Nov.–March, Mon.–Sat. 11–4. €, includes Nieuwe Kerk, above.*

The tower of this 13th-century Gothic church leans precariously, but since it hasn't toppled over yet it is presumably safe to enter for a look at the tombs of several national heroes. Among these are memorials to the great artist Johannes (Jan) Vermeer (1632–1675) and the scientist Anton van Leeuwenhoek, who is reputed to have invented the microscope. While inside, be sure to take a look at the strangely carved 16th-century pulpit and the modern stained-glass windows depicting recent Dutch history.

Now stroll over to the:

*PRINSENHOF MUSEUM ⑥, **T**: (015) 260-2358. *Open Tues.–Sat. 10–5, Sun. and holidays 1–5. Museum Card accepted. €.*

The Prinsenhof Museum is housed in a 15th-century convent that was once the residence of William the Silent. It was also the scene of his assassination, and the bullet marks are still there on the wall at the foot of the stairs. The museum that now occupies the premises is mostly devoted to the struggle for Dutch independence from Spain and also has exhibits relating to the royal House of Orange-Nassau, which has supplied Holland with its monarchs down to the present. It is well worth a visit for its elegantly decorated interior, as well as for its splendid paintings, tapestries, silverware, and porcelain.

Just across the square from this is the **Nusantara Museum** ⑦, which specializes in ethnology with an emphasis on Indonesian artifacts. **T**: *(015)*

260-2358 or **W**: *nusantara-delft.nl. Open Tues.–Sat. 10–5, Sun. and holidays 1–5. Museum Card accepted. €.*

Another nearby museum is the **Huis Lambert van Meerten** ⑧. This is of great interest for its collection of antique Delft tiles, beautiful room settings, and lovely old furniture. **T**: *(015) 260-2358 or* **W**: *lambertvanmeerten-delft.nl. Open Tues.–Sat. 10–5, Sun. and holidays 1–5. Museum Card accepted. €.*

Before heading back to the train station, you might want to take a **boat ride** through the canals of Delft. These depart from Koornmarkt, near Peperstraat, on the way to the next attraction. *Rondvaart Delft,* **T**: *(015) 212-6385 or* **W**: *rondvaartdelft.nl. Operates mid-March through Oct., daily 10–6. Rides last 45 minutes. €€.*

Close to the boat dock, facing the canal, is the small **Museum Tétar van Elven** *(9).* Named after a very obscure 19th-century painter who lived here, it is noted more for its stylish atmosphere than for the art it contains. **T**: *(015) 212-4206, Open mid-April through Oct., Tues.–Sun. 1–5. €.*

Continuing down the same street will bring you to the **Armamentarium** ⑩, a 17th-century warehouse that now houses the **Legermuseum** (Dutch Military Museum). Military buffs will enjoy the weapons on display here, ranging from ancient times to the present—along with paintings, uniforms, and displays on the House of Orange. **T**: *(015) 215-0500 or* **W**: *legermuseum.nl. Open Mon.–Fri. 10–5, Sat.–Sun. and holidays, noon–5. Museum Card accepted. €.* From here it is only a short stroll back to the station.

ADDITIONAL ATTRACTIONS:

Delft is world-famous for its traditional porcelain objects, many of which are sold—at rather steep prices—in the shops on and around the Markt. If you'd like to watch porcelain being handcrafted in the old manner, you can do so at two factories just outside the town center or a smaller one near the Markt, all of which also make sales. They are:

Royal Delftware De Porceleyne Fles at Rotterdamseweg 196, just south of the town. Founded in 1653, this is the most famous of the makers. Ask at the tourist office for current travel information. **T**: *(015) 251-2030 or* **W**: *royaldelft.nl. Open daily 9–5, closed Sun. in Nov.–March. Tour €.*

De Delftse Pauw at Delftweg 133, just north of the town. Again, inquire at the tourist office for travel details. **T**: *(015) 212-4920 or* **W**: *delftsepauw.com. Open April–Oct., daily 9–4:30; rest of year Mon.–Fri. 9–4:30, Sat.–Sun. and holidays 11–1. Free.*

Aardewerkatelier de Candelaer 14 Kerstraat, near Markt. This small studio invites visitors to watch the process of making Delftware. **T**: *(015) 213-1848 or* **W**: *candelaer.nl. Open Mon.–Fri. 9–5:30, Sat. 9–5, Sun. 10–5:30. Free.*

Rotterdam

O n May 14th, 1940, Rotterdam was practically bombed out of existence in an unprovoked attack on a neutral nation by Hitler's *Luftwaffe.* What rose from the smoldering ashes after the war was an aggressively modern city totally unlike anything else in Holland. Located at the mouth of the Rijn *(Rhine)* and Maas *(Meuse)* rivers, it is now the world's largest port, with harbor facilities extending some 20 miles west to the open sea. Having a population of over a half-million, it is also the second-largest city in the Netherlands.

Like Amsterdam, Rotterdam began in the late 13th century when a dam was erected across one of its rivers, in this case the Rotte. Full recognition as a city came in 1340, and soon after that a canal was dug, attracting commercial traffic away from nearby Delft—whose ancient harbor is now a part of Rotterdam. The war with Spain ultimately resulted in the transfer of overseas trade from Antwerp to the Dutch port. Since then, industrial development along the entire length of the Rhine has assured Rotterdam's position as the main transit point for Europe.

This intriguing daytrip covers an unusually wide variety of attractions, ranging from a cruise through the busy harbor to a look at one of the world's best art museums, and from a ride to the top of a soaring "space tower" to a stroll through the delightfully quaint village of Delfshaven.

GETTING THERE:

Trains depart Amsterdam's Centraal Station very frequently for Rotterdam's Centraal Station (CS), a ride of about one hour. Some of these go by way of Haarlem and others via Schiphol Airport. Return service operates until late evening, followed by hourly departures all night long.

By Car, take the A-4 highway southwest past Schiphol Airport to Den Haag, then the A-13 into Rotterdam. The total distance is 75 km (47 miles).

GETTING AROUND:

You may want to use public transportation for part of this trip, especially if you go all the way out to Delftshaven. Maps and information are available at the tourist office, or you might check with the transit agency, **RET**, at **T**: (0900) 9292 (toll call) or **W**: ret.rotterdam.nl.

PRACTICALITIES:

Nearly all of the museums are closed on Mondays and on April 30th (Queen's Day). The harbor cruise operates frequently from April through October, but only a few times a day during the rest of the year. Good weather is essential for enjoyment of this trip, as much of it is out of doors. The city **Tourist Office** *(VVV),* **T**: *(010) 414-0000 or* **W***: Rotterdam.info,* is at Coolsingel 67, a few blocks southeast of Centraal Station.

FOOD AND DRINK:

Rotterdam has an enormous range of restaurants in all price ranges, with the majority concentrated between Centraal Station, the Maritime Museum, and the Boymans-Van Beuningen Museum. You will also find many snack shops and fast-food outlets in the center of town. Some good restaurant choices are:

Brasserie LaVilette (160 Westblaak, 3 blocks northeast of the Boymans-Van Beuningen Museum) Superb French cuisine. **T**: (010) 414-8692. X: Sun. €€€

Old Dutch (20 Rochussenstraat, 1 block north of the Boymans-Van Beuningen Museum) A luxurious Dutch restaurant with atmosphere. **T**: (010) 436-0344. X: Sat. lunch, Sun., holidays. €€€

Engels Restaurants (45 Stationsplein, by the Centraal Station) Four restaurants in one: Brasserie Engels (Dutch/French), Beefeater (English), Tokaj (Hungarian), and Don Quijote (Spanish). **T**: (010) 411-9550. €€

Brasserie Boijmans (in the Boymans-van Beuningen Museum) Light lunches, snacks and refreshments in a stylish setting. **T**: (010) 441-9422. X: Mon. €

Museum Café (in the Maritime Museum) Lunches or just snacks, with a view of the harbor; outdoor terrace in summer. **T**: (010) 413-2680. X: Mon. €

SUGGESTED TOUR: *

Circled numbers correspond to numbers on the map.

Leave the **Centraal Station** ① and follow the map through the heart of modern Rotterdam to the first attraction. You could also get there by taking the subway *(Metro)* to the Beurs stop. Some of the streets along the way are reserved for pedestrians and form an attractive shopping area, while the broad Coolsingel is a major tree-lined boulevard with cafés. Along the way you will pass the **City Hall** *(Stadhuis),* a pre-war building that survived the bombing, as well as the World Trade Center and the Stock Exchange *(Beurs).* Streets on either side of these lead into modern shopping malls.

The **Schielandshuis** ② is the only 17th-century structure in central Rotterdam to have made it through the war intact. Today its elegant interior houses the city's **Historical Museum**, with exquisite period room settings, displays of the fine and applied arts, porcelain, costumes, toys, household equipment, and many other interesting subjects. There is also an audio-visual show on the bombardment of Rotterdam, plus a shop and a rather good restaurant. **T**: *(010) 217-6767 or* **W***: hmr.rotterdam.nl. Open Tues.–Fri. 10–5, Sat.–Sun. and holidays 11–5.*

They accept the Museum Card. €.

From here it is only a short stroll to the stunning:

MARITIME MUSEUM PRINS HENDRIK *(Maritiem Museum)* ③, **T**: (010) 413-2680 or **W**: maritiemmuseum.nl. *Open Tues.–Sat. 10–5, Sun. and holidays 11–5. Also open on Mon. in July–Aug. and on school holidays. Museum Card accepted. €. Gift shop. Café.*

Located on the edge of Rotterdam's original man-made harbor, changing exhibitions here cover the entire history of Holland's maritime exploits, with many models, artifacts, and a real periscope you can peer through. Part of the museum is outdoors on the waterfront and consists of floating ships, cranes, a lighthouse, and so on. A special treat here is to board the 19th-century warship *Buffel and* explore its fascinating interior. In the open area next to the museum is the famous *City Destroyed* monument of 1953, expressing the anguish of the 1940 bombing.

Now follow the map to one of the finest art museums in all of Europe, the:

*BOYMANS—VAN BEUNINGEN MUSEUM ④, **T**: (010) 441-9475 or **W**: boijmans.nl. *Open Tues.–Sat. 10–5, Sun. and holidays 11–5. Museum Card accepted. €€. Possible surcharge for special exhibitions. Gift shop. Café.*

The Boymans-van Beuningen Museum is unusual in that it covers a vast sweep of art over a long period of time, from medieval paintings to the most modern industrial design. You can't possibly see it all in a day, but a quick tour of the highlights can be done in an hour or so. The older part of the museum houses, naturally, the older art, while the modern Action is devoted to contemporary works. A very few of the artists represented are Rembrandt, Jan Steen, Memling, Bruegel, Dürer, Titian, Rubens, Van Dyck, Van Gogh, Picasso, Ernst, Dali, Magritte, Warhol, and Stella. Don't miss this.

The route leads through Museum Park to the **Kunsthal Rotterdam** ⑤, a superb contemporary venue for changing exhibitions covering all of the main art forms and cultural/historical themes, both intimate and monumental. **T**: *(010) 440-0300 or* **W***: kunsthal.nl. Open Tues.–Sat. 10–5, Sun. and holidays 11–5. €€.*

Now wander over to the **SPIDO landing stage** ⑥, where you can board a boat for a delightful ***harbor cruise**. Several tours are offered, ranging from 75 minutes to over two hours in length. All of them are exciting and give you close-up views of ships from all over the world, along with oil refineries and other harbor installations. A running commentary is made in English, and explanatory brochures are available. Snacks and drinks are sold on each of the boats. **T**: *(010) 275-9988 or* **W***: spido.nl. The 75-minute cruise departs at least every 45 minutes between 9:30 a.m. and 5 p.m., daily from April through October. During the rest of the year the service is less frequent, and only on Thurs.–Sun. Fares for the 75-minute cruise are €€; a combo ticket that*

Rotterdam

M = Subway stop

500 Yards

TO AMSTERDAM

Weena

Beukelsdijk

Burgemeester Meineszlaan

Gerrit van de Lindestr.

Vierambachtsstr.

Mathenesserlaan

Jan Muldersstraat

Gerrit

Hooidrift

Mathenessedijk

Aelbrechtskade

Heenraadssingel

Graaf Florisstraat

Duivenvoordstr.

Henegouwerlaan

Bloemstr.

Drievriendenstr.

West

2e Middellandstraat

1e Middellandstraat

's Gravendijkwal

Baljonstr.

Adriaanstr.

Van Speykstr.

Josephstr.

Claes de Vrieselaan

Schietbaanlaan

Mathenesserlaan

Heenraadssingel

Mathenesserlaan

Claes de Vrieselaan

Nieuwe Binnenweg

N

Nieuwe Binnenweg

Schonebergerweg

Heenraadssingel

Rochussenstraat

M

's Gravendijkwal

Schiedamseweg

M

Rochussenstraat

M

G.J. de Jonghweg

Schans

Voorhaven

Coolhaven

Coolhaven

Pieter de Hoochweg

Spanjaardstr.

⑨

Willem Buytewechstr.

Hudsonplein

Havenstraat

Westzeedijk

⑧ Euromast

Parkhaven

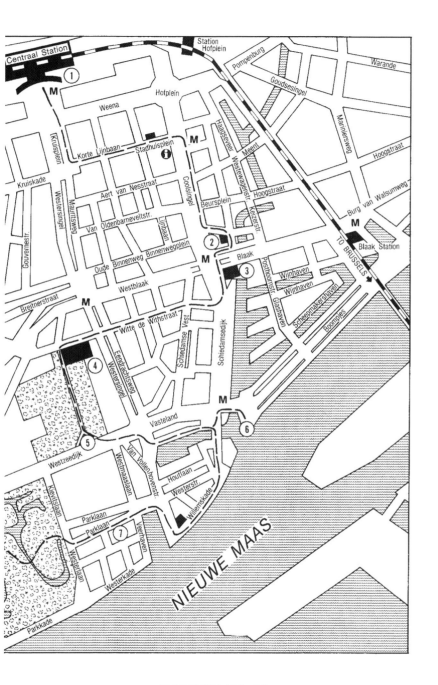

ROTTERDAM 99

includes the Euromast (below) is €€€.

Back on dry land, follow the map along the harbor and turn left on Parklaan. If you're up to it, the **Netherlands Tax and Customs Museum** *(Belasting—Douane Museum)* ⑦ has as its fascinating subject the history of taxation, complete with a section on smuggling. At least the entry won't tax you —it's free. **T**: *(010) 440-0200 or* **W**: *belasting-douanemus.nl. Open Tues.–Sun. 11–5. Closed Mon. and major holidays.*

Now follow the map through a lovely park to Rotterdam's great landmark, the ***Euromast** ⑧. Built in 1960 and later made even higher, this tower offers spectacular panoramic views of the harbor and city. An elevator takes you up to the 340-foot level, where you will find an observation platform and two restaurants. If that isn't high enough, you can board the revolving Space Cabin and blast off on a slightly unnerving ride spiraling up the Space Tower to the 600-foot level, after which a retro-rocket returns you to the platform. **T**: *(010) 436-4811 or* **W**: *euromast.com. Open April–June and Sept., daily 10–7; July–Aug., Tues.–Sat. 10 a.m.–10:30 p.m., Sun.–Mon. 10–7; Oct.–March, daily 10–5. €€.*

So far, nearly everything in Rotterdam has been modern. If you'd like to see a picturesque old corner of town that survived the war, you should head on to **Delfshaven** ⑨. Once the port for Delft, it was connected to that town by a canal dug as early as 1389. This is where the Pilgrim Fathers departed for the New World in 1620, making stops in England en route. You can get there either by walking the somewhat dreary one-mile distance, or by taking a tram from the corner near the Euromast. The tiny harbor with its restored windmill has been preserved for posterity and still looks much as it did in centuries past. A branch of the Rotterdam Historical Museum called **De Dubbelde Palmboom**, located at Voorhaven 12, is devoted to regional life in times past, shown on a series of interesting and atmospheric displays. **T**: *(010) 476-1533 or* **W**: *hmr. rotterdam.nl. Open Tues.–Fri. 10–5, Sat.–Sun. and major holidays 11–5. Museum Card accepted. €.* Close to it and facing the water is the **Oude Kerk**, a 15th-century church where the Pilgrim Fathers held their last service before departing on the *Speedwell,* which they left for the *Mayflower* in Plymouth. A plaque in English recalls the story.

The quickest way back to Rotterdam's Centraal Station is to take the subway *(Metro)* from the Delfshaven stop, changing to the northbound line at Churchillplein-Beurs.

Dordrecht

Historically one of the most important places in Holland, Dordrecht survives as a pleasant seafaring town with a strong sense of the past. Not many foreign tourists come this way, but those who do are in for a special treat as they wander through its ancient streets.

Dordrecht, or *Dordt,* as it is often called, is strategically located at what is possibly the busiest river junction in Europe. Continuous boat traffic from both the Rijn *(Rhine)* and the Maas *(Meuse)* passes by its atmospheric old harbor on the way to the North Sea. At one time this made it the major shipping center of the Netherlands, but that commerce declined as the port of Rotterdam grew.

No one knows for certain just how old Dordrecht really is, although records suggest that it was destroyed by Norsemen in 837. A castle was built here in the 11th century and the town received its charter in 1220. The disastrous flood of 1421, in which over 10,000 people drowned, took a heavy toll on Dordrecht and forever changed its landscape. Rebuilt, it was again devastated, this time by fire, in 1457. Holland's independence had its earliest beginnings here in 1572 when a meeting of the provinces declared their freedom from the king of Spain and elected William the Silent as their leader.

GETTING THERE:

Trains leave Amsterdam's Centraal Station quite frequently for Dordrecht, a run of between 80 and 95 minutes. The slower ones go by way of Haarlem, while the faster IC expresses run via Schiphol Airport. Return service operates until late evening.

By Car, take the A-4 southwest past Schiphol Airport to Den Haag, then the A-13 to Rotterdam, followed by the A-20 and the A-16 into Dordrecht. The total distance is 95 km (59 miles).

PRACTICALITIES:

Avoid going to Dordrecht on a Monday, when its attractions are closed.

The local **Tourist Office** *(VVV),* **T**: (078) 632-2440 or **W**: vvvdordrecht.nl, is just north of the train station. You might want to ask them about **boat trips** and **horse carriage rides** — and about getting to **Kinderdijk**, an outlying area noted for its many working windmills.

FOOD AND DRINK:

Marktzicht (17 Varkenmarkt, near the foot of the old harbor) Noted for its seafood and French cuisine. Open evenings. **T**: (078) 613-2584. X: Sun., Mon. €€€

Jongepier (upstairs at 8 Groothoofd, near the Groothoofdspoort) Café dining with a view. **T**: (078) 639-0855. €€

Eetcafé Bacchus (12 Blaupoortsplein, 2 blocks southwest of the Museum Mr. Simon van Gijn) An inviting place for simple Dutch food. **T**: (078) 614-9722. € and €€

De Stroper (1 Wijnbrug, halfway between De Hof and the Groothoofd-spoort) A good value in seafood, right by the water. **T**: (078) 613-0094. X: weekend lunch. € and €€

Crimpert Salm (5 Visstraat, just south of the Town Hall and Visbrug) A good value in French-inspired meals. **T**: (078) 614-5557. X: Sun. lunch. € and €€

Stationsrestauratie (in the train station) Basic food at a minimal price. **T**: (078) 613-3244. €

SUGGESTED TOUR:

Circled numbers correspond to numbers on the map.

Leave the **Train Station** ① and follow the map past the tourist office, across a canal, and through the Statenplein shopping area to the **Dordrechts Museum** ②. Located in a former asylum, this is an unusually good local art museum, whose collections focus mainly on paintings by Dordrecht artists from the 17th century to the present and include works by Albert Cuyp, Ferdinand Bol, and Ary Scheffer. It is also well known for its temporary exhibitions, particularly of recent art. *T: (078) 648-2148. Open Tues.–Sun. 11–5. Museum Cards are accepted, but there may be an extra charge for special shows. €.*

Now return to Statenplein and turn right on Hofstraat. This leads to a quiet and rather picturesque little courtyard called **De Hof** ③, where Holland's independence began in 1572 when a meeting of the provinces was held in the *Statenzaal* on the southeast side.

From here, take the narrow passageway through to Voorstraat and turn right. The *Muntpoortje,* at number 188, dates from 1555 and is all that remains of the one-time Dutch mint. Make the next left to a bridge, but don't cross it. Instead, go down the steps to a path on the Wijnhaven harbor and continue along the water's edge to the Boombrug, a small drawbridge.

Just beyond this is the **Groothoofdspoort** ④, a domed structure rebuilt in 1618 that was once the main gate to the town. Pass through it for a marvelous view of the confluence of the Oude Maas (which carries the waters of the Rhine), the Beneden Merwede, and the Noord rivers. Well over a thousand ships a day pass this point, and you can sit down and leisurely watch their progress from one of the outdoor cafe tables. **Boat trips** are also available here.

Now follow the map along Kuipershaven, a waterfront street lined with some strangely attractive old warehouses. Cross a bridge separating the two

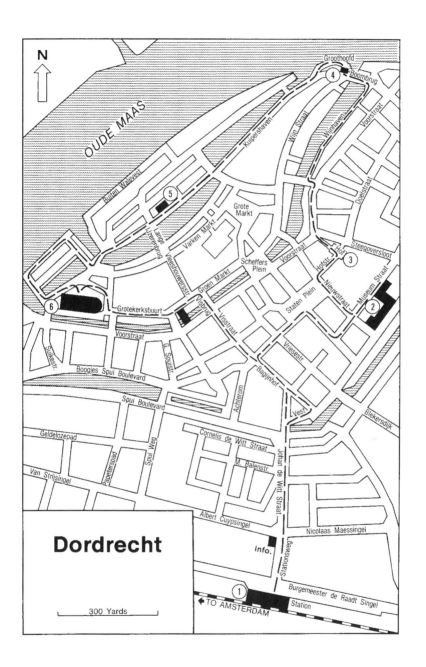

N

OUDE MAAS

Groothoofd
④ Boombrug

Kuipershaven

Wijn Straat

Wijnhaven

Voorstraat

Buiten Walevest

⑤

Doelstraat

Grote Markt

Varken Markt

Lange IJzerenbrug

Vleeshouwersstr.

Steegoversloot

Scheffers Plein

Voorstraat

Hof

③

Museum Straat

Hofstr.

Green Markt

Nieuwstraat

⑥

IJsbrug

Staten Plein

②

Grotekerksbuurt

Visstraat

Voorstraat

G. Spuistr.

Sluiskestr.

Boogjes Spui Boulevard

Vriesestr.

Baginhof

Spui Boulevard

Achterom

Vest

Blekersdijk

Geldelozepad

Spui Weg

Cornelis de Witt Straat

Papeterspad

Van Strijsingel

M. Balenstr.

Johan de Witt Straat

Albert Cuypsingel

Nicolaas Maessingel

Dordrecht

info.

Stationsweg

300 Yards

① ← TO AMSTERDAM Burgemeester de Raadt Singel

Station

DORDRECHT 103

harbors and stroll over to the ***Museum Mr. Simon van Gijn** ⑤. This is truly a gem of a provincial museum, one that should not be missed by any visitor to Dordrecht. Housed in an 18th-century mansion owned by a banker and art collector named van Gijn, its period rooms contain a fabulous collection of furnishings, tapestries, musical instruments, paintings, and the like. Be certain to visit the Toy Pavilion in the attic, where a huge assortment of children's toys are on display. **T**: *(078) 639-8200. Open Tues.–Sun. 11–5. Museum card accepted. €.* Just east of this, on the same street, the **Museum 1940–1945** concerns itself with the impact that World War II had on the region. **T**: *(078) 613-0172. Open Tues.–Sat. 10–5, Sun. noon–5. €.*

Continue along the inner harbor past the unusual Lange IJzerenbrug pedestrian bridge to the **Grote Kerk** ⑥. One of the largest and finest churches in Holland, it was begun in the 13th century but mostly dates from the 15th. Its 230-foot tower, leaning slightly to one side, is topped off with some oddly incongruous clocks and may be climbed for a magnificent view of the countryside. Step inside to see the beautiful 16th-century choir stalls, which predate the Reformation. Other features include the stained-glass windows at the east end, which depict the flood of 1421, the fire of 1457, and an historic battle scene. The white marble pulpit with its wooden canopy is outstanding, as is the 17th-century organ. An 18th-century memorial plaque in the north choir aisle is dedicated to a British officer and tells his story in English. **T**: *(078) 614-4660. Church and tower open to tourists April–Oct., Tues.–Sat. 10:30–4:30, Sun. noon–4. Church free, tower €.*

Return to the station via the route on the map, passing the **Town Hall** *(Stadhuis)* and the quaint Visbrug (bridge) along the way.

NEARBY SIGHT:

*Kinderdijk, midway between Dordrecht and Rotterdam, has the greatest concentration of working windmills in Holland. All 19 of them are operated on Saturday afternoons from 2–5 in July and August, but at least one is open to tourists on Mondays through Saturdays from April through September, from 9:30 to 5:30. **T**: *(078) 613-2800. €.* Boat trips past the mills are available. Ask at the tourist office for details on how to get there and for opening times.

Middelburg

Middelburg is an exceptionally pleasant and beautifully restored old town that offers its many visitors a chance to enjoy a different aspect of Holland. Throughout the centuries its low-lying, isolated location near the North Sea has exposed it to catastrophic flooding, but this has finally been checked by the completion of the Delta Project.

As its name suggests, Middelburg is in the middle of something. That something is Walcheren, a one-time island now connected to the mainland as a result of land reclamation projects. Much of it lies at or below sea level and is protected by dikes. It is the most historic and certainly the most interesting part of Zeeland, a watery province of which Middelburg is the capital. The island lies at the mouth of the Schelde estuary and therefore controls shipping into the Belgian port of Antwerp. This fact has always made it strategically important, especially during World War II when Middelburg was practically destroyed by the invading Germans. To flush them out, the Allies, in 1944, resorted to bombing the dikes, thus flooding the island for over a year. Tragedy struck again during the great floods of 1953, but since then all of the damage has been repaired and effective measures taken to prevent the sea from ever again claiming victory over the land.

Although this is a rather long daytrip, it is a thoroughly enjoyable one and should be particularly attractive to those traveling with a railpass.

GETTING THERE:

Trains depart Amsterdam's Centraal Station at hourly intervals for the approximately 2½-hour run to Middelburg. A change at Roosendaal is necessary for some of these trains. Return service operates until mid-evening.

By Car, take the A-4 southwest past Schiphol Airport to Den Haag, then the A-13 into Rotterdam. Crossing the river via the Maas Tunnel, take the A-29 south almost to Willemstad. From there, the N-59 and N-256 leap between the islands on long bridges to Goes, after which you follow the A-58 into Middelburg. The total distance from Amsterdam is about 192 km (120 miles).

PRACTICALITIES:

Most of the attractions are open daily between the beginning of April and late October. During other months you should check the times given for each sight to determine which day is best. An especially colorful **outdoor market** is held on Thursdays on the Markt. Good weather will make this trip much more enjoyable.

For tourist information, visit the **Tourist Shop Middelburg** at Markt 65, **T**: (0118) 674-300 or **W**: visitmiddelburg.nl

FOOD AND DRINK:

A popular tourist destination, Middelburg abounds in places to eat and drink. Some choices are:

Het Groot Paradijs (13 Damplein, 1 block east of the Abbey) French-inspired food in a classic old house. Dress well and reserve. **T**: (0118) 651-200. X: Sat. lunch, Sun., Mon. €€€

Peper & Zout (8 Lange Noordstraat, by the Town Hall) All kinds of seafood in lovely surroundings, and a good value. **T**: (0118) 627-058. X: Wed., weekend lunch. €€

Eetcafé Desafinado (Koorkerkstraat 1, just south of the Abbey) Dutch and French favorites served with a cool jazz theme. **T**: (0118) 640-767. €€

De Huifkar (19 Markt, on the square) Both a café and a restaurant, with outdoor tables on the terrace. **T**: (0118) 612-998. X: Sun. € and €€

De Kabouterhut (8 Oosterkerkplein, by the East Church) A large variety of pancakes and simple Dutch fare. **T**: (0188) 612-276. X: Mon. in winter. €

Stationsrestauratie (in the train station) Good, inexpensive food. €

SUGGESTED TOUR:

Circled numbers correspond to numbers on the map.

Leave the **Train Station** ① and follow the map past a canal and a small harbor to the **Markt** (Marketplace) ②. Lined with outdoor cafés and restaurants, this busy square is a delightful place to sit down for lunch or at least a drink. Rides through the town in a horse-drawn coach are available here at modest cost.

Completely dominating the north side of the square is the fantastically ornate **Town Hall** *(Stadhuis),* an almost magical vision of Gothic splendor. Begun in 1452, its façade is decorated with statues of the counts and countesses of Zeeland. The soaring clock tower with its needlelike pinnacles was added in the 16th century, and later additions include the wings to the rear. What is truly interesting about this magnificent structure is that it exists at all, as it was almost totally destroyed by German bombing in 1940. This is in fact a meticulous reconstruction started immediately after the last war. *Conducted tours of its interior are held Mon.–Sat. year round, and also on Sun. from April–Oct. at times posted on the sign outside.* **T**: *(0118) 674-452 or* **W**: *middelburg.nl. €.*

Now continue down Nieuwe Burg, a pedestrians-only shopping street, to

The Town Hall in the Markt

Middelburg's landmark **Abbey Tower** ③. Affectionately known as *Lange Jan* (Long John), this 280-foot octagonal belfry was originally built in the early 14th century. After a long history of fires, it collapsed during the German air raid of 1940 and wrecked the three churches at its base. Rebuilt after the war, it may be climbed for a stunning view that takes in virtually all of Walcheren. **T**: *(0118) 612-525. Open April–Oct, Mon.–Sat. 11–4, Sun. and holidays noon–4. €.*

 The tower is part of an **Abbey** *(Abdij)* founded in the early 12th century. Rebuilt several times after that, it was secularized in 1574 and thereafter used as government offices, although the now-Protestant churches remained. The entire complex has been reconstructed after being destroyed in World War II. Its three adjacent churches *(Abdijkerken)* are internally connected and are definitely worth visiting. Enter the 16th-century **Nieuwe Kerk** to see its splendid 17th-century organ, then continue through to the **Wandel Kerk**, which miraculously survived the bombs. Beyond an enormous arch is the base of the tower, and near this a doorway leads into the 14th-century **Koor Kerk**, where you can take a look at the famous 15th-century organ.

 A passageway just outside the Koor Kerk opens into the **Abbey Courtyard** *(Abdijplein)*. Guided tours of the entire abbey complex are available here in season, or you can just explore them on your own.

Another Abbey feature is the **Historama**, a multimedia show celebrating local history. **T**: *(0188) 626-655. Open year round, Mon.–Sat. 11–5, and also on Sun. from April–Oct. noon–5. €.*

Also within the Abbey Courtyard is the fascinating:

*ZEELAND MUSEUM *(Zeeuws Museum)* ④, **T**: (0188) 626-655 or **W**: zeeuwsmuseum.nl. *Closed for restoration until 2006. Opening times and admission charge to be announced. Museum Cards accepted.*

Here you can probe the history and folklore of the Zeeland district from prehistoric to modern times. Some of its more interesting displays include the skeleton of a mammoth, tapestries depicting the war with Spain, and local costumes in authentic room settings.

Now follow the map to the **Miniatuur Walcheren** ⑤, a huge outdoor model where the features and buildings of Walcheren have been reduced to a scale of 1:20. The concept is similar to that of the much larger Madurodam near Scheveningen, but here the subject is limited to the immediate region rather than encompassing all of Holland. **T**: *(0188) 612-525 or **W**: miniatuurwalcheren.nl. Open mid-March to mid-July and Sept.-Oct., daily 10–6; mid-Aug. through Aug., daily 10–7. Café. €€.*

Continue on to the **Oostkerk** (East Church) ⑥, an octagonal domed church finished in 1667. This is one of the first churches in Holland to have been built specifically for the Protestant faith. A short stroll brings you to the small harbor, on whose south side is the atmospheric **Kuiperspoort** ⑦, once the headquarters of the Coopers' Guild. Amble through the narrow alleyway behind it to examine the picturesque 16th-century warehouses. From here, you can return to the station via the route on the map, or head back to the marketplace for some well-deserved refreshments. If you do this, you may also want to see a bit of the west end of Middelburg by following the map to the **Kloveniersdoelen** ⑧. This early-17th-century structure was built as a meeting place for the Arquebus civic guard and later used by the East India Company. It is now occupied by a center for new music. The return route, by way of Lange Viele and Pottenmarkt, features a number of inviting bars and outdoor cafés.

Trip 16

*Utrecht

One of the easiest and most satisfying daytrips you can take from Amsterdam is to Utrecht, a fair-sized city noted for its engaging combination of the past and the present. The area near its train station is as contemporary as any place on Earth, yet step beyond this and you enter a world of preserved charm. Its picturesque sunken canals are unique, while some of its museums are among the most enjoyable in the nation. Home to Holland's largest university, Utrecht is alive with a youthful spirit.

The Romans built a fortification here around AD 47 to guard their crossing point on what was then the Rhine River. A town developed around this, and a church was built as early as AD 500, from which Christianity spread throughout the Netherlands. During the Middle Ages, Utrecht was frequently the residence of the Holy Roman emperors. In 1589, it was the setting for the Union of Utrecht, a pact that united the northern provinces against Spain. The troubled times that followed were finally resolved by the signing of the Treaty of Utrecht in 1713, ending the War of the Spanish Succession.

GETTING THERE:

Trains depart Amsterdam's Centraal Station at very frequent intervals for the 30-minute run to Utrecht's Centraal Station (CS). Return service operates until late evening, with reduced service all night long.

By Car, Utrecht is 35 km (22 miles) southeast of Amsterdam via the A-2 highway to the Utrecht-West exit. Convenient parking is available around the Hoog Catharijne complex.

PRACTICALITIES:

Avoid going to Utrecht on a Monday, when many of its attractions are closed.

The local **Tourist Office** *(VVV),* **T**: (0900) 128-8732 (toll call) or **W**: Holland.com/Utrecht/gb, is at Vinkenstraat 19, 2 blocks east of the Hoog Catharijne shopping center adjoining the station.

FOOD AND DRINK:

The city offers a wide choice of restaurants and cafés, especially around the Hoog Catharijne and the Oude Gracht Canal. Some choices are:

Bistro Chez Jacqueline (4 Korte Koestraat, a block north of the Hoog Catharijne, Vredenburg exit) Dutch and Continental cuisine; outdoor tables in summer. **T**: (030) 231-1089. €€ and €€€

Polman's Huis (2 Keistraat, 2 blocks northeast of the Domkerk) French-inspired fare in the old-fashioned setting of a grand café. **T**: (030) 231-3368. X: Sun. € and €€

Oudaen (Oudegracht 99, 2 blocks east of the Hoog Catharijne, Vredenburg exit) Traditional cuisine in an ancient hall, with home-brewed beer. **T**: (030) 231-1864. € and €€

Café le Journal (Neude 32, near the Town Hall) A grand café with light meals. **T**: (030) 236-4839. €

Oude Muntkelder (Oude Gracht 112, on the canal near the Town Hall) A large, popular spot for Dutch-style pancakes. **T**: (030) 231-6773. €

De Werfkring (123 Oude Gracht, on the canal near the Town Hall) Noted for its vegetarian food and young crowd. **T**: (030) 231-1752. X: Sun., holidays. €

De Soepterrine (40 Zakkendragerssteeg, 2 blocks east of the Hoog Catharijne, Vredenburg exit) Soups and salads for a hearty, healthy lunch; all squeezed into a tiny restaurant. **T**: (030) 231-7005. €

SUGGESTED TOUR:

Circled numbers correspond to numbers on the map.

Utrecht's **Centraal Station** ①, one of the busiest in Europe, is connected to the immense Hoog Catharijne complex. This climate-controlled indoor city-within-a-city, embracing some 180 shops plus theaters, restaurants, cafés, offices, a hotel, and even apartment houses, was built in the late 1970s. Spanning the streets below, it can be somewhat confusing to negotiate although there are floor plans every-where. Just follow the signs through it to Clarenburg, descend the escalators, and make your escape onto Lange Elisabeth Straat.

Make a right on Mariastraat and follow the map to the fascinating:

*NATIONAAL MUSEUM VAN SPEELKLOK TOT PIEREMENT (National Mu-seum from Musical Clock to Street Organ) ②, **T**: (030) 231-2789 or **W**: museumspeelklok.nl. *Open Tues.–Sat. 10–5, Sun. noon–5. Hourly tours. Museum Card accepted.* €€.

Located in the Buurkerk, a former church dating in part from the 13th century, this is one of the most utterly joyful museums anywhere—and a favorite with children. Its displays of mechanical musical instruments from the 18th to the 20th centuries, some of which are quite huge, don't just sit there to be admired. They make music, lots of very loud barrel-organ music, much to the delight of everyone present.

Utrecht

N

300 Yards

UTRECHT 112

UTRECHT 113

The Domtoren from the Town Hall Area

Now continue around to the **Vismarkt** ③, a market place on the Oude Gracht canal, where fishermen have been selling their catch since the 12th century. Note how the canals of Utrecht are sunk well below the level of the streets, with old warehouse entrances opening directly onto them. Many of these have been turned into restaurants, with outdoor café tables facing the water.

A left on Servetstraat brings you to the **Domtoren** ④, at 367 feet the tallest church tower in Holland. It was completed in 1382 and stands apart from the cathedral of which it was a part. The nave of the cathedral collapsed during a storm in 1674 and was never replaced, although the rest of the church is still there. The tower, luckily, can be climbed for a wonderful ***view**. **T**: *(030) 233-3036. Accompanied ascents on foot: Mon.–Fri. 1–3, Sat. 10–5, Sun. noon–5. €€.*

As you stroll across Domplein you can see the outline of the former nave, indicated by colored paving stones. The present **Domkerk** occupies the choir and transepts of the one-time cathedral, built between 1254 and 1517 on the site of a Roman settlement.

Adjoining the church is the 15th-century **Kloostergang** (Cloister) ⑤, a spot of unusual beauty and tranquility. Amble through it to a picturesque old lane behind the church, named Achter de Dom. The route on the map now takes you down some interesting streets, along the Oude Gracht canal, and through a park to Utrecht's famous:

*CENTRAAL MUSEUM ⑥, **T**: (030) 236-2362 or **W**: centraalmuseum.nl. Open *Tues—Sun. 11–5. Museum Cards accepted. €€.*

Housed in a former convent, the museum's displays cover a wide scope of interests, ranging from 20th-century Dutch art to period room settings to an unearthed 12th-century Viking ship. Upstairs, there is an excellent collection of Utrecht Old Master paintings, applied arts, and historical artifacts. Ask about visits to the nearby **Rietveld-Schroder House**, an early 20th-century triumph of the *De Stijl* movement, and a real treat for anyone with an interest in architecture, design, and décor. Reservations for this are needed, and there is a substantial extra charge.

Return toward the center of town on Lange Nieuwstraat and turn right on Zuilenstraat to the:

*RIJKSMUSEUM HET CATHARIJNECONVENT ⑦, **T**: (030) 231-7296 or **W**: catharijneconvent.nl. Open *Tues.–Fri. 10–5, Sat.–Sun. and holidays noon–5. Museum Cards accepted. €€.*

The Rijksmuseum het Catharijneconvent is located in a former 16th-century convent, whose entrance is at Nieuwe Gracht 63. Its modern interior contains nothing less than the largest collection of medieval art in Holland, along with a vast amount of religious artifacts and a sweeping survey of Christianity in the Netherlands.

Continue across the town moat to the thoroughly enjoyable and very popular:

*DUTCH RAILWAY MUSEUM (Nederlands Spoorwegmuseum) ⑧, **T**: (030) 230-6206 or **W**: spoorwegmuseum.nl. *Open Tues.–Fri. 10–5, Sat.–Sun. and some holidays 11:30–5, closed Mon., New Year's Day, and some holidays. Museum Cards accepted. €€.*

One of Europe's best railway museums, recently renovated, is appropriately located in a former train station from the 19th century. Along its platforms and in its yards is a magnificent collection of locomotives, cars, and trams. Model trains speed along miniature tracks in the station itself, much to the delight of railfans young and old. Indoors, there is also a collection of railroading artifacts, and you can get refreshments in the museum's restaurant.

A rather interesting route back to the center is to follow the canal and turn left into Kromme Nieuwe Gracht, a narrow street with a tiny canal. Another left brings you to **St. Pieterskerk** ⑨, an 11th-century Romanesque church that hasn't changed very much over the ages. Continue on Achter St. Pieter and Keistraat to Janskerkhof, then follow the map to the **Town Hall** *(Stadhuis)* ⑩ on the Oude Gracht canal. This area is particularly rich in outdoor cafés, mostly on the water's edge. ***Boat trips** through the canals are offered nearby, at the corner of Potterstraat and the canal, and make a fine way to finish off your trip to Utrecht before returning to the station.

Gouda

F ew towns are more typically "Dutch" than Gouda, whose cheese is renowned throughout the world but whose name is usually mispronounced. Correctly said, the word is *How-dah*. Surprisingly, its marketplace is the largest in Holland, and its Gothic Town Hall is easily among the most impressive anywhere. Although a weekly market attracts huge crowds, most of these come from the local area and the event is not in any sense staged for tourists. What does bring visitors is the splendid St. Janskerk and the delightful Het Catharina Gasthuis museum, as well as the picturesque canal-lined streets.

Gouda began in the 12th century and received its charter in 1272. Early prosperity came with the development of a cloth industry and was later expanded by the manufacture of clay tobacco pipes, candles, pottery, and cheese. These later trades continue to play an important role in the economy today, and add a touch of Old World charm to a venerable town.

GETTING THERE:

Trains depart Amsterdam's Centraal Station at one-hour intervals for the 50-minute ride to Gouda. These are locals *(stoptrein)* marked for Rotterdam CS, but travel a strange route via the original Breukelen. Return service operates until late evening.

By Car, leave Amsterdam on the A-4 highway past Schiphol Airport, then turn south on the N-207 into Gouda. The total distance is 53 km (33 miles).

PRACTICALITIES:

The famous Cheese Market is held on Thursday mornings from mid-June through mid-August. There are also general outdoor markets all year round on Thursday mornings and all day on Saturdays. The church is closed to tourists on Sundays.

The local **Tourist Office** *(VVV)*, **T**: (0900) 4683-2888 (toll call) or **W**: vvv.gouda.nl, is on the Market Square.

FOOD AND DRINK:

Gouda has a nice selection of restaurants and cafés, especially on and around the marketplace. Some choices are:

Restaurant Scheeps (Westhaven 4, near the De Moriaan Museum) Local specialties, including vegetarian, indoors or out in the garden. **T**: (0182) 517-572. €€€

De Zalm (Markt 34, on the Markt) Light and full meals overlooking the action. **T**: (0182) 525-345. €€

Café In de Gouwe Geit (Achter de Kerk, behind St. Janskerk) Light meals, snacks, and beverages right by the main attractions. **T**: (0182) 528-885. €

SUGGESTED TOUR:
Circled numbers correspond to numbers on the map.

Leave the **Train Station** ① and follow the map across a canal and down Kleiweg, a pedestrians-only shopping street. This will bring you to the **Markt**, the largest marketplace in Holland. At its north end is the **Waag** ②, a handsome 17th-century weigh house for cheese, where you can watch cheese being made, sample some, and learn all about this local industry. Note the carved relief above the doorway, which clearly depicts the building's function. **T**: *(0182) 529-996. Open Apr.–Oct., Tues.–Sun. 1–5, opening at 10 on Thurs. market days. €.*

In the center of the square stands the magnificent **Town Hall** *(Stadhuis)* ③, a late Gothic structure that was once surrounded by a moat. Built around 1450, it has an unusually fine southern façade embellished with statues of the counts and countesses of Burgundy. A carillon along its east side plays every half-hour, accompanied by moving figures acting out the granting of the town's charter. Its stone scaffold at the north end offers a good view of the market—the last view enjoyed by criminals who were once hanged here.

Stroll down to **St. Janskerk** ④, which has the curious distinction of being the longest church in Holland. It was begun in the 13th century but was almost totally destroyed by fire in 1552. What you see today is primarily a 16th-century reconstruction, famed for its extraordinary stained-glass windows. With a total surface area of about half an acre, all but 3 of the 70 windows were installed between 1555 and 1603, and so represent both the Roman Catholic and Protestant periods. The last three are from the 20th century, of which the Liberation Window of I947—graphically recalling the horrors of World War II —is truly striking. An illustrated brochure that describes the windows and suggests a sequence for viewing them is available in English. *Open March–Oct, Mon.–Sat. 9–5; Nov.–Feb. Mon.–Sat. 9–4. Closed to tourists on Sun. €.*

Just across from the church, on Achter de Kerk, is the fascinating:

MUNICIPAL MUSEUM "ST. CATHERINE'S HOSPITAL" *(Stedelijk Museum "Het Catharina Gasthuis")* ⑤, **T**: (0182) 588-441. *Open Mon.–Sat. 10–5, Sun. noon–5. Museum Card accepted. €.*

Occupying the 14th-to-17th-century buildings of a former hospice, this museum's displays cover a wide scope of local history shown in a series of authentic room settings. There is, of course, a great deal of religious art as well as an excellent collection of 19th- and 20th-century paintings. An entire 18th-century

Gouda

300 Yards

The Town Hall

dispensary has been reconstructed along with a kitchen and various domestic rooms. Don't miss the gruesome torture instruments and cells in the dark basement, or the room full of toys and dolls.

Leave via the entrance on Oosthaven and cross the canal. In a few yards you will come to the **De Moriaan Museum** ⑥, where an unusual collection of tobacco pipes, tiles, and ceramics is displayed in a merchant's home of 1617. The building alone is worth a visit, and as a bonus there is a restored antique tobacco shop complete with inventory. **T**: *(0182) 588-444. Open April–Sept., Wed.–Sat. 1–6. Free.*

Continue along the canal to the river. About two blocks to the right are moored several traditional sailing barges and other old vessels, which can be seen from the street. Turning left brings you to the 18th-century **'t Slot Windmill** ⑦. This is private and cannot be visited, but it makes a pretty sight as you turn left into a small park. From here, follow Spieringstraat back to Achter de Kerk and exit onto Wijdstraat.

Lage Couwe leads along a canal to the 17th-century **Corn Exchange** and **Fish Market** *(Korenbeurs en Visbank)* ⑧, two colonnaded areas on either side of the water. Turn right into a narrow lane called Vissteeg, along which is a small artisan's shop where you can watch the traditional clay pipes being made and perhaps purchase one. From here you can follow the map back to the station.

Trip 18

Het Loo Palace

For nearly three centuries, the magnificent Palace of Het Loo was a favorite country seat of the House of Orange-Nassau, the family that continues to provide Holland with its sovereigns to this day. In the grand tradition of France's Versailles, Bavaria's Nymphenburg, and Austria's Schonbrunn, it is set on the edge of a large estate and is bordered by fabulous gardens. Until 1975, it was still occupied by members of the royal family, but after that it was transformed into a national museum and opened to the public in 1984.

The Het Loo Palace was begun in 1685 by William III, a descendant of William the Silent and later *stadhouder* of the Netherlands—the title "king" was not used by the House of Orange-Nassau until 1814. In 1689, William III and his wife, Mary Stuart, became joint sovereigns of England and ruled that country as William III and Mary II. William continued his position of leadership in Holland, however, and used Het Loo until his death in 1702. The palace remained in the family and has been used by all of the sovereigns of the Netherlands through the reign of Queen Wilhelmina, who abdicated in 1948 and died in 1962. Her granddaughter, Princess Margriet, lived there until 1975.

Seven years of expensive restoration work have returned the palace and its grounds to their original 17th-century appearance, with some of the interior rooms representing the centuries since then. A visit here, while very enjoyable in itself, will also leave you with some insight into the relationship between the House of Orange-Nassau and the nation as a whole.

GETTING THERE:

Trains leave Amsterdam's Centraal Station at half-hour intervals for the 65-minute ride to Apeldoorn, where the palace is located. Some of these require a change at Amersfoort and at least one does not run on Sundays and certain holidays. Return service operates until late evening.

By Car, take the A-1 highway east from Amsterdam to Apeldoorn, a distance of 90 km (56 miles), and then follow local signs to Het Loo.

PRACTICALITIES:

Avoid going on a Monday, when everything is closed. Fine weather will make this trip much more enjoyable. Buses to the palace run less frequently on

Sundays and holidays.

The local **Tourist Office** *(VVV),* **T**: (055) 526-0200 or **W**: vvvapeldoorn.nl, is two blocks north of the train station at Deventerstraat 18, in Apeldoorn.

FOOD AND DRINK:

There are a few good restaurants near the palace and a couple of cafeterias within its grounds. The town of Apeldoorn has several restaurants. Some suggestions are:

De Keizerskroon (7 Konigstraat, near the palace) A comfortable small hotel with a well-regarded restaurant. **T**: (055) 521-7744. €€ and €€€

Poppe (7 Paslaan, 7 blocks northwest of the Apeldoorn train station) French-inspired food in the center of town, with outdoor tables in season. **T**: (055) 522-3286. X: Mon. €€

Theehuis (opposite the stables in the palace grounds) A self-service cafeteria for light meals and snacks, indoors or out. **T**: (055) 577-2487. X: Mon. €

Restaurant Balzaal (in the west wing of the palace) A self-service cafeteria in the ballroom; outdoor tables in summer. **T**: (055) 577-2417. X: Mon. €

SUGGESTED TOUR:

Circled numbers correspond to numbers on the map.

From the **Apeldoorn Train Station** ① you have a choice of taking a bus, a taxi, or walking to the Het Loo Palace. The distance is a bit less than two miles via the route shown on the map. Buses number 102 and 104 leave from the square in front of the station and go directly to Het Loo ②, while the number 11 goes to a bus stop ③ within walking distance of it.

*RIJKSMUSEUM PALEIS HET LOO ④–⑥, Amersfoortsweg, Apeldoorn, **T**: (055) 577-2400 or **W**: paleishetloo.nl. *Open Tues.–Sun. 10–5; wings from 1–5. Closed Mon. except on holidays, and New Year's Day. Museum Card accepted. €€. Gift shop. Restaurants.*

A visit to the Rijksmuseum Paleis Het Loo begins at the **Royal Stables** ④, opposite which there is a cafeteria with outdoor café tables. Built around 1910, the stables hold an interesting collection of carriages, coaches, and even sleighs used by the royal family. Their automobiles, ranging from some real old-timers to relatively recent models, are especially fascinating.

From here, a path leads to the **Royal Palace** ⑤ itself. In a wing to the left of the courtyard, you can watch an introductory video show that lasts under 30 minutes and is given—on different screens—in English, Dutch, German, and French. Just beyond this, in a small courtyard, is another cafeteria where you can get light lunches or drinks. Again, outdoor café tables are available.

The **East Wing**, across the main courtyard, houses a collection of paintings, costumes, medals, and personal effects relating to the royal family.

Het Loo Palace at Apeldoorn

500 Yards

The Royal Palace from the Gardens

Enter the **palace** proper and follow a well-marked route through its many rooms. This usually begins with the Entrance Hall, the old and new Dining Rooms, and the Chapel. It then goes upstairs to the Library, the Long Gallery, several apartments of various kings and queens, the Grand Staircase, and the Great Hall. Returning to the ground floor, the route leads through the Sitting Room and Workroom of Queen Wilhelmina, the last sovereign to reside at Het Loo.

A basement door at the rear of the palace brings you into the fabulous ***Gardens** ⑥, now restored to their 17th-century appearance. With over 200 varieties of plants, several working fountains, and colonnaded pavilions at its north end, there is enough here to delight your senses for quite a while before you return to the station in Apeldoorn.

Giethoorn

W ater, water everywhere—that's Giethoorn, an improbable Dutch village that calls itself the "Venice of Holland." The only way to get around this strange and wonderful place is by boat, on foot, or by bicycle. There are no roads at all, just narrow tree-shaded canals, paths, and tiny wooden bridges connecting the quaint thatched-roof cottages and lovely flower gardens.

Giethoorn has not exactly gone unnoticed by Dutch and German vacationers, but it is still an unusual destination for North American visitors. Fortunately, its charms are spread over a fairly large area, so crowding should never be a problem. Boat trips through its dreamy canals and on its lake are offered everywhere, or you can rent a hand-propelled punter or electric "whisper boat" and explore on your own. The entire area can also be seen on foot by following the walking tour described.

This unique place was first settled around 1230 by a sect of flagellants who came to escape religious persecution. They earned their living by digging peat in what was then bog country, and in so doing uncovered countless horns of goats who had presumably drowned during some of the periodic floods. Thus the name *Geytenhoren,* or goats' horns, which was eventually corrupted into Giethoorn. The peat digging, in time, caused many ponds and lakes to form, and these were connected by canals to facilitate transport.

GETTING THERE:

Trains marked for Groningen depart Amsterdam's Centraal Station hourly for the direct 92-minute ride to Meppel, where you get bus number 79 to Blauwe Hand, then bus number 72 to Giethoorn. Return train service operates until late evening, but check the local bus schedule. Alternatively, you can take a train to Steenwijk instead. This involves a change at either Zwolle or Amersfoort, but it's a bit quicker and the bus ride is short and direct.

By Car, leave Amsterdam on the A-1 highway, heading east toward Amersfoort, then take the A-28 northeast to the first Zwolle exit. From there, follow local roads via Hasselt and Zwartsluis to Giethoorn. The total distance is 135 km (84 miles).

PRACTICALITIES:

Those coming by train should avoid Sundays, when there is no connecting bus service. This is strictly an outdoor trip, so good weather is absolutely essential. You will encounter fewer tourists during the spring and fall, and in winter the canals may freeze over to produce an ice-skater's paradise. The Monday-to-Saturday bus service is reduced during the off season.

The local **Tourist Office** *(VVV),* **T**: (0900) 567-4637 (toll call) or **W**: vvvgiethoorn.nl, is on the Beulakerweg, near the bus stop at the south end of the village.

FOOD AND DRINK:

Being a popular vacation spot for the Dutch and the Germans, Giethoorn has a wide selection of restaurants and cafés in the moderate-to-low price range. A few choices are:

Hollands Venetië (Beulakerweg 167, near Petersteeg) Dutch and German food, popular with tourists. Indoor/outdoor dining. X: mid-October through March. **T**: (0521) 361-231. €€

De Rietstulp (Ds. T.O. Hylkemaweg 15, near the church) Dutch food, served indoors or out on the terrace. **T**: (0521) 361-833. € and €€

Smit's Paviljoen (Binnenpad 29, on the lake) A nice pavilion restaurant with a great view, with outdoor tables in summer. **T**: (0521) 361-215. X: winter. €

SUGGESTED TOUR:

Circled numbers correspond to numbers on the map.

Leave the **Meppel Train Station** and turn left into the bus departure area. Here you can board the hourly NWH bus for a 20-minute ride through lovely countryside to Giethoorn, making an easy change enroute at Blauwe Hand. If you came via **Steenwijk** instead, take a bus for a very short ride direct to Giethoorn. Note that the buses do not run on Sundays.

Get off at the **bus stop** ① near the **Giethoorn Tourist Office** *(VVV)* on Beulakerweg. Those with cars will find plenty of parking nearby. Enter the village on Frensensteeg and turn left at the canal onto a footpath called Zuiderpad. This crosses the water several times on tiny bridges, passing delightful country houses as it heads north. All along the way there are places that offer **boat rides** or rentals.

The simple **Village Church** ② overlooks an especially picturesque junction of three canals. Continue north on Binnenpad, passing the tiny ***Museum de Oude Aarde** ③. Exhibits here include crystals, semiprecious stones, and various minerals glowing under special illumination. There are also displays of local fauna. **T**: *(0521) 361-313. Open March–Oct., daily 10–6; Nov.–Feb., Wed.–Sun. 10–5. Museum Cards accepted.* €.

Now head out to **Smit's Paviljoen** ④ on the Bovenwijde lake. Various boating activities are offered here, along with light lunches and drinks in a beautiful setting.

Giethoorn

N

500 Yards

BOVENWIJDE

Beulakerweg

De Deukten

Kanaaldijk

Binnenpad

⑥

⑤

Bus

Ds. T.O. Hylkemaweg

Binnenpad

Bartus Warnersweg

Beulakerweg

Langesteeg

Vosjacht

Petersteeg

Zuiderpad

Info.

Frensensteeg

Bus

Maaiensteeg

TO MEPPEL

GIETHOORN 126

Along the Canals of Giethoorn

Return to the church and follow Ds. T.O. Hylkemaweg past several shops and restaurants to the **north bus stop** ⑤ on Beulakerweg. From here you can get a bus directly back to Steenwijk, or to Meppel with a change at Blauwe Hand.

ADDITIONAL ATTRACTION:

If you have time left, continue on from the north bus stop ⑤, cross the canal, and turn down Cornelisgracht to the **Histo-Mobil Automuseum** ⑥. Here you can see a good collection of very old and sometimes strange automobiles, bicycles, mopeds, farm wagons, and other things on wheels. **T**: *(0521) 361-498. Open April–Oct, Tues.–Sun. 10–6. €.*

Trip 20

Leeuwarden
(Ljouwert)

Throughout history, Frisia has been a world apart—speaking its own language, waving its own flag, singing its own anthem, and stubbornly clinging to its fierce sense of individuality. These traditions live on in the ancient city of Leeuwarden, or *Ljouwert* as it is called in Frisian. Today the capital of Friesland Province, Leeuwarden offers its visitors the chance to experience a very different side of the Netherlands.

The economy of Frisia revolves around dairy farming, so it is perhaps not surprising that Leeuwarden's most striking public monument is a statue of a fat cow. The city's favorite daughter is remembered by a statue, too. Born here in 1876 as Margaretha Zelle, she was known to the world as the spy Mata Hari, and is depicted as an exotic dancer.

Frisian is regarded as the language most akin to English, and it is thought by some scholars that the "Anglo-Saxons" who invaded England after the fall of the Roman Empire were in fact Frisian adventurers. Leeuwarden has strong connections to the United States as well, for it was here, in 1782, that the first official recognition of the new American nation was declared, leading to a much-needed loan from the Dutch government. The local ties go back further than that, however, as this area also produced Peter Stuyvesant, an early governor of New York when it was still called New Amsterdam.

GETTING THERE:

Trains depart Amsterdam's Centraal Station at hourly intervals for Leeuwarden, a direct ride of just under 2½ hours. Be sure to get on the correct set of cars, as these trains split at Zwolle. In addition, there are other trains that require a change at Amersfoort. Return service operates until mid-evening.

By Car, head north from Amsterdam on the A-7/E-22 highway and cross the IJsselmeer on the famous enclosing dike *(Afsluitdijk)*. When you reach the mainland, take the A-31 into Leeuwarden. The total distance is 138 km (86 miles).

PRACTICALITIES:

Leeuwarden may be visited at any time, but note that most of the attractions are closed on Mondays.

The local **Tourist Office** *(VVV),* **T**: (0900) 202-4060 (toll call) or **W**: vvvleeuwarden.nl (in Dutch), is at Sophia Laan 4, 2 blocks north of the train station.

FOOD AND DRINK:

Some good choices of places to eat in Leeuwarden are:

Het Binnenhof (Weerd 18, a block north of the Waag) Dutch and Continental cuisine in a grand café setting. **T**: (058) 213-1514. €€

Spijs Lokaal (Eewal 54, 2 blocks east of the Stadhuis) A popular place for contemporary dishes. **T**: (058) 216-2214. €€

Het Leven (Druifstreek 57a, 3 blocks south of the Fries Museum) Traditional Dutch specialties, among others. **T**: (058) 212-1233. € and €€

SUGGESTED TOUR:

Circled numbers correspond to numbers on the map.

Leave the **Train Station** ① and walk straight ahead down Sophia Laan past the tourist office, crossing a canal. Just beyond this is the Wilhelminaplein, where an outdoor market is held on Fridays. Continue on and turn right at the next canal to a busy open square called Waagplein. In the center of this stands the **Waag** ②, an attractive 16th-century weigh house in the Frisian Renaissance style. Once used as a cheese market, it is now home to a restaurant and a bank.

From here follow a narrow canal to the small **Mata Hari Statue** ③. Curiously, this depicts the famous courtesan, entertainer, and alleged World War I spy as an exotic dancer — here clothed although she usually performed in the buff. A native of Leeuwarden, she was shot by a French firing squad in 1917 for giving secrets to the Germans, although she may actually have been a double agent working for the Allies.

Stroll down Korfmakersstraat and turn left to the:

*FRIES MUSEUM ④, **T**: (058) 255-5500 or **W**: friesmuseum.nl. *Open Tues.–Sun. 11–5. Closed Jan.1, Dec. 25. Museum Cards accepted. €.*

This is one of the very best provincial museums in Holland. Housed in an 18th-century mansion, it is devoted to a sweeping survey of Frisian culture from prehistoric to modern times. Among the highlights are period room settings, 19th-century shops, costumes, and the famous painted furniture from Hindeloopen. There is a painting by Rembrandt of his wife, Saskia, who was born in Leeuwarden. Other treasures include ancient pottery, Roman coins dating from their occupation of the area, medieval sculptures, and a room full of old printing presses. A particularly interesting exhibition focuses on the life and times of Mata Hari.

Now follow the map to the **Grote Kerk** ⑤, also known as the Jacobijnerkerk.

The most important church in Leeuwarden, it was originally erected in the 13th century and was largely rebuilt in the 15th. Its simple but rather elegant interior houses some splendid tombs of the Frisian branch of the House of Orange-Nassau.

Grote Kerkstraat leads to the **Mata Hari House** ⑥, home of the renowned spy from 1883 until 1890. This is now occupied by the Frisian Literary Museum *(Frysk Letterkundich Museum)*, which promotes the use of Frisian in literature and every-day speech. You are most welcome to step inside and learn all you wanted to know about the Frisian language. **T**: *(058) 212-0834. Open Mon.–Fri. 1:30–5. Closed weekends and holidays.* €.

Continue down the street to the:

*MUSEUM HET PRINCESSEHOF ⑦, **T**: (058) 294-8958 or **W**: princessehof.nl. Open Tues.–Sun. 10–5. €.

Devoted primarily to ceramics from all over the Earth, the displays in this marvelous museum are so fascinating that you will surely enjoy a visit—even if you have no burning passion for pottery. Among the many features are the world's largest collection of tiles; Chinese ware from prehistoric to modern times; Art Nouveau and contemporary ceramics; and Indonesian puppets, weapons, and fabrics. Don't miss this special treat.

In just a few more steps you will come to the **Oldehove** ⑧, the famed leaning tower of Leeuwarden. Rising rather forlornly at the end of a parking lot, this lopsided pile is 130 feet high and was begun in 1529 as part of a cathedral that never got built. Alas, the soil sank, the Reformation intervened, and the project ran out of money. You can climb to the top for an aerial view of the town, extending in clear weather all the way to the West Frisian Islands. *Open May–Sept., Tues.–Sat. 2–5.* €.

The park to the immediate north of this is a nice place to relax before carrying on. Looking across the canal, you'll see a strange statue of a cow called **Us Mem** (Our Mother), the symbol of Frisian prosperity. Now follow the map past the **Stadhuis** ⑨, a town hall built in 1715, then turn down St. Jacobsstraat and Wirdumerdijk to the Zuiderplein. From here it's only a short stroll back to the station.

Leeuwarden

N

300 Yards

Boterhoek
Noordersingel
Noorderweg
Hoekster End
Nieweburen
Groeneweg
Pijlsteeg
Breedstr
Perkstr
Sacramentsstr
Tuinen N.Z.
Tuinen Z.Z.
Grote Kerkstraat
Speelmansstr
Eewal
Voorstreek
Turfmarkt
Plantage
Bagijnestraat
Hofplein
St. Jacobsstr
Grote Hoogstr
Kelders
Over de Kelders
Korfmakersstr
Droevendal
Oosterkade
K. Kerkstr
Nieuwestad N.Z.
Nieuwestad Z.Z.
Weerd
Naauw
Heerestr
Tweebaksmarkt
Haniasteeg
Doelesteeg
Peperstr
Oude Oosterstr
Groot Schavernek
Ruiterskwartier
Waagplein
Keizersgracht
Druifstreek
Schoolstr
Prins Hendrikstr
Wilhelminaplein
Zaailand
Zuiderstraat
Wirdumerdijk
Nieuweweg
Willemskade N.Z.
Zuidergrachtswal
info.
Willemskade Z.Z.
Romkeslaan
Lange Marktstraat
Sophia Laan
Zuider Plein
Zuidersingel
Stationsweg
TO AMSTERDAM
Station
Schrans

Trip 21

Netherlands Open-Air Museum at Arnhem

Outdoor folk museums have become increasingly popular in Europe and throughout the world as more of the countryside succumbs to modern development and the traditional ways of life disappear. In many cases they are the only realistic way of saving a nation's domestic heritage from being paved over to make way for yet more shopping malls. Typically, threatened structures ranging from thatched farm cottages to early industrial buildings are moved into a protected park setting and reassembled in village groupings according to the region they represent. Trained personnel, often in folk costumes, carry on the old crafts and farm the fields in the traditional way, while reconstructed country inns continue to serve age-old recipes. A visit to one of the better open-air museums can be a lot of fun, and may be the only chance you'll ever get to experience some aspects of the Old World.

There are several open-air museums in Holland, notably at Zaanse Schans and Enkhuizen, but this one, at Arnhem, is by far the largest and most complete. Spread over an area of about 75 acres, it was begun in 1912 and now contains roughly 100 structures. All of these have been restored to their original appearance, and many are filled with period furnishings. Besides the farmhouses and barns, there are workshops, windmills, bridges, inns, a school, a church, and even some urban buildings.

The museum suggests several routes; the one described here is a modified version of them. In addition to walking, there are historic trams operating all over the park that you can ride. At the entrance pavilion is a special exhibition called the Holland*Rama*, showing regional costumes and historical material. Food and drinks are offered at several places along the way, as are rest rooms.

By getting off to an early start, it is entirely possible to combine this trip in the same day with one to the Hoge Veluwe National Park with its famous Kröller-Müller Museum. This is described in the next chapter. To do this by public transportation, you must first return to the bus stop in front of the Arnhem train station. Those with cars can drive directly there.

The Drawbridge to the Village

GETTING THERE:

Trains leave Amsterdam's Centraal Station frequently for the 68-minute ride to Arnhem. In addition to the regular 1C expresses, there are EuroCity trains that require a supplementary fare unless you are using a Eurailpass. Return service operates until late evening.

By Car, head south from Amsterdam on the A-2 highway past Utrecht, then take the A-12 east to the Arnhem-Apeldoorn exit and follow local signs to the Openlucht Museum. The total distance is 99 km (62 miles).

PRACTICALITIES:

The museum is open daily from late March through October. Good weather is essential for enjoyment of this trip. The **Tourist Office** in Arnhem *(VVV)*, **T**: (026) 370-0226 or **W**: vvvarnhem.nl (in Dutch), is at Willemsplein 8, a few blocks east of the station.

FOOD AND DRINK:

There are several places to eat and drink at the outdoor museum as well as restaurants and cafés in Arnhem. Some choices are:

AT THE MUSEUM:

Pavilion Restaurant (at the entrance pavilion) Sandwiches and light refreshments. €

De Hanekamp (near the far end) Pancakes and snacks. €

IN ARNHEM:

Hotel Haarhuis (1 Stationsplein, across from the station) Good-value meals in a small hotel. **T**: (026) 442-7441. €€

NETHERLANDS OPEN-AIR MUSEUM   133

Netherlands Open Air Museum

Not to scale

De Hanekamp Inn

Village

Info.

Entrance

TO ARNHEM

NETHERLANDS OPEN-AIR MUSEUM   134

SUGGESTED TOUR:

Circled numbers correspond to numbers on the map.
The easiest way to get from the **Arnhem Train Station** to the open-air museum is to take bus number 3 in the direction of Alteveer. During the summer months there is also the direct bus number 13. Both depart frequently from the square in front of the station, and the ride takes 10 minutes. Otherwise, it's a 2½-mile taxi ride or walk.

*NETHERLANDS OPEN-AIR MUSEUM *(Nederlands Openlucht Museum)* (①–⑬), Schelmseweg 89, Arnhem, **T**: (026) 357-6111 or **W**: openluchtmuseum.nl (mostly in Dutch). *Open late March through October, daily 10-5, variable schedule in winter. Museum Card accepted. €€€, includes HollandRama. Historic trams provide transportation in the park. An illustrated guide booklet in English is sold at the gate.*

At the entrance ① is an exhibition pavilion called **Holland*Rama***, where you can see regional costumes, historic material, and special shows in a multimedia spectacular. Just beyond this turn left and stroll down to the **Horse-Drawn Oil Mill** ② from the province of Gelderland. Converted from a farmhouse around 1830, it was used to extract lighting and cooking oils by crushing seeds such as rape or flax. Close to this is a small thatched-roof **Veluwe Farmhouse** ③ from around 1850, whose furnished interior may be visited.

The route now passes a small exhibition of beekeeping on the way to the **Betuwe Farmhouse** ④, a rather large structure originally built in 1646. Also from Gelderland Province, it has an attached barn and a nicely-furnished interior.

Return past the bees and turn left to the romantically sited **Farmhouse from Giethoorn** ⑤, which of course is partially surrounded by water. Built in 1832, much of it was used for the storage of hay, with attractive living quarters at one end. Down the road from it stands the large **Staphorst Farmhouse** ⑥, a type still found in that conservative part of Holland. Most of this is devoted to the storage of hay, but the small living quarters are beautifully decorated with tiles and painted furniture. Behind it is the **Farmhouse with a Pyramid Roof**, erected in 1745 in North Holland province, and associated with the making of Edam cheeses.

The route now enters a small village over a typical wooden drawbridge from around 1800. The **Merchant's House** ⑦ from Koog on the Zaan (near Zaanse Schans) partially dates from 1686 and has the sort of comfortable interior favored by the 19th-century bourgeoisie. Adjacent to this is a tradesman's house from the same area, which now serves as a souvenir shop.

Turn left and stroll through the village to the **Fisherman's Cottage from Marken** ⑧, which is similar to the ones you find today on the island in the IJsselmeer just north of Amsterdam. Its tiny interior has excellent examples of the traditional cupboard beds then popular in the north.

Continue on past an early-!9th-century **Laundry** ⑨ that was brought here from an area near Haarlem. Close to it is a refreshment stand, where you can take a break before admiring the unusual **Post Windmill** ⑩. This was once used to grind grain in North Holland, and parts of it are over 300 years old.

The **Paper Mill from theVeluwe** ⑪ is in a beautifully wooded location between two ponds. Powered by an overshot waterwheel, its mechanisms still work and are used to give demonstrations of hand paper-making.

Although it is a re-creation and not an original, the **Parlor from Hindeloopen** ⑫ is quite interesting for the stylized painted furniture that has come to be associated with that former Zuider Zee town.

Now follow the map past the lovely Herb Garden to the **Frisian Farmstead** ⑬, whose rather elegant living quarters reflect the prosperity of that dairy region. Near this is the **Farmhouse from Beerta** ⑭, an area in Groningen province. Its living section has been restored to the state it was in around 1935, after electrification provided such luxuries as lighting, kitchen appliances, and a radio. In contrast, the **Drenthe Farmhouse** ⑮ is a large but rather primitive affair dating from around 1700.

Continue on to the **De Hanekamp Inn** ⑯, an 18th-century country inn from Zwolle. It now functions as a delightful café for museum visitors, with both indoor and outdoor tables.

Limburg province, in the south and much hillier than the rest of Holland, is represented by the **Krawinkel Farmstead** ⑰ and other nearby structures. From here the route passes a grouping of various **Windmills** ⑱ on the way back to the entrance.

Hoge Veluwe National Park and the Kröller Müller Museum

Y ou may be surprised to discover a genuine wilderness area in a country as jam-packed as Holland, but this 22 square miles of nature preserve is only part of the attraction. The other is the magnificent Kröller-Müller Museum located right in its heart. Easily counted as one of the very best modern art museums in the world, it is certainly worth a daytrip in itself. The park has other features as well, which can be explored by car, by bus, on foot, or on one of the 1,300 white bicycles that are available free for your use.

Both the park and the museum were a gift to the nation, made in 1935 by a wealthy businessman named Anton Kröller and his art-collecting wife, Helene Müller. The museum's collections are absolutely first-rate, with no less than 278 paintings by van Gogh alone. Adjacent to it is a sculpture garden where over 60 contemporary pieces adorn some 26 acres of gorgeous land-scape.

It is possible—by getting off loan early start—to combine this daytrip with one to the Netherlands Open-Air Museum at Arnhem, described in the previous chapter.

GETTING THERE:

Trains depart Amsterdam's Centraal Station frequently for the 68-minute ride to Arnhem, from which you take a bus into the Hoge Veluwe. This bus runs from April through October, at least 4 times a day, hourly in July-August. In addition to the regular IC expresses, there are EuroCity trains that require a supplementary fare unless you are using a Eurailpass. Return service operates until late evening. An alternative route is to take a train to Apeldoorn (see trip 18), then an hourly bus to the park.

By Car, take the A-2 highway south from Amsterdam to a point just beyond Utrecht, then the A-12 east to the Hoge Veluwe exit just before Arnhem. From there follow local signs to the entrance at Schaarsbergen. The total distance is about 96 km (60 miles).

PRACTICALITIES:

The Kröller-Müller Museum is open every day except on Mondays and New Year's Day. The direct bus service from Arnhem runs from April through October. *Note that there is also year-round daily bus service from the Apeldoorn train station (see Het Loo Palace) instead of Arnhem, should you want to come out of season.* Good weather is essential unless you plan to spend the entire time in the museum.

The **Tourist Office** in Arnhem *(VVV)*, **T**: (026) 370-0226 or **W**: vvvarnhem.nl (in Dutch), is a few blocks east of the station.

Free "White" bicycles may be obtained at any entrance, or at the museum or visitor center. If you get one at the Rijzenberg entrance, be aware that it is about 10 km (6 miles) of pedaling to the museum, and even more to the other attractions. **"Blue" bicycles** may be rented at the visitor center, € per day or €€ for tandems.

FOOD AND DRINK:

Some places to eat and drink in the Hoge Veluwe National Park are:

Rijzenburg (17 Koningsweg, at the south entrance to the park) Superb dining in an old farmhouse or out on the terrace. **T**: (026) 443-6733. €€ and €€€

De Koperen Kop (near the Visitor Center) Pancakes and other light meals, indoors or out. **T**: (0318) 591-289. €

Café Monsieur Jacques (in the museum) Self-service with light meals, snacks, and drinks. **T**: (0318) 591-657. €

Recommendations for Arnhem are shown in the previous chapter.

SUGGESTED TOUR:

Circled numbers correspond to numbers on the map.

Those coming by rail will begin at the Arnhem Train Station and take a bus to the Hoge Veluwe park. From April to the end of October there is a direct bus, which takes 30 minutes to reach the Kröller-Müller Museum. *At other times you might come via train to Apeldoorn instead, from which there is an hourly bus that runs daily all year round (route 110).*

If you came by car you should enter the park via the Rijzenburg Gate ① at Schaarsbergen, which is where bus enters. The museum is about 8 miles northwest of central Arnhem.

*HOGE VELUWE NATIONAL PARK AND THE KRÖLLER-MÜLLER

MUSEUM ①–⑤. Park **T**: (0318) 591-627 or **W**: hogeveluwe.nl; museum **T**: (0318) 591-241 or **W**: kmm.nl. *Park open daily in April 8–8, in May 8–9, June–July 8–10, Aug. 8–9, Sept. 9–8, Oct. 9–7, Nov.–March 9–5:30. Museum open Tues.–Sun. and bank holidays, 10–5. Museum closed Mon. and New Year's Day. Park admission only €€, combined admission with museum €€€.*

The Hoge Veluwe National Park covers an area of some 13,500 acres. A vast variety of wildlife lives in these woods and heathlands, including deer, mouflons, wild boars, foxes, badgers, hawks, and buzzards. During the rutting season (early September to mid-October), visitors are not allowed to leave the road in the game preserve area.

Begin your visit at the *Kröller-Müller Museum ②, where an extraordinary collection of art from the late 19th and 20th centuries is displayed in two adjoining structures. The first of these was built in 1938 and the second in 1977. The nucleus of the museum is a collection of 278 works by Vincent van Gogh, several of which are among the finest and most famous ever done by that renowned Dutch painter. Among the other artists represented are Picasso, Mondrian, Léger, Redon, Seurat, and Ensor. To emphasize the universality of all art, the displays are interspersed with paintings from the 16th and 17th centuries, notably by Gerard David and both Cranachs; and with pottery from China and ancient Greece. Not everything is on view at any one time, as the collections are far larger than the size of the galleries allows, and space must be made for temporary shows.

From the south wing of the museum you can step out into the fabulous *Sculpture Garden ③, one of the largest in Europe. More than 60 works are spread over a lovely area of some 26 acres. A few of the sculptors represented are Rodin, Moore, Lipchitz, Marini, and Oldenburg. The most spectacular piece, by far, is the enormous *Jardin d'Email by Jean Dubuffet—an abstract landscape so huge that hundreds of people can crawl over it at the same time. Climb the steps into it and join the fun!

Now stroll over to the Visitor Center *(Bezoekers Centrum)* ④, where you can learn all about the rest of the park and perhaps make reservations for a tour of the St. Hubertus Lodge, below. *Open daily 10–5.* Nearby is the Museonder, offering a glimpse of life beneath the earth's surface and an underground stroll beneath the entire root system of a 135-year-old beech tree. Some 1,300 white bicycles are available without charge to all park visitors. You can borrow one of these and pedal over nearly 25 miles of special bicycle paths. Or you might prefer to rent a blue bicycle or tandem bike.

The best place to head for is the St. Hubertus Lodge *(Jachtslot Sint Hubertus)* ⑤, a country home built for the Kröller-Müllers in 1920. You can also get there by car, by bus, or on foot.

Buses back to Arnhem depart (in season) from the Koperen Kop restaurant by the Visitor Center and the museum.

Maastricht

Take one look at a map of Holland and you'll understand why Maastricht is the least Dutch city in the Netherlands. Located at the bottom of a narrow finger of land that pokes its way between Belgium and Germany, this ancient and remarkably well-preserved provincial capital is practically next door to Liège and Aachen, and lies as far south as Brussels. The typically flat landscape and canals disappear as the surrounding "Alps" soar to heights of over 1,000 feet. This is where the Dutch often go when they feel the urge for an exotic "foreign" vacation, and when they yearn for a superlative French meal.

Maastricht was founded by the Romans, possibly as far back as 50 BC, which accounts for the Latin strain in its temperament. Located at a point where the Maas *(Meuse)* River could be crossed, it became a strategic fortification along the road linking Cologne with the coast. From AD 382 until 720, Maastricht was the seat of a bishop, and was later ruled jointly by the prince-bishops of Liège and the dukes of Brabant. Throughout the Middle Ages and up until the late 18th century, it was frequently under siege by the French, the Spaniards, the Austrians, and anyone else who wanted to march through. When Belgium declared its independence in 1830, a strong Dutch military presence kept the city a part of Holland, which it remains today despite any sense of geographic logic.

Maastricht can be visited as a daytrip from Brussels just as easily as from Amsterdam.

GETTING THERE:

Trains depart Amsterdam's Centraal Station at hourly intervals for the 2½-hour ride to Maastricht. Return service operates until mid-evening.

Trains leave Brussels' three major stations at hourly intervals for the ride about 2 hours, via Liège. Return service runs until mid-evening.

By Car, it's the A-2/N-2 highway all the way. Maastricht is 212 km (132 miles) southeast of Amsterdam.

By Car from Brussels, take the A-3 east to exit 29, then the N-69 and N-79 northeast through Tongeren to Maastricht. The total distance is 106 km (66 miles).

PRACTICALITIES:

The various attractions of Maastricht follow complex schedules, but generally everything is open daily between mid-April and late September. Note that the Bonnefanten Museum is closed on Mondays and some holidays. An outdoor market is held on Wednesday and Friday mornings.

The local **Tourist Office** *(VVV)*, **T**: (043) 325-2121 or **W**: vvvmaastricht.nl, is in the 15th-century Dinghuis on Kleine Staat, a block south of the Markt. Ask them about visits to the Caves of Mount St. Peter.

FOOD AND DRINK:

Maastricht is noted for its fine dining, much of which meets Belgian and French standards. The outdoor cafés on the Vrijthof square are especially appealing. Some restaurant choices are:

Toine Hermsen (2 St. Bernardusstraat, just south of the Church of Our Lady) Elegant French cuisine of the highest quality. Dress well and reserve, **T**: (043) 325-8400. X: Sat. lunch, Sun., Mon. €€€

't Plenske (6 Plankstraat, near the Church of Our Lady) Classic French cuisine, with gardens seating offered in summer. **T**: (043) 321-8456. X: Sun. €€€

Au Coin des Bons Enfants (4 Ezelmarkt, 3 blocks south of St. Servatius Church) French and regional cuisine, indoors or out on the terrace. **T**: (043) 321-2359. X: Tues. €€ and €€€

't Klääoske (20 Plankstraat, near the Church of Our Lady) A small restaurant with French-accented fare and outdoor tables in season. **T**: (043) 325-8553. €€ and €€€

Gadjah Mas (Rechtstraat 42, a block southeast of the St. Servatius Bridge) Wonderful Indonesian cuisine, including vegetarian dishes and rijsttafel, served in elegant surroundings. **T** (043) 321-1568. €€ and €€€

Bistro 't Orgelke (Tongersestraat 42, near the western end of the town walls) Hearty Dutch food, either meaty or veggie. **T**: (043) 321-6982. €€

Tapperij De Poshoorn (Stationsstraat 47, 3 blocks west of the station) Inexpensive Dutch meals, and a great selection of beers. **T**: (043) 321-7334. €

In den Ouden Vogelstruys (Vrijthof 15) A popular café with light lunches and tasty beer. **T**: (043) 321-4888. €

SUGGESTED TOUR:

Circled numbers correspond to numbers on the map.

Leave the **Train Station** ① and walk down Stationsstraat to the Maas River. The St. Servatius Bridge *(St. Servaasbrug)* was originally erected in 1280 and rebuilt several times since then. Cross it and follow the map to the tourist office *(VVV)* in the ancient Dinghuis ②, a former court of justice dating from around 1470. Here you can get current information about visits to the Caves of Mount St. Peter ⑧ and about short cruises on the river ④.

Continue around to the **Markt** (Marketplace) ③, where a colorful outdoor market is held on Wednesday and Friday mornings from 8 a.m. to 1 p.m. In its center stands the **Stadhuis**, a rather impressive 17th-century town hall whose interesting interior may be visited. **T**: *(043) 350-5050. Open Mon.–Fri. 8:30–12:20 and 2–5:30. Free.* The statue at the north end of the square commemorates a local son, Jan Pieter Minckelers, who invented gas lighting and is shown holding one of his flames.

Now return to the river via Hoenderstraat. Cruises lasting about one hour can be taken from the **Stiphout Pier** ④ between mid-April and late September. There are also longer cruises that include a visit to the Caves of Mount St. Peter, and others to Liège in Belgium. *Rederij Stiphout,* **T**: *(043) 351-5300 or* **W***: stiphout.nl.*

Continue down Kesselkade into the charming Stokstraat Quarter, lined with restored 17th- and 18th-century houses. A left on Plankstraat brings you to the Romanesque **Church of Our Lady** *(Onze Lieve Vrouwe Basiliek)* ⑤. Begun around AD 1000 as a cruciform basilica, it has been altered through the centuries but still maintains much of its medieval atmosphere. Its Treasury contains a wealth of ecclesiastical arts and crafts, well worth a visit. **T**: (043,) *325-1851. Church open daily except during services. Treasury open Easter to mid-Sept., Mon.–Sat. 11–5, Sun. 1–5. €.*

The route now leads to the massive **Helpoort** (Gate of Hell) ⑥, the oldest surviving town gate in Holland. It was built in 1229 and still looks terribly ominous. Walk through it, not to hell, but to the **Pesthuis**, which is almost as bad. The present building is actually a paper mill built along the water in 1775, but on this site was once a house for dying victims of the plague. The fortification just across from this is called **De Vijf Koppen** ⑦ after the five severed heads that once decorated it. Their previous owners had been convicted of treason in 1638. You can climb up on the ramparts for a nice view.

From here you can make a side trip by following the map to the most famous attraction of Maastricht, the:

*CAVES OF MOUNT ST. PETER *(Grotten St.-Pietersberg)* ⑧, **T**: (043) 325-2121. *Open on a complex schedule, generally daily from late April through Oct., and on Wed., Fri., Sat. and Sun. the rest of the year. Tours (some in English) are most frequent in July–Aug., otherwise at specified times; ask first at the tourist office. €, with boat trip €€.*

The northern entrance to the caves is about one mile to the southwest, and involves a not-too-difficult uphill climb. *It is also possible to see them from the southern (Zonneberg) entrance (off the map), which can be reached by bus or car, or as part of some river cruises.* Be sure to bring a jacket or sweater as the interior temperature is about 50° F. A flashlight would be helpful but is not really necessary.

The Caves of Mount St. Peter are man-made, and not the result of nature. For the past 2,000 years or so the local inhabitants have been digging into this mountain to obtain marl, a stone particularly suitable for construction. In the process of

Maastricht

400 Yards

MAASTRICHT 144

MAASTRICHT 145

Inside the Caves of Mount St. Peter

doing this they have left behind one of the strangest sights in Europe—over 20,000 interconnecting cave-like passages honeycombing the entire mountain and extending for miles in all directions, even into Belgium.

It is extremely easy to get lost in this subterranean labyrinth; more people have gone into it than have ever come out. For this reason **you must take a guided tour**, which leaves on schedule from a little café opposite the fortress of St. Peter. If you arrive early, you can sit at one of the outdoor tables and enjoy a snack or drink while looking out over the city.

Once inside the caves, you will pass many carvings and charcoal drawings on the soft limestone walls, the work of theology students who came her to meditate between the late 19th century and the 1960s. There is also graffiti left behind by several famous people. Twelve different kinds of bats live here, and there are a variety of fossils to be found. Such an underground maze naturally found military significance as a place of refuge in times of war, a role it played as recently as 1944.

Return via Luikerweg and St. Hubertuslaan. You can continue the town walking tour at Begijnenstraat near the Vijf Koppen fortification ⑦. Follow the map through some old streets and climb up onto the town walls at Zwingelput. A stroll along here provides good views, after which you descend onto Heksenstraat, passing an old watermill and a charming little house straddling the Jeker stream on Bonnefantenstraat.

From here, the route goes slightly uphill to the 10th- century:

A Section of the Old Fortifications

*BASILICA OF ST. SERVATIUS *(Sint-Servaasbasiliek)* ⑨, entrance on Keizer Karelplein, **T**: (043) 325-2121 or **W**: sintservaas.nl. Open *April–Oct, daily 10–5, closing at 6 in July–Aug.; Nov.–March, Sun. 12:30–5. Closed during services. Church free. Treasury €.*

Often regarded as the oldest church in the Netherlands and much altered over the years, this former cathedral in the Romanesque style is dedicated to the first Bishop of Maastricht, who transferred his seat here in AD 382. You can visit the church and its fabulous **Treasury** *(Schatkamer)*. On display here is the 12th-century ***Reliquary of St. Servatius**, along with a vast collection of outstanding medieval religious artifacts.

Stroll down to the **Vrijthof** ⑩, a large and very pleasant square lined with trees and outdoor cafés. This is the perfect place to relax before finishing your tour. On the way back to the station, after crossing the bridge, you might want to make a little side trip by strolling south along the river to the:

*BONNEFANTEN MUSEUM ⑪, 250 Ave. Céramique, **T**: (043) 329-0190 or **W**: bonnefanten.nl. *Open Tues.–Sun. 11–5. Closed Mon. except public holidays, New Year's Day, Carnival, and Christmas. Museum Cards accepted. €€. Possible surcharge for special exhibitions.*

This is the major museum of Limburg Province and displays such treasures as local archaeological finds and superb paintings by such Flemish masters as Bruegel, Van Dyck, and Rubens. There is also a good collection of modern art as well as changing exhibitions.

Section III

Daytrips in
BELGIUM

Yes, there really is a magical kingdom of Belgium, and it lies just outside Brussels. You won't find much of the national character in this modern all-European headquarters city, but venture a few miles beyond and you step back in time to a world filled with art treasures; a land imbued with a lusty zest for life. So compact is this kingdom that nearly all of its wonders can easily be explored on daytrips from Brussels. Thirteen of the most fascinating destinations are described in the next section, preceded by a "get acquainted" walking tour of Brussels itself. The Flemish towns come first, followed by the French-speaking towns.

THE COUNTRY

An imaginary line running from east to west just south of Brussels divides Belgium into two distinctly different worlds. To the north, but excluding the capital, lies the land of the Flemings, famous for its medieval art cities as well as for its seacoast. Here the Germanic influences are strong, and the culture somewhat related to that of Holland. Take one step south of the line, however, and you have entered the Latin-based world of the Walloons, where a more French way of life dominates the ancient towns and forests.

This division results from a tumultuous history extending over two millennia, beginning with the Roman conquest of the *Belgae* tribes by Julius Caesar in 57 BC. Almost five centuries of peace as an imperial province ensued, until the fall of the empire brought on an invasion by Germanic tribes of Franks. A kingdom was established that eventually led to the 9th-century empire headed by Charlemagne, an empire later partitioned among his grandsons.

By the 12th century, the great Flemish towns had risen to positions of nearly unrivaled importance and were usually able to avoid domination by the French. The Hundred Years War between England and France made a battleground of Flanders, relieved in 1384 by the transfer of power to the dukes of Burgundy, whose lands eventually extended to cover most of the Low Countries. Nearly a century later, these were turned over to the Austrian Hapsburgs, and through them to the king of Spain.

The Low Countries prospered greatly under Spanish rule, but the rise of Protestantism in the north soon brought on repression. A long period of conflict followed, with the south remaining loyal to Catholic Spain. In time, the Dutch won. What is now Belgium reverted to Austrian rule, and later to France. Napoleon's final defeat at Waterloo, in 1814, led to amalgamation with Holland. In 1830 the Belgians, by now tired of foreign domination, declared their independence. After a brief struggle, the Dutch bowed to the inevitable and let the troublesome Belgians go their own way.

The new kingdom prospered with the Industrial Revolution of the 19th century, particularly in the French-speaking south, which had most of the natural resources. An invasion by Germany in 1914 helped bring about a feeling of national unity, and in the aftermath of World War I the Flemish north began to gain its share of political power. In 1940 the Germans struck again, this time under Hitler. The Belgian king, Leopold III, surrendered, and the country suffered under Nazi tyranny until being relieved by Allied forces in 1944. Post-war reconstruction led to great prosperity, with Brussels emerging as the "capital" of Europe.

PRACTICALITIES

TRANSPORTATION:

All of the daytrips in Belgium described in this book can be made by rail, and all by car. Your choice depends on purely personal factors, but you may want to consider some of the following information before deciding.

BY RAIL:

Belgium was the first country in continental Europe to have passenger-train service, inaugurated in 1835 between Brussels and Mechelen. Today it boasts the densest rail network in Europe, with tracks radiating out from a Brussels hub to just about everywhere in the country. Service is so frequent that reference to a schedule is rarely necessary. With the short distances involved, trains are almost invariably the fastest way of getting around.

Much improved in recent years, the Belgian National Railways *(Societe Nationale des Chemins de Fer Belges* or *SNCB/Nationale Maatschappij der Belgische Spoorwegen orNMBS)* has introduced an IC/IR system of departures at repeating intervals, which greatly simplifies knowing what time the train leaves. Fares are reasonable and can be considerably reduced by using one of the economical rail-passes described later on.

There are very few places of tourist interest in Belgium that cannot be reached directly by train. Stations are usually located right in the heart of town, so close to the major attractions that all of the Belgian walking tours outlined in this book start right at the station.

Seasoned travelers often consider riding trains to be one of the very best ways of meeting the local people and making new friends. It is not at all unusual to strike up an engaging conversation that makes your trip all the more enjoyable. You will also get a marvelous view of the passing countryside from the large windows, and you will have time to catch up on your reading.

All trains operated by the Belgian National Railways belong to one of the following categories, as indicated on schedules and departure platforms:

EC—*EuroCity.* A category of international expresses with special comforts. Both first- and second-class seating is offered, and there is a supplementary fare that is covered by most railpasses. These trains really are not intended for trips solely within Belgium.

INT—*International Express,* an older category of long-distance trains intended for travel to other countries. Both first- and second-class seating is available.

EXT—Special relief trains run on busy days.

1C—*Intercity.* These comfortable expresses are usually your best bet for travel within Belgium. Most of them are made up of very modern cars and operate on frequently recurring schedules. There is no supplementary fare, and both classes are provided for.

IR—*InterRegion.* Connecting the smaller towns and other localities with large cities and the 1C network, these modern trains have their schedules coordinated with the Intercity expresses. Both classes are available.

L—Locals making many stops, often used in commuter service.

High-speed service to Amsterdam, Paris and Cologne is provided by **Thalys, T**: 02-528-2828 or **W**: thalys.com. **High-speed service to London** via the Channel Tunnel is provided by **Eurostar, T**: 02-528-2828 or **W**: eurostar.com. Both of these services depart from Brussel's Midi/Zuid station and require advance reservations. The trip to Paris takes 85 minutes, to London 2 hours and 45 minutes.

Brussels has quite a few **train stations**. Only the three shown on the map are of interest to tourists, and it doesn't matter which of these you use as virtually all trains, except for a few international expresses, stop at all three. They are *Nord/Noord, Central/Central,* and *Midi/Zuid.* Pick the one closest to your hotel.

Most **destinations** in Belgium have both a French and a Flemish name, which might at first confuse you. This book uses the name most familiar to English-speaking people, followed by the alternative name(s) in parentheses. Thus,

MAJOR RAILWAY STATIONS IN BRUSSELS

Gare du Nord
Noord Station

Boulevard d'Anvers

Boulevard Emile Jacqmain

Boulevard de Nieuport

Boulevard Barthélemy

Boulevard du Jardin

Bd. A. Max

Botanique

(Train in tunnel)

Centre Monnaie
Theatre-Royal

Boulevard Anspach

St. Nicholas
Bourse
Grand' Place

Cathedral

**Gare Centrale
Centraal Station**

Boulevard M. Lemonnier

Chaussée de Mons

Rue Royale

Boulevard de l'Abattoir

(Train in tunnel)

Art Museums

Royal Palace

Boulevard du Midi

Rue de la Régence

Boulevard du Régent

Bd. Jamar

Palace
of Justice

**Gare du Midi
Zuid Station**

Boulevard de Waterloo

Avenue Louise

Chaussée d'Ixelles

N

Antwerp can be *Antwerpen* or *Anvers;* Bruges, *Brugge;* Mechelen, *Malines;* and Tournai, *Doornik!* Schedules and signs in Brussels are bilingual, but those in the provinces often use only the local spellings. Be sure you know each of the possible variations before beginning any rail trip, or you just might stay on the train past a station marked *Brugge* when you wanted to get off at Bruges. All of the different names are shown on the heading to each daytrip.

Schedules are really not necessary, as you will seldom have more than a half-hour wait for a train going your way. Tables of departure are posted on yellow boards in each station, and times are expressed in terms of the 24-hour clock; thus a train at 4:52 p.m. would be marked as 16.52. A condensed schedule booklet listing most services of interest to tourists is available free at the information counters. The booklets are in either French or Flemish, but not both. The information personnel almost invariable speak English and will be only too pleased to help you. Real railfans will, of course, want to add the complete schedule book, called an *Indicateur/Spoorboekje,* to their collection. There is a modest charge for this.

Full travel information, including schedules, fares, passes, and so on, is available in English at **W**: b-rail.be.

Reservations are neither necessary nor possible for travel within Belgium, although you might want to consider them for long international journeys.

Some trains split en route to their destinations. Be sure to get on the right set of cars and ask the conductor, to be certain. Destinations are sometimes —but not always —marked on the cars themselves. First-class cars are indicated with the numeral "1" near the door, and with a yellow stripe above the windows.

There is little in the way of **food service** on trains within Belgium, although many have a roving mini-bar offering snacks and beverages. You are better off purchasing refreshments in the station, or nearby, and bringing them on the train.

All but the most local of trains carry both first- and second-class accommodations. First class is, of course, a bit more comfortable and a whole lot less crowded during peak travel times, but most people will find second class to be perfectly adequate for the short journeys involved.

RAILPASSES can be a bargain if you intend to do any real amount of train travel. The Belgian National Railways *(SNCB or NMBS)* accepts the following passes:

EURAILPASS
EURAIL SAVERPASS
EURAIL FLEXIPASS
EURAIL YOUTHPASS
EURAIL SELECTPASS
EURAIL GERMANY 'N BENELUX PASS
BENELUX TOURRAIL PASS

All of these are described in Section II. In addition, Belgium offers its own national passes, sold at stations:

BELGIUM RAIL PASS—Allows 10 trips inside Belgium (but not to border towns) within a six-month period, subject to certain limitations. It may be used by more than one person, but cannot be used on weekends or in July–August. If you can live with these restrictions, it is a terrific bargain.

GO-PASS—For youths under 26, allows ten 2nd-class trips within 6 months. It may be used by more than one person, but subject to the same limitations as the Belgian Rail Pass, above.

Ask at the station about other bargain plans; these are always changing but can be good deals.

Remember that all railpasses must be used in accordance with the rules and instructions accompanying them, and that you must always be prepared to show your passport. When having passes validated, be certain that you agree with the dates before allowing the agent to write them in.

If you intend to take several of the daytrips in this book, and especially if one or two of them are to more distant places such as Oostende, a railpass will probably wind up saving you a considerable amount of money. Even if the savings are less than that, a pass should still be considered for the convenience it affords in not having to line up for tickets, and for the freedom of just hopping aboard trains at whim. Possession of a rail-pass will also encourage you to become more adventurous in seeking out offbeat destinations. It allows you to take longer and more circuitous routes, which might be more interesting. Should you ever manage to get on the wrong train by mistake, your only cost will be your lost time. Railpasses can even be used to cut your dining expenses just by riding to a nearby small town for dinner, where restaurants are usually less expensive than in large cities.

Those who have decided against a railpass may still be able to save some money on their train fares. The Belgian National Railways offers a variety of **excursion tickets** to popular tourist spots, some of which include entry to the various attractions. These are usually called **B-Dagtrips** or some similar name. Ask about them at the train information counters.

While English is commonly spoken by most of the railway employees you are likely to come in contact with, the signs in stations and on trains, as well as the words used on schedules, are in either French or Flemish. The glossaries in Section V should help you with both.

Passengers flying in or out of **Brussels International Airport** (Zaventem) will be happy to know that there is direct, frequent rail service from the terminal itself to all three stations in downtown Brussels.

BY CAR:

Driving on Belgium's superb highways and dense network of secondary roads is essentially the same as in North America, but there are a few national peculiarities. First, there is the confusing matter of place names. Many towns have both a Flemish and a French name, to say nothing of the English one you're familiar with. Thus Brussels is either *Bruxelles* or *Brussel*. This can be absolutely baffling when

Tournai suddenly becomes *Doornik,* or Liège is spelled *Luik.* Road signs are usually only in the language of the region you happen to be in at the moment. You will have to learn both names for each town you intend to drive to, and be on the lookout for signs leading to them. Good road maps show the official local name in heavy type and the alternate name in parentheses. The chapter headings in this book use the name most familiar to English speakers, with other name(s) following in parentheses.

Another problem is that strange traffic rule imported from France called *priorité à droite,* by which vehicles coming in from the right have the right-of-way. This leads to cars dashing into the main stream of traffic from side streets without stopping or slowing down. The rule does not apply when you are on a highway marked with a black arrow inside a red triangle, but you must still be on your guard at all times, especially in built-up areas.

The maximum speed limit on four-lane highways is 120 kph (75 mph), on other roads 70 kph (43 mph), and in urban areas 50 kph (31 mph). Seat belts must be worn at all times, and children under 12 are confined to the rear seat, if there is one. All that's needed to drive in Belgium is a valid driver's license from your own country, a passport, registration for the car, and evidence of insurance (Green Card). Although not required, an International Driver's Permit, issued in the U.S.A. by the A.A.A. and by other motor clubs in other countries, is recommended. Should you have a breakdown or an accident you can summon help from the roadside emergency telephones or, if you're on a main highway, by opening your hood and waiting for a patrol car to come by.

WHEN TO GO:

Any time is a good time to visit Belgium, as most of the attractions are open year-round. A few, however, close between about mid-autumn and early spring. Specific details are given for each daytrip. The best time to come is undoubtedly between mid-spring and early autumn. June, with its longer days, offers the most sunshine. Whatever the season, be prepared for changing weather, and always carry protection against an unexpected brief shower. A light jacket or sweater will come in handy, even in summer.

HOLIDAYS:

Public holidays *(Jours Fériés/Openbare Feestdagen)* in Belgium are:
New Year's Day
Easter Sunday
Easter Monday
Labor Day (May 1st)
Ascension Day (6th Thursday after Easter)
Whitsun
Whit Monday (7th Monday after Easter)
National Day (July 21st)

Assumption (August 15th)
All Saints' Day (November 1st)
Armistice Day (November 11th)
Christmas Day

When any of these fall on a Sunday, the holiday is observed on the following Monday. Expect trains to operate on holiday schedules.

LANGUAGE:

As you are undoubtedly aware of by now, Belgium is primarily divided into French- and Flemish-speaking zones. Brussels, although located within the Flemish area, is officially bilingual and is in fact predominantly French. There is also a small German-speaking zone in the east. Much has been made of Belgium's linguistic problems, but somehow the people have adapted to it and actually get along with each other rather well.

A surprisingly large number of Belgians speak excellent English, and do so willingly. This is especially true in Brussels and in the Flemish areas. Flemish, by the way, is actually Dutch, with identical spellings and slightly different pronunciations. The French spoken in Belgium is almost the same as that in France, even if the Parisians don't think so. Again, English is widely understood by the Walloons, as the French-speakers call themselves. A little knowledge of French will be helpful in ordering meals in the south, although you can get along quite well without it.

MONEY:

Price ranges for attractions are shown in *euros* (€), the currency for both Belgium and most of Western Europe. These are for full adult admissions; discounts are usually available for seniors, students, and children:

€	Up to 5 euros.
€€	6-10 euros.
€€€	11-20 euros.
€€€€	21 or more euros.

The value of the euro varies daily, but is usually in the range of US $1.20 to US $1.40. Banknotes are issued in values of 5, 10, 20, 50, 100, 200, and 500 euros; and coins in values of 1, 2, 5, 10, 20, and 50 cents as well as 1 and 2 euros. The design of banknotes is the same in all countries, but the coins vary by nationality — however all coins are valid in all Eurozone countries. Currently, besides Belgium these include Austria, Finland, France, Germany, Greece, Holland, Ireland, Italy, Luxembourg, Netherlands, Portugal, and Spain.

It is always advisable to do your money exchange transactions at a commercial bank, where you will get the best rate. Some tourist information offices are handy places to change money when the banks are closed. Other money changers often charge outrageous commissions.

Traveler's Checks are the safest way to protect your money while abroad.

They often, however, entail service charges both when you buy them and again when you convert them into euros in Belgium.

Automated Teller Machines (ATMs) offer the best exchange rates to be found anywhere, and allow you to take money directly out of your home bank account as you need it. They are usually open 24 hours a day, are conveniently located all over Belgium, and yield cash in euros. Check with your issuing bank before leaving home to make sure that your PIN code will work in Belgium. Bear in mind that these machines don't always work, so always have a backup plan (or starve).

Credit cards are widely accepted at the more expensive establishments throughout Belgium, but less often by budget hotels and restaurants. They may also be used to yield cash advances from ATM machines, provided you have a compatible PIN code. The most commonly accepted cards are **Visa** *(Carte Bleue)* and **MasterCard** *(EuroCard),* with **American Express** a distant third.

TELEPHONES:

Most public telephones in Belgium use use the convenient Telecard, a pre-paid debit card in which the cost of each call is subtracted until its face value is all used up. These cards are available in €5, €10, and €25 denominations at post offices, train stations, newsstands and other merchants.

To phone ahead from another town in Belgium (or even to make local calls) you must first dial the area code, which always begins with 0, followed by the number. If calling from outside Belgium, dial the international access code for the country that you're in, then the country code for Belgium (32), then the area code without the 0, followed by the number.

You may wish to rent or purchase a **cell phone** while in Belgium, which is certainly a convenience if you're staying for a few weeks or longer. Most American cellular (mobile) phones will not work in Belgium unless they are of the tri-band (900/1800/1900 MHz) variety on the GSM system with a compatible SIM card. Even then, you may be billed at very high rates by your American service provider. Check with them first. One source of rentals is **W**: cellularabroad.com. Purchases of prepaid phones can be made at specialty shops in Brussels and other Belgian cities.

FOOD AND DRINK:

Belgian cuisine is renowned throughout the world, and is one of the major reasons for visiting that country. Although basically French, it has its own specialties that you're almost certain to enjoy. To help you do that, several choice restaurants are listed for each destination in the next section of this book. Most of these are longtime favorites of experienced travelers and serve typically Belgian dishes, except where otherwise noted. Their relative price range, based on the least expensive full meal offered, is indicated by these symbols:

€ — Inexpensive, but may have fancier dishes available.

€€ — Reasonable. These establishments may also feature daily specials.

€€€— Luxurious and expensive.

X: — Days or periods closed.

Those who take dining very seriously should consult an up-to-date restaurant and hotel guide such as the classic red-cover *Michelin Benelux,* issued annually around the beginning of each year. It is always wise to check the posted menus before entering, paying particular attention to any daily set-meal specials.

Belgians demand good food almost as a birthright, and get it at a bewildering variety of restaurants. Regular meals tend to be enormous and lengthy, perhaps as compensation for the small "continental" breakfasts. A great deal of fat is often used in traditional Belgian cooking, so you will probably want to limit yourself to one full meal a day. This is no hardship, since light meals are always available at cafés, and there are plenty of street vendors for snacks.

A handy **menu translator** for both Flemish and French dishes will be found in Section V.

Some typically Belgian **meat dishes** are: *Carbonnades flamandes* (beef cooked in beer), *Biftek et frites* (beefsteak with French fries), *Jambon d'Ardennes* (smoked ham), *Rognons de Veau à la Liègeoise* (roast veal kidneys), and *Boudins Liège* (sausage). A wide choice of game dishes is available in season. The favorite **seafood** seems to be *moules* (mussels), served in such huge quantities that you won't have room for anything else. Shrimp is often prepared as *Tomates aux Crevettes* (stuffed in tomatoes) or as *Croquettes aux Crevettes* (deep-fried in cakes). A great many other fish dishes are commonly found on menus. *Waterzooi,* a famous Flemish specialty, is either chicken or fish, stewed in a sauce with vegetables. Another **fowl** treat is *Oie a l'instar de Visé* (goose boiled and then fried). Among the **vegetables** usually featured are *Chicorée-witloof* (Belgian endive), *Asperges à la flamande* (white asparagus with egg sauce), and the ever-popular *Choux de Bruxelles* (Brussels sprouts). The most common **snack**, sold everywhere, is *frites* (French fries, most often eaten with mayonnaise). Be sure to try *gaufres* (the famous Belgian waffles), and don't forget the sinfully rich chocolates.

Belgium is the land of glorious **beer**. No one, not even the Germans or the Dutch, make a better brew. Hundreds of different brands are produced in this small country, and there is a fantastic range of tastes and strengths (up to 12%!) available. Relatively little of this is exported, so here is your chance to try something different. A few of the more common types are: *pils* (similar to Dutch and other European beers), *gueuze* (with a strong winey taste), *kriek* (with a hint of cherries), *trappiste* (dark, malty, and often very strong, once made by monks), and *rodenbach* (bitter). No wines are made in Belgium, but Luxembourg is not far away and their white Moselles are both excellent and unusual. All kinds of French wines are available at quite reasonable prices. Finally, if you just want mineral water, you won't find a better one than the Belgian *Spa*.

SUGGESTED TOURS:

The do-it-yourself walking tours in the next section are relatively short and easy to follow. On the assumption that most readers will be traveling by train, they always begin at the local station. Those going by car can make a simple adjustment. Suggested routes are shown by heavy broken lines on the maps, while the circled numbers refer to attractions or points of reference along the way, with corresponding numbers in the text. Remember that in Brussels the streets have names in both French and Flemish.

Trying to see everything in any given town could easily become an exhausting marathon. You will certainly enjoy yourself more by being selective and passing up anything that doesn't catch your fancy in favor of a friendly café.

Information such as the opening times of various attractions is as accurate as was possible at the time of writing, but nothing is more certain in travel than change. You should always check with the local tourist office if seeing a particular sight is crucially important to you.

The amount of time that any segment of a walking tour will take can be estimated by looking at the scale on the map and figuring that the average person covers about 100 yards/meters per minute.

TOURIST INFORMATION:

Virtually every town of any tourist interest in Belgium has its own information office, which can help you with specific questions. Known by a variety of names, they are almost always identified by the small letter "i." Their locations are shown on the town maps in this book by the word "info.," or the letter "i" and repeated along with the phone number and website address under the "PRACTICALITIES" section for each trip.

ADVANCE PLANNING INFORMATION:

The Belgian Tourist Office has branches throughout Western Europe and in a few other parts of the world. They will gladly provide maps and brochures as well as help in planning your trip. You can contact them at:

780 Third Ave., **New York**, NY 10017, U.S.A., **T**: 212-758-8130, FAX 212-355-7675, **W**: visitbelgium.com

PO Box 760, Succursale NDG, **Montréal**, PQ H4A 3S2, Canada, **T**: 514-457-2888, FAX 514-489-8965, **W**: visitbelgium.com

31 Pepper St., **London** E14 9RW, United Kingdom **T**: 0906-302-0245 (toll call) or **W**: visitflanders.co.uk. This office handles only Brussels and Flemish-speaking Belgium.

The most useful **tourist-information websites** for Belgium are: **W**: visitbelgium.com, **W**: opt.be, **W**: wallonie-tourisme.be, and **W**: visitflanders.com

Brussels

(Bruxelles, Brussel)

Brussels is more than just the capital of Belgium. As the seat of the European Union, numerous other international agencies, and hundreds of multi-national corporations, it is truly regarded as the *de facto* capital of all Europe. Perhaps more to the point, Brussels is also the perfect base for exploring the entire country on one-day excursions. Before setting out on daytrips, however, you should really take a look at this lively and often surprising city. While only a few of its sights can be called spectacular, there are many interesting attractions that lie hidden away amid the bustle of modern commerce. The "get acquainted" walking tour described in the next few pages will take you to some of the best of these, after which you might want to probe other sights beyond the city center.

Located at the strategic point where the ancient Cologne-Bruges road crossed the Senne River, Brussels developed into an important trading center as early as the 10th century. Then known as *Bruocsella,* the town had its origins in a much earlier settlement, of which little is known. It was granted its first charter in 1312, growing rapidly to a population of 43,000 by the 15th century, by which time it was ruled by the dukes of Burgundy. In the years to come, power shifted back and forth between the French, the Spaniards, the Austrians, and the Dutch. Belgium finally declared its independence in 1830, and Brussels became its capital.

GETTING THERE:

Trains connect Brussels' three major stations (see map on page 151) with nearly every other place in Belgium, and they run so frequently that reference to schedules is rarely necessary. Some typical running times are: Ghent—33 minutes, Antwerp—35 minutes, Bruges—58 minutes, and Liège —78 minutes. There are also good international services to Amsterdam, Luxembourg City, and Paris—each less than 3 hours away— and to other European cities as well. The South Station *(Gare du Midi)* offers high-speed Eurostar service to London via the channel tunnel, and high-speed Thalys service to Paris, Rotterdam, Amsterdam, and Cologne.

By Car, Brussels is only 48 km (30 miles) from Antwerp, 55 km (34 miles) from Ghent, 77 km (48 miles) from Liège, and 96 km (60 miles) from Bruges—all by superb modern highways. Recommended routes are shown in the chapters for these and other towns.

By Air, Brussels is served with direct flights from every corner of Europe and the world. Its modern Brussels International Airport at Zaventem, **T**: 02-753-4221, **W**: brusselsairport.be, is only 14 km (9 miles) from the city center and has its own train station right in the terminal, with frequent departures for the short ride to all three of Brussels' major stations.

GETTING AROUND:

You won't need public transportation for this walking tour, but it is essential for some of the outlying attractions that you might want to visit later. Consisting of subways *(Métro),* trams, and buses, the system operates from 6 a.m. until midnight. Information can be had at **T**: 02-515-2000 or **W**: stib.irisnet.be. One single fare takes you anywhere in the city, and you can save money by purchasing a 5- or 10-trip ticket or a One-Day Card; the latter costs less than three trips. Maps and information are available at the tourist office or in the subway stations. Be warned that taxis are quite expensive, although a tip is included in the metered fare.

PRACTICALITIES:

Any time is a good time to visit Brussels, which is rarely overcrowded with tourists. The city is much more alive on a working day, but note that most of the major museums are closed on Mondays.

The local tourist office, **Brussels International Tourism and Congress** *(B.I.T.C.),* **T**: 02- 513-8940 or **W**: brusselsinternational.be, is in the Town Hall on Grand' Place. For information on all of Belgium, consult the **Belgian Tourist Office** at Rue du Marché aux Herbes 63, one block northeast of the Grand' Place, **T**: 02-504-0390 or **W**: visitbelgium.com

FOOD AND DRINK:

One of the great rewards of a trip to Brussels is the opportunity of dining well. The restaurants listed below are mostly in the area of the Grand' Place, with a few near the Place du Grand Sablon. Many superb establishments are not shown here because they are located well off the walking-tour route. For details on these you should consult a reliable restaurant guide such as the annual *Michelin Benelux.* Those on a tighter budget will be happy to know that a large variety of inexpensive cafés serving light lunches, cafeterias, and fast-food outlets are located along most of the suggested route.

Maison du Cygne (Grand' Place 9) Elegant dining in one of Brussels' better restaurants. Dress well and reserve, **T**: 02-511-8244. X: Sat. lunch, Sun. €€€

L' Ogenblik (Galerie des Princes 1, 3 blocks northeast of Grand' Place) Excellent French cuisine in a simple setting. **T**: 02-511-6151. X: Sun. €€€

't Kelderke (Grand' Place 15) A cellar restaurant right in the heart of things. **T**:

02-513-7344. €€

Aux Armes de Bruxelles (Rue des Bouchers 13, 2 blocks northeast of Grand' Place) Traditional Belgian cuisine in a friendly, rather old-fashioned setting. **T**: 02-511-5598. X: Mon. €€

In 't Spinnekopke (Place du Jardin-aux-Fleurs, near Rue Van Artevelde, 4 blocks west of the Stock Exchange) A really old and traditional Belgian restaurant— out of the way but a genuine experience. **T**: 02-511-8695. X: Sat. eve., Sun. €€

La Roue d'Or (Rue des Chapeliers 26, 2 blocks south of Grand' Place) An inviting old brasserie with good-value lunches. **T**: 02-514-2554. € and €€

Taverne du Passage (Galerie de la Reine 30, 1 block northeast of Grand' Place) Fine Belgian dishes in an arcade. **T**: 02-512-3732. € and €€

Chez Léon (Rue des Bouchers 18, 2 blocks northeast of Grand' Place) A popular bistro noted for its Belgian cuisine. **T**: 02-511-1415. €

Le Roi d'Espagne (Grand' Place 1) A great casual place for snacks and beer, outdoor tables. **T**: 02-513-0807. €

SUGGESTED TOUR:

Circled numbers correspond to numbers on the map.

The **Gare Centrale/Centraal Station** ① is a convenient place to start this tour, although you may prefer to begin right at the ***Grand' Place**, just a short walk away. Regarded by many as the most beautiful square in Europe, it has been the center of life in Brussels since the 12th century. Without exception, all of the buildings surrounding it are extraordinary pieces of architecture, ranging in style from the Gothic to the baroque. With its many outdoor cafés, markets, and street entertainments, the square is a magnet attracting both visitors and residents alike.

The west side of the Grand' Place is totally dominated by the monumental **Town Hall** *(Hôtel de Ville)* ②, whose exquisite, delicate tower soars to a height of 314 feet and is topped by a copper weathervane of the Archangel Michael. Construction of this masterpiece began in 1402 and was completed by 1480, although a few alterations have been made since. The entrance under the tower is off-center, as it is actually part of an earlier 14th-century building. In 1695, the Town Hall was badly damaged during an artillery bombardment ordered by France's Louis XIV, which destroyed the other houses in the square. Everything was quickly rebuilt, however, accounting for the exuberantly baroque structures in what is otherwise a medieval setting. The splendid interior of the Town Hall, noted especially for its tapestries, may be visited on guided tours in English, French, Dutch, German, and sign language. ☎ *02- 279-4365. Tours Apr.–Sept., Tues.–Wed. at 3:15 and Sun. at 10:45 & 12:15; Oct.–March, Tues.–Wed. at 3:15. €.* You may prefer to come back for this. The city tourist office is also in the Town Hall.

Directly across the square stands the:

MAISON DU ROI ③, **T**: 02-279-4350. Open *Tues.–Fri. 10–5, and Sat.–Sun. and holidays noon–5. €.*

Brussels

300 Yards

BRUSSELS 163

Façades on the Grand' Place

Despite its name, the Maison du Roi was built as a law court and never had anything to do with sheltering kings. First erected around 1515, it was severely damaged in the invasion of 1695, only partially repaired, and then neglected until the late 19th century, when it was completely reconstructed using old pictures as a guide. Today it houses the **Museum of the City of Brussels** *(Musée de la Ville de Bruxelles).* Although this is devoted to the history of Brussels and contains a number of outstanding works of art, its most popular attraction is undoubtedly the **Manneken-Pis Room** on the top floor. Here you can see a vast collection of exotic costumes worn on different occasions by that world-famous statue of an impish little boy, whom you'll be meeting soon.

The rest of the square is lined with magnificent **guild houses** erected between 1696 and 1700 after their predecessors had been demolished during the bombardment of 1695. Many of these now house restaurants and cafés, where you can sit outdoors while relishing the whole scene. You may want to stop in at number 10, which belonged to the brewers' guild and now contains the **Brewery Museum** *(Musée des Brasseurs Belges).* Step inside to discover how Belgium's favorite liquid was made in times gone by, and to learn about the new high-tech methods of today. **T**: *02-511-4987 or* **W**: *beerparadise.be. Open April–Nov., daily 10–5; Dec.–March, Sat.–Sun. noon–5. €.*

Right next door, at number 13, is the Museum of Cocoa and Chocolate, a tasty introduction into one of Belgium's great pleasures. **T**: *02-514-2048 or* **W**: *mucc.be. Open July–Aug., daily 10:30–4; Sept.–June, Tues.–Sun. 10:30–4. €.*

Now leave the Grand' Place and follow the map to what is surely the most famous sight in Brussels. The **Manneken-Pis** ④ tells a lot about the Belgians and

The Manneken-Pis

what they think of foreign invaders. Who else would have erected a two-foot-high statue of a little boy peeing? First carved in stone, "Little Julian" was redone in bronze in 1619 and has been periodically stolen, but always replaced. People from all over the world continue to follow the example of France's King Louis XV, who donated a splendid costume to keep the lad warm. The entire wardrobe, now numbering some 654 outfits, is on display in the Maison du Roi in the Grand' Place *(above)*. These are worn on special occasions throughout the year, but most of the time Julian remains his happy naked self. The inevitable souvenir shops near the statue offer an imaginative range of slightly perverted gifts, some of which squirt wine.

Head back to the town center on Rue du Midi and stop at the delightful little **Church of St. Nicholas** ⑤. Almost completely abutted by shops, this strangely appealing church, dedicated to the patron saint of merchants, was begun in the 12th century and greatly altered throughout the centuries. Its atmospheric interior has a collection of minor art works. **T**: *02-513-8022. Free.*

Rue de la Bourse leads past the **Stock Exchange** *(Bourse),* built in 1873 in the classical manner. Turn right on Boulevard Anspach, a busy shopping street, to Place de Brouckere. Surrounded by modern office buildings, this is the commercial heart of today's Brussels. From here stroll around to Place de la Monnaie, a vast open pedestrian area bordered by the **Théâtre Royal de la Monnaie** ⑥, the National

Opera House. Opened in 1819 and later rebuilt, this was the scene in 1830 of a mass demonstration that led to Belgium's declaration of independence from Holland.

Return along the busy shopping street called Rue des Fripiers and turn left on Rue du Marché aux Herbes. This brings you into the center of medieval Brussels, a preserved area of antiquity known as **L'Ilôt Sacré** (The Sacred Isle). Practically next door to the Grand' Place, its colorful narrow streets and passageways are lined with picturesque restaurants and craft shops.

Follow the map through the maze and enter the **Galeries Saint-Hubert** ⑦, a complex of glass-vaulted shopping arcades whose different sections are known as the Galerie des Princes, the Galerie du Roi, and the Galerie de la Reine. Opened in 1847, these were the first such structures in Europe, the concept later spreading to Paris, Milan, London, and other cities. In reality, it was the forerunner of the modern indoor shopping mall. Within its sunlit passages you will find several "outdoor" cafés and restaurants.

The route now leaves the Lower Town and begins a slight climb to the Upper Town. Along the way you will pass the massive ***Cathedral of Saints Michael and Gudule** *(Cathédrals St.-Michel et Ste.-Gudule)* ⑧, which serves as the national church of Belgium and which only achieved cathedral status in 1962. That was after a long wait, as construction of the present structure began in 1226 and was pretty well completed by the 15th century. Its somewhat austere interior is noted for the exceptionally fine 16th-century **stained-glass windows** in the choir, depicting Brussels' Burgundian, Austrian, and Spanish rulers. Some other features to look for are the **Chapel of the Holy Sacrament** to the side of the choir, and the fabulous 17th- century **pulpit** in the nave. **T**: *02-217-8345 or* **W***: kathedraalstmichiel.be. Open Mon.–Fri. 8–6, Sat.–Sun. 8:30–6. Church free, crypt and treasury €.*

Continue uphill to Place du Congrés, where the tall 19th-century **Congress Column** ⑨ honors the national gathering that proclaimed a Belgian constitution after the 1830 revolution. An eternal flame marks the grave of unknown soldiers from both world wars. Step out onto the huge esplanade just beyond this for a splendid panoramic view across Brussels, with a close-up look at the modern administrative complex.

Now follow Rue Royale and turn left on Rue de la Loi. The 18th-century **Palace of the Nation** houses both chambers of the Belgian parliament and overlooks the **Parc du Bruxelles** ⑩, a rather formal public park in the French manner. Once a hunting preserve of the dukes of Brabant, it was the scene of fierce fighting between Dutch troops and the rebellious Belgians in 1830. Stroll through it to the **Royal Palace** ⑪, the official town residence of the king. Some of its interior, particularly the Throne Room, is usually open to the public in late summer. **T**: *02-551-2020. Open late July–late Sept., Tues.–Sun. 10:30–4:30. Free.*

Just downhill from this is the Place Royale, where two of the finest art museums in all of Europe are located:

*ROYAL MUSEUMS OF FINE ARTS *(Musées Royaux des Beaux-Arts de Belgique)* ⑫, **T**: 02-508-3211 or **W**: fine-arts-museum.be. *Open Tues.– Sun. 10–5, closed Mon. and major holidays. Classic Art closed for lunch noon–1, Modern Art from 1–2. €. Gift shop. Cafeteria.*

These two outstanding museums are connected internally at the basement level and share a joint admission, so you can wander back and forth between them. The larger one, with its entrance on Rue de la Régence, is the **Museum of Classic Art** *(Musée d'Art Ancien).* Its extensive collections are particularly rich in works by the Flemish masters such as Bruegel, Rubens, Memling, and Van der Weyden. The Dutch schools are represented by, among others, Bosch, Frans Hals, and Van Dyck. There are also masterpieces of the Italian, French, German, and Spanish schools from the 15th through the 18th centuries. An underground passage connects this museum with the **Museum of Modern Art**, much of which is housed in spectacular subterranean galleries first opened in 1984. The collections here cover the entire scope of 19th- and 20th-century art, with special reference to works by Belgian artists such as Ensor, Magritte, and Delvaux. Don't miss this special Brussels treat!

Continue down Rue de la Régence to the **Square du Petit Sablon** ⑬, a delightful area lined with small bronze statues representing the medieval trade guilds. Across from this stands the **Notre-Dame du Sablon Church** ⑭. Dating from the 15th century, this is one of the most beautiful late-Gothic structures in Belgium. Step inside to see its famous 17th-century baroque **pulpit** and the magnificent stained-glass windows. **T**: *02-511-5741. Open Mon–Fri. 9–5, Sat.–Sun. 10–6:30. Free.*

The square below this, known as Place du Grand Sablon, is noted for its outdoor antiques market held on Saturdays from 9 a.m. to 8 p.m. and on Sundays from 9 a.m. to 2 p.m. There is also a large variety of cafés and restaurants around here.

You can return to the central train station, or to Grand' Place, via the route shown on the map.

ADDITIONAL SIGHTS:

Brussels is reputed to have a hundred museums, give or take a few. In addition, there are several other sights that you might want to visit on another day. Complete details on these are available at the tourist office or by purchasing a special guidebook to the city. Some of the more outstanding attractions are:

Waterloo. The site of the famous battle where Napoleon met his final defeat in 1815 has an enormous monument you can climb, and several museums explaining the battle. Get there by a local train leaving all three stations at half-hour intervals in the direction of Charleroi, or by bus route "W" from South Station *(Gare du Midi).*

Atomium. A remnant from the 1958 World's Fair, this strange structure represents an iron crystal molecule magnified 165 billion times. Consisting of nine spheres, each about 60 feet in diameter and connected by tubes to reach a height of 335 feet, it houses displays on nuclear energy and space travel as well as a restaurant. Travel within it is by elevator and escalators. More than a wee bit dated today, it is a great place to reminisce about the 1950s. Take the Métro to Heysel, or tram 23 or 81 to the north end of the line. **T**: *02-475-4777 or* **W***: atomium.be. Open late March-June and Sept., daily 9:30–5; July–Aug., daily 9:30–7, Oct.– early Jan., daily 10–5. Closed for renovation until early 2006. €€.*

Royal Museum of Art and History. Located in the Parc du Cinquantenaire to the east of the center city, this museum has an enormous collection of classical antiquity and artifacts of mixed ages from all over the world. **T**: *02-741-7211 or* **W**: *kmkg-mrah.be. Open Tues.–Fri. 9:30–5, Sat.–Sun. 10–5. €.* While there, you can also visit the **Royal Museum of the Army and Military History**—a major collection of weaponry including aircraft and World War II artifacts. **T**: *02-733-4493 or* **W**: *klm-mra.be. Opwn Tues.–Sun. 9–noon and 1–4:45. Closed major holidays. Free.* Another adjoining treat, for car enthusiasts at least, is **Autoworld**. **T**: *02-736-4165 or* **W**: *autoworld.be. Open April–Sept., Mon.–Fri. 9:30–6, Sat.–Sun. 10–6.; Oct.– March, daily 10–5. €.* Take the Métro to the Merode stop, or tram 81, or bus numbers 20, 28, 36, 61, 67, or 80.

Horta Museum. Brussels' favorite architect was Victor Horta, whose work in the Art Nouveau style is renowned throughout the world. You can see its splendors in his former home at Rue Américaine 25 in the southern part of the city. Bus number 54 or 60, or trams 81, 82, 91, or 92 go there. **T**: *02-543-0490 or* **W**: *hortamuseum.be. Open Tues.–Sun. 2–5:30. Closed major holidays. €.*

Ghent

(Gent, Gand)

Histroy may live on in Ghent, but this great Flemish industrial city most certainty does not dwell in the past. Although it may possess more venerable buildings than any other place in Belgium, it is hardly a preserved museum. Indeed, its medieval treasures have become an integral part of a dynamic urban center where the Middle Ages blend right into the 21st century.

Ghent began as an abbey founded by St. Bavon about AD 630. During the 9th century, a castle was built at the confluence of the rivers Lieve and Leie, around which a town developed. By the 13th century, a growing textile industry made Ghent one of the largest cities in northern Europe, and a force to be reckoned with. Its economy declined after the Spaniards came to power in the 16th century, but was revived with the introduction of cotton-spinning machinery during the Industrial Revolution. A new canal opened the way to seagoing vessels, and today Ghent is the third-largest port in Belgium. The city has a curious connection with American history, for it was here that the treaty ending the War of 1812 was negotiated and signed.

GETTING THERE:

Trains depart Brussels' three major stations at half-hour intervals for the 33-minute ride to Ghent's St. Pieters Station. Return service operates until late evening.

By Car, Ghent is 54 km (34 miles) northwest of Brussels via the A-10/E-40 highway. Park as close to the cathedral as possible and drive to the Bijloke Museum and the Fine Arts Museum to avoid a long walk.

PRACTICALITIES:

Avoid visiting Ghent on a Monday, when many of its most important sights are closed.

The local **Tourist Office**, **T**: 09-266-5232 or **W**: visitgent.be, is in the crypt of the Belfy on Botermarkt.

FOOD AND DRINK:

Some good restaurant choices are:

Graaf van Egmond (St. Michielsplein 21, 3 blocks west of the Belfry) Flemish specialties in a 13th-century townhouse on the river. **T**: 09-225-0727. X: Sun. eve., Mon. €€€

Auberge de Fonteyne (Gouden Leeuwplein 7, by the Town Hall) Traditional Flemish fare, including Waterzooi and mussels, all in a 16th-century house. **T**: 09-224-2454. X: Sat. eve., Sun. eve. €€ and €€€

't Klokhuys (Corduwaniersstraat, a block north of the Folklore Museum) A brasserie with both Flemish and French dishes. **T**: 09-223-4241. X:Mon. lunch. €€

Keizershof (Vrijdagmarkt 47, on the Vrijdag Markt) Both contemporary European and traditional Belgian dishes, served in a casual atmosphere, indoors or in the garden. **T**: 09-223-4466. X: Sun. € and €€

Brooderie (Jan Breydelstraat 8, near the Design Museum) A pleasant, casual place for light and healthy veggie meals. **T**: 09-225-0623. X: Mon. €

Ghent is famous (or notorious!) for its traditional beer taverns *(kroegen),* which serve up to several hundred different varieties of brew—some of which are very high in alcohol content. Among the more interesting places are:

Dulle Griet (Vrijdagmarkt 50) A highly atmospheric place with snacks as well as beer. **T**: 09-224-2455. €

Waterhuis aan de Bierkant (Groentenmarkt 9, on the water 2 blocks southeast of the castle) Popular with visitors; outdoor tables. €

SUGGESTED TOUR:

Circled numbers correspond to numbers on the map.

From **St. Pieters Station** ① it is an uninteresting 1½-mile walk to the center of town, following the route on the map. You can avoid this by taking tram number 1, 11, or 12 to Korenmarkt or Centrum.

Begin at the **Belfry and Cloth Hall** (Belfort *en Lakenhalle)* ②, two adjoining medieval structures in the middle of a large open square. At one time these were hemmed in by houses, which have long since disappeared. The Belfry soars to a height of 312 feet and can be seen for miles around. Begun in 1321 and completed in 1339, it contains one of the best carillons in Belgium, a bell museum, and the local tourist office. You can visit these, and ride an elevator to the top for a splendid **view* of the city. A ten-foot copper dragon, first cast in 1377 and twice replaced, tops the spire, while next to its base stands a 17th-century former jail called the *Mammelokker.* The adjacent Cloth Hall dates from the early 15th century and was originally an assembly room for wool and cloth merchants. **T**: *09-233-9922. Open mid-March to mid-Nov., 10–12:30 and 2–5:30. €, includes free guided tours from May–Sept, at 2:10, 3:10, and 4:10.*

Step across the square to:

*ST. BAVO'S CATHEDRAL *(Sint-Baafskathedraal)* ③, **T**: 09-269-2045. *Church open April–Oct., daily 8:30–6; rest of year, daily 8:30-5. Closed mornings on Sun., church holidays, and during services. Free. Mystic Lamb exhibition open April–Oct., Mon.–Sat. and holidays 9:30–4:45, Sun. 1–4:30; rest of year Mon.–Sat. and holidays 10:30–3:45, Sun. 1–3:30. €.*

This magnificent Gothic structure was built between the 13th and 16th centuries on the foundations of an earlier Romanesque church. St. Bavo's is renowned throughout the world for the quality of its art treasures. Foremost among these is the **Adoration of the Mystic Lamb,* a large 15th-century altarpiece widely regarded as being one of the most important paintings in the history of art. It is supposedly a joint creation by Jan van Eyck and his older brother Hubert, but this is disputed by historians, as there is no evidence that the famous Flemish painter ever had a brother by that name. That the work exists at all is a miracle in itself. Phillip II tried to take it to Spain, and in 1566 it barely escaped destruction by the Calvinists, who considered it a symbol of idolatry. During the 18th century, its naked Adam and Eve proved offensive to the eyes of the Hapsburg emperor Josef II, who had those panels replaced by clothed figures. The French stole the painting in 1794 and didn't return it until after Napoleon's defeat at Waterloo, after which parts of it were sold to a Berlin museum. It was not until 1920 that all of its sections were reunited in Ghent, only to be partially stolen again. During World War II, the Nazis grabbed the whole thing and hid it in an Austrian salt mine, where it was discovered in 1945 by American soldiers. Happily, it is now in one piece, except for a small panel that has never been recovered and was replaced by a copy.

Other major masterpieces in the cathedral include the *Conversion of St. Bavo* by Peter Paul Rubens, the *Triptych of the Calvary* by Justus of Ghent, and a fabulously carved pulpit by Laurent Delvaux. Be sure to visit the 12th-century **crypt** with its famous frescoes and church treasures.

Return to the Belfry and turn right to the **Town Hall** *(Stadhuis)* ④, a peculiar jumble of architectural styles if ever there was one. Begun in the 15th century, its construction dragged on until the 18th. Part of it is flamboyant Gothic, another is sober Renaissance, a third Flemish baroque, and the final fourth is in the rococo style. Oddly enough, it all works, and the entire structure is actually quite handsome. *Guided visits depart from the nearby tourist office, May–Oct., Mon.–Thurs., at 3. €.*

Now follow the map to the **Vrijdag Markt** ⑤, where a goods market is held on Fridays, hence the name. The same market is also held on Saturdays, and there's a bird market on Sundays. Traditionally the meeting place of the townspeople, this large square has seen more than its share of political violence and skirmishes between the trade guilds since at least the 14th century.

Continue on Meerseniersstraat to the Leie River, near which you can see **"Mad Meg"** *(Dulle Griet),* an enormous 15th-century cannon once used in

Ghent

500 Yards

GHENT 173

The Castle of the Counts

Ghent's interminable wars. Cross the little bridge and turn left past some interesting facades to the **Museum of Folklore**, also called the **Huis van Alijn** *(Museum voor Volkskunde)* ⑥. Housed in a beautifully restored 14th-century children's home, the museum re-creates life among the common people of Ghent during the 19th century. Its picturesque courtyard is lined with 18 typical Flemish houses, complete with replica shops and period room settings. **T**: *09-269-2350 or* **W**: *huisvanalijn.be. Open Tues.–Sun., 11–5. €.*

The route now leads to the:

*CASTLE OF THE COUNTS *(Het Gravensteen)* ⑦, **T**: 09-225-9306 or **W**: gent.be/gravensteen. Open *April–Sept., daily 9–6; rest of year, daily 9–5. Last admission 45 minutes before closing. €€.*

Built in 1180 on the foundations of the original 9th-century castle, the massive and foreboding Castle of the Counts was primarily used to keep the local citizens in line through sheer intimidation. You can climb all over its perfectly restored battlements for a great view, and visit (if you dare!) the terrifying torture chambers, where a vast assortment of hideous instruments of pain and death —including a rather efficient-looking guillotine—are on display in the **Museum of Court Paraphernalia**. Don't miss this chilling adventure!

The square in front of the castle was used as a place of public execution, by burning or beheading, until the late 18th century. It also served as a fish market and is lined with impressive old buildings.

Cross the bridge and turn left to the **Design Museum Gent** *(Museum voor Sierkunst en Vormgeving)* ⑧, where exhibitions of handicrafts and design from the Renaissance to modern times are displayed in a fine 18th-century mansion. There are various furnished interiors and a section filled with 20th-century works including Art Nouveau and Art Deco items. **T**: *09-267-9999. Open Tues.–Sun. 10–6.* €.

Just a short stroll from this is the medieval harbor, bordered by a lovely stretch of old buildings called the **Graslei** ⑨. Short **boat trips** through the city's streams and canals are offered near the bridge on either side of the river. **T**: *09-266-0522 or* **W**: *gent-watertoerist.be. The cruises last about 40 minutes.* €€.

Cross the bridge and stroll along the Graslei for a wonderful look at some marvelous ***guild houses** dating from the 13th through the 17th centuries. The bridge at its south end, the St. Michielsbrug, offers a stunning view of the urban scene.

From the nearby center of town you can return to St. Pieters Station by tram or continue walking along the river's edge to the **Archaeological Museum of the Bijloke** *(Oudheidkundig Museum van de Bijloke)* ⑩. Housed in a still-functioning medieval abbey, the museum has a superb collection of the religious and applied arts, weapons, clothes, musical instruments, and so on, displayed in lovely room settings. **T**: *09-225-1106. Open Thurs. 10–1 and 2–6, Sun. and holidays 2–6.* €.

Those traveling on foot may want to return to the station via the **Fine Arts Museum** *(Museum voor Schone Kunsten)* ①, located in Citadel Park. Here you will find an excellent collection of Flemish and Dutch works by such masters as Bosch, Rubens, Van Dyck, Bruegel, and Frans Hals. There are also quite a few modern pieces by James Ensor, Rouault, Delvaux, Magritte, and others. **T**: *09-240-0700 or* **W**: *mskgent.be. Closed for restoration until early 2006.*

Practically adjacent to this is the **Municipal Museum for Contemporary Art** *(Stedelijk Museum voorActuele Kunst),* which focuses on Belgian and international art since 1945. The exhibitions here are constantly changing as the art scene evolves. **T**: *09-221-1703 or* **W**: *smak.be. Open Tues.–Sun. 10–6.* €, *higher prices for special exhibitions.*

From here it is a short walk back to the train station.

Bruges
(Brugge)

Time has long stood still in medieval Bruges, a romantic city that went to sleep in the Middle Ages and didn't wake up until the 19th century. Virtually all of the events of modern history have passed it by, leaving behind a perfectly preserved gem that is today among the loveliest places in Europe. No visitor to Belgium should miss seeing it.

In its heyday Bruges was a very wealthy town, attracting great artists and erecting splendid houses. Built around a 9th-century castle, its position near the Zwin estuary made it an ideal inland port, well protected from the storms of the North Sea. By the 12th century it was one of the most important trading centers in Europe. Shiploads of wool from England arrived daily to be woven into cloth at Bruges.

Gradually, however, the Zwin began to silt up and at first, expensive efforts were made at dredging it. Around the same time, the English started to make their own cloth for export. The weavers at Bruges—defending their own privileges—prohibited this from entering their harbor, and so the trade naturally shifted to rival Antwerp. This was the beginning of the end. Investment in a canal, new harbor facilities, and a change in the guild rules might have saved the day, but the merchants of Bruges balked at the price, with the result that the town slowly declined and became known as "Bruges-la-Morte," or "the dead city."

Ironically, the necessary canal finally got built, and it opened in 1907, along with the splendid modern harbor of Zeebrugge. By then, however, the citizens of Bruges had discovered a gold mine in their own past and took steps to insure that the town's medieval appearance would forever remain intact to delight the tourists.

And Bruges does get more than its share of visitors. Everything is so well organized, though, that even in the peak travel season it remains an extraordinarily pleasant place and never seems overcrowded. The suggested walking tour, besides covering the basics, also takes you into parts of town that relatively few tourists ever get to see.

Incidentally, the town is known locally by its Flemish name of *Brugge,* even if the English-speaking world continues to call it by the French Bruges.

GETTING THERE:

Trains depart Brussels' three major stations at half-hour intervals for the one-hour ride to Bruges *(Brugge)*. Return service operates until late evening.

By Car, Bruges is 96 km (60 miles) northwest of Brussels via the A-10/E40 highway to exit 9. Park in the lot near the train station and avoid driving in the Old Town.

PRACTICALITIES:

Any time is a good time to visit Bruges, but note that many of the major attractions are closed on Mondays.

The highly organized local **Tourist Office** has moved to 't Zand 34, a half-mile north of the train station and 2 blocks west of the Cathedral. Contact them at **T**: 050-448-686 or **W**: brugge.be

FOOD AND DRINK:

Being a major tourist area, Bruges offers a wide range of restaurants and cafés in every possible price range. Some choices are:

De Karmeliet (Langestraat 19, 3 blocks south of the Jerusalem Church) World-renowned French cuisine in an 18th-century mansion. Dress nicely and reserve, **T**: 050-338-259. X: Sun. eve., Mon. €€€+

Due de Bourgogne (Huidenvettersplein 12, a block southeast of the Basilica of the Holy Blood) A world-famous inn with classic French cuisine. **T**: 050-332-038 for reservations. X: Mon., Tues. lunch. €€€

't Pandreitje (Pandreitje 6, 2 blocks southeast of the Basilica of the Holy Blood) Classic French and Belgian cuisine. **T**: 050-331-190. X: Sun., Wed. €€€

't Bourgoensche Cruyce (Wollestraat 41, close to the Basilica of the Holy Blood) A small and very popular restaurant overlooking a canal. **T**: (050) 337-926. X: Tues., Wed. €€€

Erasmus (Wollestraat 35, just south of Markt) A bright, modern place with garden seating in summer, serving traditional Flemish dishes and over 155 kinds of beer. **T**: 050-335-781. X: Thurs. €€

Grand Kaffee de Passage (Dweerstraat 26, 2 blocks northwest of the cathedral) Traditional Belgian cuisine on a modest budget. **T**: 050-340-232. € and €€

De Belegde Boterham (Kleine St.-Amandstraat 5, a block west of the Markt) Healthy light lunches, but no dinner. X: Sun. €

Het Dagelijks Brood (Philipstockstraat 21, 2 blocks north of the Town Hall) Light lunches, including salads, soups, sandwiches, and quiches. **T**: 050-336-060. X: Tues. €

Lotus (Wapenmakersstraat 5, 2 blocks northeast of the Town Hall) Vegetarian delights in a modern setting. **T**: 050-331-078. Open for lunch only. X: Sun. €

Bruges
(Brugge)

500 Yards

SUGGESTED TOUR:

Circled numbers correspond to numbers on the map.

Leave the **Brugge Train Station** ① and follow the map through a park to the **Minnewater** ②, popularly known as the "Lake of Love." During the Middle Ages this was the commercial harbor of the town, defended in part by the powder tower of 1398 at its south end.

Stroll along this peaceful scene and turn left into the ***Beguinage** *(Begijnhof)* ③, a sheltered world of meditation that has hardly changed since its foundation in the 13th century. In those days its tiny houses were occupied by single lay women, or widows who wished to live a religious life without taking formal vows. Today it is inhabited by Benedictine nuns wearing 15th-century costumes. Amble quietly through its courtyard and visit the small church, first erected in 1245 and rebuilt in 1605. The **house** at the northeast corner has been restored to its 17th-century condition and is open to visitors. Don't miss this unusual treat. If the south gate to the Beguinage is closed, you can usually get in via the main north gate. **T**: *050-330-011. Beguinage free. House open March–Nov., Mon.–Fri. 10–noon and 1:45–5:30, Sat. 10–noon; Dec.–Feb., Mon.–Fri. 11–noon, also 1:45–4:15 on Wed.– Thurs., and on Sat. 10–noon. €.*

Cross the little bridge and walk two blocks east to the **Diamond Museum** *(Diamantmuseum Brugge)* ④. With a history dating back some five centuries, Bruges is Europe's oldest diamond center. Now this romantic and somewhat mysterious story is told in a sparkling gem of a museum. **T**: *050-342-056 or* **W**: *diamondmuseum.be. Open daily 10:30–5:30. €€.*

Now follow the map to the bridge on Katelijnestraat. This is one of the four places where you can take a delightful half-hour ***boat ride** through the town's picturesque canals. These depart whenever there are sufficient customers, and are a "must" for all visitors to Bruges. *Operates March to mid-Nov., daily 10–6, plus weekends in late Nov. and Dec. Rides: €€.*

Just across the bridge stands the **Church of Our Lady** *(Onze Lieve Vrouwekerk)* ⑤. Built in a variety of styles between the 13th and 15th centuries, it has the tallest spire in the Low Countries. Step inside to see the famous ***Virgin and Child** statue by Michelangelo, one of the few pieces by that renowned artist to have left Italy during his lifetime. Among the many other works of art are the 16th-century monumental tombs of Mary of Burgundy and Charles the Bold. High above the north ambulatory there is an enclosed balcony that opens into the adjacent Gruuthuse Museum. The balcony was put there in the 15th century so the wealthy merchant who lived in that mansion could attend services without leaving home. **T**: *050-345-314. Open Mon.–Fri. 9–12:30 and 1:30–5, Sat. 9–12:30 and 1:30–4, Sun. 1:30–5. €.*

Directly across the street from the church is the:

HOSPITAL OF ST. JOHN & *MEMLING MUSEUM *(St. Janshospitaal)* ⑥, **T**: 050-448-711. *Open Tues.–Sun. 9:30–5. Closed Mon. and major holidays. €€.*

Founded in the 12th century to care for Bruges' sick and indigent, this former hospice contains a stunning collection of works by Hans Memling, a 15th-century German-born painter who became the leading artist of medieval Bruges.

The most outstanding pieces are the *Reliquary of St. Ursala,* in which the legend of the saint and her 11,000 virgins being massacred in Cologne is depicted on the sides of an oak reliquary, and the *Mystical Marriage of St. Catherine,* a sublimely beautiful altarpiece dedicated to St. John the Baptist and St. John the Evangelist, the patron saints of the hospital. While there, be sure to visit the restored 17th-century **Dispensary** *(Apotheek),* which remained in use until 1971.

Continue along Mariastraat and Heilige Geeststraat to **St. Savior's Cathedral** *(St.-Salvator's Katheddraal)* ⑦, an essentially Gothic structure grafted onto an earlier Romanesque base. Architecturally undistinguished, it has suffered much during the centuries of its existence and was only elevated to cathedral status in 1834. Nevertheless, its interior does have some exquisitely carved choir stalls and misericords, splendid tapestries, and a lovely baroque rood screen. The adjoining **Cathedral Museum** features some works by the old Flemish masters Dirk Bouts and Hugo van der Goes. **T**: *050-336-841. Church open Sun.–Mon. 2–5:45, Tues.–Fri. 8:30–11:45 and 2–5:45, Sat. 8:30–11:45 and 2–3:30, Sun. 9–10:15. Closed to tourists during services. Museum open Sun.–Fri. 2–5. Church free, Museum €.*

The route now follows a complicated but colorful path to the **Markt** and its rather extravagant and slightly askew 13th-century **Belfry** *(Belfort)* ⑧, the very symbol of Bruges. Soaring some 270 feet above the old marketplace, it may be climbed for a truly spectacular *view. On the way up you can glimpse the famous 47-bell carillon that plays tunes every quarter-hour. At the base of the belfry tower is the Halle, a 13th-century covered market that now houses local government agencies. *Belfry open Tues.–Sun. 9:30–5; last admission at 4:15. €.*

Stroll through the lively Markt, an unusually attractive square lined with restaurants and outdoor cafés. From here, the walking tour leaves the tourists behind and explores a quiet part of town where the atmosphere of the Middle Ages remains more intact. Follow the map through a series of narrow streets and alleyways to **Jan van Eyckplein** ⑨, named after the great 15th-century Flemish painter. This neighborhood was the center of commercial activities during the 13th and 14th centuries, and still retains much of that ambiance.

Continue along the canalside Spinolarei until you come to a bridge. At this point you could cut the tour short by turning right and following the map to the Basilica of the Holy Blood ⑲. If you prefer to see some more sights of an unusual nature, however, you should cross the bridge and turn down Carmersstraat to the outer ring canal. Here you will find several restored **windmills**, one of which may be visited. Known as **St. Janshuismolen** ⑩, it is of the stilt type and was rebuilt in 1770. You can climb up into its working mechanism for a good look as some flour is ground. Open *April–Sept., daily 9:30–12:30 and 1:30–5.*

Now amble through the park to the early-15th-century **Cross Gate** *(Kruispoort)* ⑪, once a part of the ramparts that were largely demolished during the late 18th century. Head back into town on Langestraat and Peperstraat, which will take you to the 15th-century **Jerusalem Church** ⑫, supposedly built to the same plans as the Holy Sepulchre in Jerusalem. It is especially noted for its 15th-century stained-glass windows and its interesting crypt. *Open Mon.–Fri. 10–noon and 2–6, Sat. 10–noon and 2–5.*

Just north of this, in the medieval almshouses, is the popular **Lace Center** *(Kantcentrum).* Sponsored by the state, this is where the ancient skills of lace making are passed on to younger generations. **T**: *050-330-072 or* **W**: *kantcentrum.com. Open Mon.–Fri. 10–noon and 2–6, Sat. 10–noon and 2–5. Closed Sun. and holidays. €.*

Across the street is the **Folklore Museum** *(Museum voor Volkskunde),* which you might also want to see for its period room settings, worksops, and artifacts. In case you're thirsty, there's also a little tavern called De Zwarte Kat. **T**: *050-448-764. Open Tues.–Sun. 9:30–5. €.*

The route now continues on past St. Anne's Church and crosses a small canal. Turn left and follow around to one of the prettiest sights in Bruges, the **Groenerei** ⑬. From here you get a lovely view down the canal and into the old part of town. Stroll along the water and turn right on Blinde Ezelstraat to the flamboyant **Town Hall** *(Stadhuis)* ⑭. Begun in the 14th century, its magnificent façade is a veritable forest of statuary. Step inside to see its splendid **Gothic Hall** *(Gotische Zaal),* decorated with murals depicting the history of Bruges, and its fantastic vaulted ceiling. Very close to this, in a nearby building, is the **Renaissance Hall** *(Renaissancezaal 't Brugse Vrije),* another interesting historic site that is included in the same admission as the Gothic Hall. *Both open Tues.–Sun. 9:30–5. Combined admission €.*

The large open square known as Burg, in front of the Town Hall, occupies the site of the original 9th-century castle around which Bruges developed. Also facing this is the **Basilica of the Holy Blood** *(Heilig Bloedbaziliek)* ⑮, where what is said to be blood washed from the body of Christ is venerated. The 12th-century basilica consists of a lower and an upper chapel, the lower being a dark Romanesque structure that remains virtually unchanged. The sacred relic is in the upper chapel, which was rebuilt in the Gothic style during the 16th century. On Ascension Day, it is carried through the city streets in a colorful procession. *Open daily 10–noon and 2–4. Closed Wed. afternoons. €.*

Return across the canal and follow the map to the world-famous:

The Bonifacius Bridge

*GROENINGE MUSEUM ⑱, **T**: 050-448-711. *Open Tues.–Sun. 9:30–5.* €€.
Covering the entire scope of Flemish art from the 15th through the 20th centuries, this superb museum displays works by Jan van Eyck, Hans Memling, Rogier van der Weyden, Hugo van der Goes, Breugel, Bosch, and such moderns as Magritte and Delvaux. If you like art, you'll love this collection—easily one of the best in the world.

Leave the museum by a side passage and stroll around to the tiny ***Bonifacius Bridge**, beyond which lies one of the most enchanting and evocative corners of old Bruges. From here it is only steps to the **Gruuthuse Museum** ⑰, housed in a fabulous 15th-century merchant's mansion. In it are displayed several thousand antiques of all sorts, covering the entire sweep of Bruges' history. As you wander through the complex of rooms, you may be startled to look out directly into the interior of the Church of Our Lady, reminding you that this tour has come full circle. **T**: *050-448-711. Open Tues.–Sun. 9:30–5.* €€.
Game for a little bit more before heading for some well-deserved refreshment? Practically adjacent to this is the **Arenthuis-Brangwyn Museum**, housed in an 18th-century mansion. The ground floor features a collection of historic lace, while the upper floor is devoted to the works of Frank Brangwyn (1867–1956), a British painter who lived in Bruges and created many of his finest works here. **T**: *050-448-711. Open Tues.–Sun. 9:30–5.* €.

Trip 27

Oostende

(Ostende, Ostend)

The sparkling seaside resort of Oostende neatly bundles most of its considerable attractions into a compact area overlooking the North Sea. A busy passenger port with constant ferries to England's Dover, a colorful fishing harbor and yacht marina, miles of sandy beaches, Belgium's largest casino, and a thriving shopping district all vie for the attention of visitors —many of whom come over from Britain. Connoisseurs of modern art will see a different aspect of Oostende, however, as this was the lifelong home of James Ensor, one of the major pioneers of Expressionism. Many of his strange works may be seen here, along with his fully restored home.

Although Oostende was founded in the 11th century and was a main departure point for the Crusades, it is today a thoroughly modern town, since little of its past survived the wars of this and previous centuries.

GETTING THERE:

Trains depart Brussels' three major stations at hourly intervals for the 80-minute ride to Oostende. Return service operates until mid-evening. Expect crowds on summer weekends.

By Car, it's the A-10/E-40 highway all the way. Oostende is 115 km (72 miles) northwest of Brussels.

PRACTICALITIES:

Oostende is best visited between June and the end of September, when all of its attractions are open. Some of the museums are closed on Tuesdays, another on Monday. Good weather will make this trip much more enjoyable.

The local **Tourist Office, T**: 059-701-199 or **W**: toerisme-oostende.be, is at Monacoplein 2, opposite the casino. During July and August there is a branch in the train station.

FOOD AND DRINK:

Being a popular seaside resort, Oostende has a great variety of restaurants and cafés in all price categories. Quite a few of these specialize in seafood. Some choices are:

Villa Maritza (Albert I Promenade 76, 2 blocks southwest of the casino)

Exquisite French cuisine in a villa overlooking the sea. **T**: 059-508-808 for reservations. X: Sun. eve, Mon., Tues. €€€

David Dewaele (Visserskaai 39, by the fish market) This renowned seafood restaurant also has a few meat dishes. **T**: 059-704-226. X: Mon. in off-season. €€ and €€€

James Taverne (Ensor Galerij, off Vlaandernstraat, near Ensor House) A cozy old favorite for traditional cuisine. **T**: 059-705-245. X: Tues. €

Cardiff (St. Sebastiaanstraat 4, a block west of the Folklore Museum) A small hotel with a fine dining room. **T**: 059-702-898. X: Tues. off-season. €

Taverne Koekoek (Langestraat 38, 2 blocks southwest of the Ensor House) Chicken on a spit, 24 hours a day. **T**: 059-708-970. €

SUGGESTED TOUR:

Circled numbers correspond to numbers on the map.

The **Train Station** ① is right on the harbor and connects directly with ferries to England. From here, stroll down along the old fishing harbor and the Visserskaai, a delightful fishermen's quay lined with seafood restaurants and cafés. Near its end is the **North Sea Aquarium** *(Noordzeeaquarium)* ②, where living fish may be seen in a natural environment along with a fine collection of seashells. **T**: *059-321-669. Open April–Sept., daily 10–noon and 2–5, remaining open until 6 on weekends; rest of year weekends only, 10–noon and 2–6. €.*

A walk out on the **Western Jetty** *(Westerstaketsel)* ③ affords good views and the opportunity of taking a **short cruise**. **T**: *059- 706-294. Cruises July–Aug., daily each hour from 11–5. Also on weekends from Easter–June and in Sept.*

Return to the Visserskaai and continue along the broad Albert I Promenade, which looks out over the sea. This leads to the modern **Casino** *(Kursaal)* ④, complete with a concert hall, nightclub, restaurant, and gambling rooms. **T**: *059-705-777. Gaming begins daily at 3 p.m. and requires payment of a membership fee of €.*

Now follow the map to the:

*JAMES ENSOR HOUSE *(Ensorhuis)* ⑤, Vlaanderenstraat, **T**: 059-805-335. *Open June–Sept., Wed.–Mon. 10–noon and 2–5; rest of year weekends only, 2–5. Closed Tues. €.*

One of the most original artists of modern times, James Ensor was born in Oostende in 1860 and died there in 1949, having seldom left the town. His father was English, thus the name. The house was previously used by his aunt and uncle as a souvenir shop, the ground floor of which is now preserved. Upstairs, the studio and living quarters have been maintained as they were in his time, although the works of art on display are all copies, as the originals are in major museums. What is most striking about his work is its sense of grotesque satire, a legacy that can be traced back to earlier Flemish painters such as Bruegel and Bosch. You may

Oostende

400 Yards

N

Beach

love or hate these paintings, but you will never forget them.

Continue straight ahead to **Wapenplein**, the main square of Oostende. This is dominated by the **Festival and Culture Palace** *(Stedelijk Feest en Kultuurpaleis)* ⑥, which houses two interesting museums. The first of these is the **"De Plate" Folklore Museum**, where the history of the town from prehistoric to relatively recent times is on display, with artifacts and period room settings. **T**: *059-805-335. Open in summer season, Wed.–Sun. 10–noon and 2–5; rest of year on Sat. only. €.*

On the floor above this is the **Fine Arts Museum** *(Museum voor Schone Kunsten)*, devoted primarily to the artistic trends of the last hundred years. Pride of place is naturally given to Oostende's own James Ensor, who is represented by a large collection of his earlier works. **T**: 059-519-830. *Presently closed; may move to a new location. Ask at the Tourist Office.*

The route now goes through an attractive pedestrians-only shopping area and turns left to the **Church of St. Peter and St. Paul** ⑦. First built in the 14th century, it was rebuilt in the neo-Gothic style in 1907 and contains the tomb of Belgium's first queen, who died in Oostende in 1850. Behind it stands the Peppermill Tower, the only remaining part of the original medieval church.

A stroll westward on Josef II Straat soon brings you to the **Leopold Park** ⑧ with its flower clock, pond, bandstand, and miniature golf course. Continue through this and follow Spilliartstraat and Romestraat to the **Provincial Museum for Modern Art** *(Provinciaal Museum voor Moderne Kunst)* ⑨, which explores contemporary Belgian art in all of its aspects, including sculpture, film, and video. **T**: *059-508-118 or* **W**: *pmmk.be. Open Tues.–Sun. 10–6. €, higher during special exhibitions.*

Return on Alfon Pieterslaan to what is perhaps Oostende's most exciting attraction. Moored at the end of the yacht basin is the:

MERCATOR ⑩, **T**: 059-705-654. *Open April–June and Sept., daily 10–12:30 and 2–5:30; July–Aug., daily 10–5:30; Oct.–March, weekends 10–12:30 and 2–4:30. €.*

This splendid three-masted training ship formerly belonged to the Belgian Merchant Navy. Launched in 1932, she made voyages throughout the world until 1960, when she was retired as a museum. You can climb all over the proud vessel and explore below decks as well, examining the items collected during her many adventures to exotic ports.

From here it is a short walk back to the station.

Trip 28

Kortrijk

(Courtrai)

Although it boasts no world-famous tourist attractions, Kortrijk does offer the opportunity to get off the beaten path and enjoy a thoroughly delightful Flemish town with a rich history. This easy daytrip includes a visit to what may be the most charming *beguinage* in the Low Countries, to an important 13th-century church with two outstanding works of art, to a splendid town hall, and to excellent museums of local history. More than that, Kortrijk is an unusually pleasant shopping center for the region, with recently renovated, pedestrianized streets and a good selection of places to eat and drink. The town lies just six miles from the French border.

Known as *Cortoriacum* in Roman times, Kortrijk was always an important road junction. Ever since the Middle Ages it has prospered as a result of the unusually soft water in its river, the Leie. This was ideal for making linen from the locally grown flax, and set the stage for the town's textile industry of today.

Kortrijk will always be remembered in history as the site of the Battle of the Golden Spurs, which occurred in 1302, marking the beginning of the end of the Age of Chivalry. Fought between the Flemish weavers and a large army of French knights, it was the first time that ordinary citizens had ever defeated a professional force in armor.

GETTING THERE:

Trains leave Brussels' three major stations at hourly intervals for the 70-minute ride to Kortrijk (Courtrai). Return service operates until mid-evening.

By Car, leave Brussels on the A-10/E-40 highway west towards Ghent to exit 15, then take the A-14/E-17 southwest to Kortrijk exit 3. The total distance from Brussels is 90 km (56 miles).

PRACTICALITIES:

Kortrijk may be visited at any time, but note that most museums are closed on Mondays. Some other sights are closed or have shorter hours during the off-season, especially on weekends.

The local **Tourist Office**, **T**: 056-277-840 or **W**: kortrijk.be/toerisme, is at St.-Michielsplein 5; a few steps from the Grote Markt. Ask them about the nearby National Flax Museum, accessible by bus or car.

FOOD AND DRINK:

You will find a good selection of restaurants and cafés in Kortrijk. Among them are:

Broel (Broelkaai 8, near the Broelmuseum) Both indoor and outdoor meals by the river. **T**: 056-218-351. X: Sat. lunch. €€

Center Broel (Craanmarkt 6, a block south of the Town Hall) Good-value meals in a small hotel, indoors or out. **T**: 056-219-721. € and €€

César (Grote Markt 2) This tavern with indoor/outdoor seating offers good-value lunches right in the center of town. **T**: 056-222-260. X: Tues. € and €€

Belfort (Grote Markt 52) A small hotel with a recommended restaurant, Bistro 't Kopke. **T**: 056-222-220. € and €€

SUGGESTED TOUR:

Circled numbers correspond to numbers on the map.

Leave the **Train Station** ① and follow the map past the theater hall to the **Grote Market** ②. In the middle of this large open market square stands the 14th-century **Belfry** *(Belfort),* the only remaining part of a medieval cloth hall that was destroyed by bombing during World War II. The two figures under its center pinnacle strike the hours on the town clock.

Facing the northwest corner of the square is the **Town Hall** *(Stadhuis)* ③, of 14th-century origin but rebuilt around 1520 with both Gothic and Renaissance elements. Several alterations have occurred since, the latest being a complete renovation in 1962. The many statutes of the counts of Flanders that embellish its facade are modern reproductions. Step inside to see the Aldermen's Chamber *(Schepenzaal)* on the ground floor, which has a splendid 16th-century fireplace in the flamboyant Gothic style. The room is now used for weddings and receptions. Upstairs, the Council Chamber *(Oude Raadzaal)* has an even more magnificent 16th-century mantlepiece, decorated with figures of the virtues and the vices of mankind. All around, the sculptures, murals, and stained-glass windows merit close examination, as some of the scenes depicted are more than a little satirical. *Ask at the nearby tourist office about admission.*

Now stroll through the square to the **Church of St. Martin** *(St.-Maarten-skerk)* ④, begun in the 13th century and rebuilt at the beginning of the 15th. In its choir, there is a beautifully carved gilded stone tabernacle, and in the center nave a baroque pulpit. *Open Mon.–Fri. 7:30–5, Sat. 9:30–5, Sun. 10:30–6. Free.*

Close to this is the entrance gate to the **Béguinage** *(Begijnhof)* ⑤, a place of surprising calm in the center of a busy town. These tiny spiritual communities were founded in the Middle Ages and were especially prevalent in Belgium, which at one time had 94 of them. The *Beguines* were lay women who lived devout lives

Kortrijk

200 Yards

In the Béguinage

of chastity, simplicity, and obedience, but who did not take perpetual vows. Their numbers were high as a result of the surplus of women caused by constant wars, which killed off many of the available men to whom they would otherwise have been married.

Although it was founded in 1238, the 40 tiny houses that still exist in the Beguinage are mostly from the 17th century. Near the entrance is a chapel, dating perhaps from the 15th century, that has a nice interior with an air of restrained elegance. The Mother Superior's House contains a small **museum** of life in the Béguinage in former times. Stroll through the narrow winding streets, and be sure to notice the minuscule Chapel of Our Lady of the Snow, where pious people come to pray for relief from mental stress. *Museum:* **T**: *056-244-802. Open daily 2–6. €.*

Continue on to the *Church of Our Lady *(Onze Lieve Vrouwkerk)* ⑥, the oldest building in town and once part of its fortifications. Built in the 13th century, it was altered several times since and is noted for its two great artistic treasures. One of these is the 14th-century alabaster statue of St. Catherine, and the other is the masterful *Raising of the Cross* of 1631, one of the last paintings done by Van Dyck before he left Flanders for England. **T**: *056-244-800. Open weekdays 8–6, Sat. 9–4:30, Sun. 11–6. Free.*

A right turn on Groeningestraat leads to the **Groeninge Abbey** *(Groeningeabdij)* ⑦. Built in the late 16th century, it now houses a museum of Kortrijk's colorful past from prehistoric times up to the eve of the First World War, with a special focus on the Battle of the Golden Spurs—a crucial event in European history that occurred here in 1302. **T**: 056-277-850. *Open Tues.–Sun. 10–noon and 2–5. Free.*

The Broel Towers

Continue on to the **Broel Towers** ⑧, two fortifications from the 12th and 15th centuries that once guarded the river crossing. In the center of the bridge stands a statue of St. Nepomucenus, the patron saint of the drowned.

Beyond this is the **Broel Museum** ⑨, located in an 18th-century mansion. Its rich collections include paintings and sculptures by artists who lived or worked in Kortrijk from the 16th century up to the present. The museum is especially noted for its hall of ceramics. **T**: *056-277-780. Open Tues.–Sun. 10–noon and 2–5. Free.*

Return to Grote Markt and its attractive cafés, where you can relax before returning to the station. Just southeast of this is a renovated shopping area that you might want to explore before heading back to the station.

NEARBY ATTRACTION:

Less than two miles south of the town center, and easily reached by bus or car, is the **National Flax Museum** and its adjoining **Lace and Linen Museum** *(Nationaal Vlas, Kant en Linnenmuseum)* ⑩. Due to the softness of the water in the Leie River, Kortrijk has been a center for flax cultivation since medieval times, and a modern industry based on it thrives to this day. The two museums here celebrate this past with some 26 tableaux, historic artifacts, and samples of lace and linen through the ages—all housed in a 19th-century Flemish farmhouse. **T**: *056-210-138. Open March–Nov., Tues.–Fri. 9–12:30 and 1:30–6, Sat.–Sun. 2–6. Closed on holidays. Each museum: €. Discounted combination tickets for both available.*

Mechelen

(Malines)

Travelers with a particular interest in cathedrals and churches in general will surely enjoy a visit to Mechelen, the religious capital of Belgium and the seat of its archbishop primate. Located just a few miles north of Brussels, it is a thoroughly Flemish town that has preserved a great deal of its medieval atmosphere.

Mechelen grew around an 8th-century abbey, founded by St. Rombout, and soon became part of the Bishopric of Liège. After a period of independence it passed to the dukes of Burgundy, reaching a peak of prosperity in the early 16th century when it was chosen as the residence of Margaret of Austria, who governed the Low Countries as regent for the infant Charles V. A brilliant court of artists and scholars lived in Mechelen in those days, but the glory faded in 1531 when the government moved to Brussels. During World War I it held out heroically against the invading Germans, finally succumbing and suffering much damage. This and the ravages of World War II have since been repaired, with the town today being an exceptionally pleasant place to visit—and one not exactly overrun with tourists.

GETTING THERE:

Trains depart Brussels' three major stations frequently for the 20-minute ride to Mechelen *(Malines)*. Return service operates until late evening.

By Car, Mechelen is 27 km (17 miles) north of Brussels on the A-1/E-19 highway.

PRACTICALITIES:

You can stroll around Mechelen at any time in good weather, but don't plan on seeing the churches before afternoon. The Cathedral opens at 9:30, but the other churches are open on Tuesdays through Sundays only, from 1:30 to 4:30 p.m. The museums are closed on Mondays, and an outdoor market is held in the Grote Markt on Saturday mornings.

The local **Tourist Office**, **T**: 015-297-655 or 070-222-800 (toll), **W**: inenuitmechelen.be, is in the Town Hall on Grote Markt. Ask about tours in the cathedral tower, and any other attractions.

FOOD AND DRINK:

Some good restaurant choices in Mechelen are:

D'Hoogh (Grote Markt 19, upstairs) Classic French cuisine in the grand manner. Reservations suggested, **T**: 015-217-553. X: Sat. lunch, Sun. eve., Mon., Aug. €€€

Mechelse Mangerie (Grote Markt 23, near the tourist office) Indoor/outdoor dining, with seasonal specialties, both meat and fish. **T**: 015-201-952. €€

Gulden Anker (Brusselsesteenweg 2, a block southwest of the Brussels Gate) Noted for its seafood. **T**: 015-422-535. X: Sat. lunch, Sun. eve, late July. €€

There are quite a few cafés on the Grote Markt.

SUGGESTED TOUR:

Circled numbers correspond to numbers on the map.

Express trains from Brussels stop at Mechelen's **main station** ①. From there, follow the map to the **Grote Markt** ②, a lovely market square lined with gabled houses from the 16th through the 18th centuries. In its center stands a statute of Margaret of Austria, whose 16th-century regency briefly brought fame to Mechelen, then the effective capital of the Low Countries. A colorful outdoor market is still held here on Saturday mornings.

The east side of the square is totally dominated by the **Town Hall** *(Stadhuis),* composed of two very different buildings. The larger one to the right, which houses the tourist office and whose Gothic arch leads to a nice inner courtyard, is the former *Lakenhal, or* Cloth Hall. Begun in 1320, it was rebuilt after a fire in 1342 and acquired its octagonal turrets only in the 16th century. At the same time, its left wing was torn down to make space for a palace, but work on this soon ceased when the court moved to Brussels. The flamboyant structure you see here today, which appears to be many centuries old, was actually built in 1911 to the original plans. Together, the ensemble makes a dramatic sight.

While at the Town Hall, stop in at the tourist office to ask about which of the town's several small (and unusual) museums are open today, and how to get to them.

Leave the square and follow Befferstraat to the **Palace of Margaret of Austria** ③, erected in the Gothic and Renaissance styles during the 16th century. It now serves as a law court. Try to get a look at its magnificent inner courtyard. Across the street is the 17th-century **Church of St. Peter and St. Paul**, whose interior is graced with lovely oak confessional boxes, carved with allegorical sculptures.

The route now leads to a beautiful early-16th-century mansion that houses the **Museum Hof Van Busleyden** ④. Its collections are concerned with local history and especially with the musical art of the carillon, for which Mechelen is famous. Another display here is the original 1647 figure of *Op-Signoorke,* a town mascot that was always taken for a ride during festivals. In 1775, a citizen of rival Antwerp was falsely accused of trying to steal it, and he was beaten by the mob. Since then, Antwerp has made various attempts at revenge, and actually succeeded in kidnap-

Mechelen

500 Yards

N

ping the figure in 1949, returning it the next year. **T**: *015-294-030. Open Tues.–Sun. and holidays, 10–5. €.* Adjacent to it is the **Carillon School**, whose students come from all over the world.

Just around the corner stands **St. Janskerk** ⑤, a 15th-century church noted for its exquisite triptych, the **Adoration of the Magi,* one of the finest works by Rubens. Unfortunately, the church is often closed, but if it's open be sure to stop in.

Now follow the map to **St. Catherine's Church** *(St. Katelijnekerk)* ⑥, built in 1336. Its rather austere interior is quite lovely and features some exceptional confessionals and an interesting pulpit. Continue on through an old part of town to the baroque **Béguinage Church** ⑦. Built in 1629, it contains a number of superb art works, but is rarely open.

The route on the map soon brings you to the ***Cathedral of St. Rombout** *(Sint-Romboutskathedraal)* ⑧, a truly remarkable Gothic structure whose 15th-century tower soars to a height of 318 feet and contains two carillons. The older of these is partly from the 15th century, while the newer is a recent addition. Construction on the cathedral itself began in 1217 and continued into the 16th century. Step inside to see the 17th-century high altar and the tombs of the archbishops. A series of paintings in the ambulatory depicts the life of St. Rombout, while other works of art in the south transept include Van Dyck's magnificent **Crucifixion* of 1627. *Open daily 9:30–5. Free.*

Stroll over to the Grote Markt and turn right on the IJzerenleen, an attractive shopping street that begins at the handsome 14th-century *Schepenhuis,* Mechelen's first town hall. The bridge on the Dijle River, known as the Grootbrug, dates from 1298 and has three irregular arches. Once across it, you could make an interesting little side trip down Van Beethovenstraat, a small street named for the composer's grandfather, who was born in Mechelen. It leads through a brewery to the river's edge, where some 16th-century houses grace the area near the next bridge.

A left turn at the Grootbrug brings you to **De Zalm** ⑨, the House of the Salmon, a handsome Renaissance structure built in the 16th century for the Fishmongers' Guild. The nicest way back to the train station takes you past the imposing 14th-century **Brussels Gate** *(Brusselpoort)* ⑩, the only remaining part of the medieval town walls. It now houses a museum of local history, from prehistoric times to the recent past. **T**: *015-294-030. Open Tues.–Sun. 1–5. €.* From there just follow the map to the station.

Antwerp

(Antwerpen, Anvers)

If you haven't already discovered it, a visit to Antwerp should come as a wonderful surprise. Belgium's second-largest city and major seaport is not only a great cultural center, it is also a highly entertaining, beautiful, vital, and immensely likeable place. Don't miss this urban Flemish treat!

Legend has it that Antwerp began during the Roman era with the riverside castle of a giant named Druon Antigon, who extracted tolls from passing ships and cut off the hands of sailors who refused to pay, which he then threw into the Schelde—thus the name *Handwerpen,* meaning "to throw a hand." Historians, however, offer a less picturesque theory, insisting that the name derives from *Aan de Werpen,* literally "at the wharf." Whatever the truth of the matter, Antwerp's reason for existence has always been its strategic location on a deep river that runs through Dutch territory to the North Sea.

Actually, there has been a settlement here since the 2nd century AD, and it acquired a fortress in the 9th century. Towards the end of the 15th century, Antwerp took over much of the trade of rival Bruges, whose outlet to the sea had silted up. The city was sacked by the Spaniards in 1576, and its economy was later ruined by the Dutch, who blocked access to the Schelde estuary for nearly 150 years, an act of aggression that ended only under Napoleon's assumption of power in 1795. Belgium's declaration of independence in 1830 led to Holland charging a toll for "their" river, but this was settled in 1863. Since then, Antwerp has regained its position and is once again one of the leading ports of Europe.

Antwerp's most famous citizen was Peter Paul Rubens (1577–1640), the German-born painter who spent most of his life in Antwerp and left behind an astonishing legacy of art that graces the city today. You'll be seeing much of this along the walking tour, although the city possesses far more masterpieces than can possibly be seen in one day. For this reason, and for the other attractions as well, it may be a good idea to stay over for a few days, or to come back at a later time to continue your exploration of this magnificent place.

GETTING THERE:

Trains depart Brussels' three major stations frequently for the 35-minute ride to Antwerp's Centraal Station. A few other trains stop only at Antwerpen-

Berchem Station, which would involve making a change. Return service runs until late evening.

By Car, the easiest route is to take the A-1/E-19 highway through Mechelen. Antwerp is 51 km (32 miles) north of Brussels. Park as close to the Rubens House as possible, to cut down your walking distance.

PRACTICALITIES:

Antwerp is a pleasure to visit at any time, but note that most of the museums are closed on Mondays and on some major holidays. The harbor cruises operate from May through October, but not every day—check the listing.

The local **Tourist Office** is located at Grote Markt 13, **T**: 03-232-0103 or **W**: visitantwerpen.be.

FOOD AND DRINK:

There are a great many wonderful restaurants and cafés all over Antwerp. A few of the better choices in the areas covered by this walking tour are:

BETWEEN CENTRAAL STATION AND THE CENTER:

Rimini (Vestingstraat 5, 2 blocks west of Centraal Station) Italian cooking. **T**: 03-226-0608. X: Sun. €€

Terminus (Fr.-Rooseveltplaats 9, 4 blocks northwest of Centraal Station) Local specialties at good prices. **T**: 03-231-4795. €€

The Bistro (Wapper 1a, next to the Rubens House) International cuisine in a delightful location. **T**: 03-232-3675. €€

De Foyer (Komedieplaats 18, 2 blocks east of the Mayer van den Bergh Museum) An elegant old place with light meals and buffet lunches. **T**: 03-233-5517. X: Sun. eve. € and €€

IN THE CENTER OF TOWN:

't Fornuis (Reyndersstraat 24, 2 blocks southwest of the cathedral) Superb traditional food in a rustic atmosphere. Dress nicely and reserve. **T**: 03-233-6270. X: Sat., Sun. €€€+

In de Schaduw van de Kathedraal (Handschoenmarkt 17, opposite the cathedral) Delicious Belgian specialties, indoors or out. **T**: 03-232-4014. X: Tues., Mon. in winter. €€€

Neuze Neuze (Wijngaardstraat 19, 3 blocks northeast of the cathedral) A rambling, cozy restaurant with gourmet-level French cuisine. **T**: 03-232-2797. X: Sun., Wed. noon, Sat. noon. €€ and €€€

De Gulden Beer (Grote Markt 14) Italian and French cuisine right on the main square, both indoors and out. **T**: 03-226-0841. €€ and €€€

Dock's Café (Jordaenskaai 7, a block west of St. Pauluskerk) This riverside brasserie is just north of the Steen. **T**: 03-226-6330. X: Sat. lunch. € and €€

SUGGESTED TOUR:

Circled numbers correspond to numbers on the map.

The Town Hall in the Grote Markt

Centraal Station ① is located about one mile east of the Old Town's center, where the sights begin. The entire distance from station to center is along a series of attractive shopping streets, but if you prefer to ride you can take the underground tram *(Pre Métro)* to Groenplaats. Just north of here stands the:

*CATHEDRAL OF OUR LADY *(Onze Lieve Vrouwekathedraal)* ②, Handschoenmarkt, **T**: 03-213-9951 or **W**: dekathedraal.be. *Open weekdays 10–5:30, Sat. 10–3, Sun. 10–4. Closed during services. €.*

Although it is the largest Gothic church in Belgium, Antwerp's great cathedral is so hemmed in by houses, built right up to its walls, that its immense size does not become immediately apparent. The present cathedral was begun in 1352 and was essentially finished during the 16th century. Its fantastically ornate north tower soars some 404 feet above the street, while the south tower was never completed.

The cathedral's spacious, luminous interior has recently undergone a 20-year restoration and can now once again be seen in its full splendor. Three masterpieces by Rubens to be on the lookout for are his *Elevation of the Cross,* the *Descent from the Cross,* and the *Assumption.*

Continue on to the nearby **Grote Markt** ③, the impressive main square of Antwerp. In its center stands the **Brabo Fountain**, atop which the legendary hero Silvius Brabo tosses the hand of Antigon into the Schelde, thus saving the town from the evil giant's tyranny. The entire west side of the square is occupied by the magnificent 16th-century **Town Hall** *(Stadhuis)*, whose essentially 19th-century

ANTWERP 200

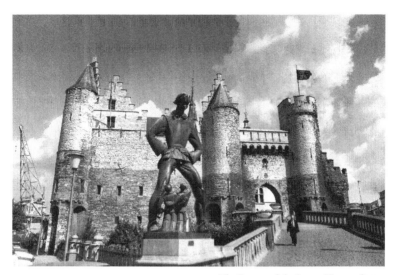

The Steen and the Lange Wapper Statue

interior may usually be visited on any day except Sundays. **T**: *03-220-8020. Guided tours ore offered on Mon.–Thurs. at 2 p.m. €.* Ornate guild houses, mostly from the 16th century, line the other sides of the square. Many of these now contain restaurants or cafés, contributing to the generally festive atmosphere.

A short stroll down Suikerrui brings you to the Schelde River. ***Harbor cruises** offered by the Flandria Company depart from the landing stage at **Steenplein** ④. These are a lot of fun, although only the longer trips get into the modern port, as it is quite a distance downstream. Still, the views are interesting, and refreshments are available on board. Most of the cruises are for about 50–90 minutes. **T**: *03-231-3100 or* **W**: *flandriaboat.com. Operates May–Sept., on Tues. and Thurs.-Sun. (daily in July–Aug.); and on weekends in Oct. Departures at 1, 2, 3, and 4 p.m. €€ and €€€.*

At the north end of Steenplein stands a forbidding medieval fortress called the **Steen** ⑤, whose foundations date from the 9th century. The remaining parts of the castle itself were built around 1250 and have been altered many times since. Originally the residence of the ruling counts, it was later used as a notorious prison and now houses the **National Maritime Museum** *(Scheepvaartmuseum Steen)*. The modern statue at its entrance is of the "Lange Wapper," a giant who was the scourge of drunkards. Inside, the museum has a fascinating collection of nautical artifacts, ship models, and displays concerning Antwerp's maritime development. There is an outdoor collection of real boats and barges adjacent to the castle. **T**: *03-201-9340 or* **W**: *museum.antwerpen.be/sheepvaartmuseum. Open Tues.–Sun. 10–5, closed major holidays. €.*

Now follow the map to the **Vleeshuis** ⑥, a masterful gabled and turreted mansion, built for the Butchers' Guild in 1503. Its elegant interior today houses an excellent museum for the applied arts that is especially noted for its collection of old musical instruments. **T**: *03-233-6404 or* **W***: museum.antwerpen. be/vleeshuis. Closed for renovation until sometime in 2006.*

Continue on to **Veemarkt**, the former cattle market, and **St. Pauluskerk** ⑦, a late Gothic church of the 16th century ornamented with a 17th-century baroque tower. Its lovely interior contains some fine woodcarvings, choir stalls, and confessionals. There are also several paintings by Rubens and other local artists. **T**: *03-232-3267. Open for tourists Easter–Sept., daily 2–5. Closed during services. Free.*

The route now leads through a charming old part of town and returns to the Grote Markt. Head south on Oude Koornmarkt and follow around to Vrijdagmarkt, where an antiques market is held on Wednesday and Friday mornings. Facing this is the:

*PLANTIN-MORETUS MUSEUM ⑧. **T**: 03-221-1450 or **W**: museum.ant werpen.be/plantin_moretus. *Open Tues.–Sun. 10-5. Closed some major holidays.* €€.

This is an absolutely essential stop for anyone who loves books. The publishing firm founded in 1555 by Christopher Plantin grew to become the most important in Europe, was taken over by his son-in-law Jan Moretus, and remained in business until 1867. The complex of buildings in which it is housed served as both the family mansion and as printing shops. Step inside to see the vast collection of publishing artifacts, including examples of the development of alphabets, a type foundry, printing presses, many rare volumes, and a Gutenberg Bible. There are also several paintings by Rubens, who was a family friend. Don't miss this special treat.

From here, you can make a side trip on foot or by bus or tram to the Royal Museum of Fine Arts, or you could skip that and head straight for the Mayer van den Bergh Museum.

*ROYAL MUSEUM OF FINE ARTS *(Koninklijk Museum voor Schone Kunsten)* ⑨, **T**: 03-238-7809 or **W**: museum.antwerpen.be/kmska. *Open Tues.–Sat. 10–5, Sun. 10–6. Closed Mon. and some major holidays.* €€, *includes audio guide. Higher prices for special exhibitions.*

This is easily among the most impressive art museums in the Low Countries. Its monumental collections include works by such masters as Van Eyck, Van der Weyden, Memling, and Quinten Matsys, among others. Rubens gets two entire galleries to himself, and his contemporaries, such as Van Dyck and Jordaens, are well represented. You'll also find paintings by Bruegel, Cranach, and Frans Hals. Modern art is well covered with works by such Belgian luminaries as Ensor, Magritte, and Delvaux.

Return via the route on the map and turn east to the **Mayer van den Bergh Museum** ⑩, where a small but absolutely exquisite collection of medieval and Renaissance art is displayed in a reconstructed 16th-century town house. The most important piece here is Bruegel's *Dulle Griet* (Mad Meg), an astonishing painting that touches on the supernatural. **T**: *03-232-4237 or* **W***: museum. antwerpen.be/mayervandenbergh. Open Tues.–Sun. 10–5. Closed Mon. and some major holidays.* €.

Continue on to what is probably Antwerp's most popular attraction:

*RUBENS HOUSE ⑪, **T**: 03-201-1555 or **W**: museum.antwerpen.be/rubenshuis. Open *Tues.–Sun. 10–5. Closed Mon. and some major holidays.* €€, *includes audio guide.*

The great painter Peter Paul Rubens began construction on this large townhouse and studio around 1610 and lived there until his death in 1640. After that it deteriorated badly, and by the time it was acquired by the city in 1937 there was not much left beyond the framework. A meticulous reconstruction was finished and it opened to the public in 1946. None of its present furnishings actually belonged to Rubens, but they are all authentic antiques from his time and show just how well this prosperous artist, diplomat, and scholar really lived. Be sure to get out into the **garden**, laid out as it appeared in his paintings.

While on the subject of Rubens, you may want to visit the nearby **St. Jacobskerk** ⑫, a patrician church where the artist and his family are buried. Above the altar in the Rubens Chapel is one of the master's last works, *Our Lady Surrounded by Saints,* in which he depicted himself as St. George, his two wives as Martha and Mary, his father as St. Jerome, and his son as Christ. **T**: *03-225-0414. Open April–Oct, daily 2–5; Nov.–March, Wed.–Mon. 2–5. Closed to tourists during services.* €.

From here, you can walk or take a tram back to the station. Antwerp has many other attractions, such as the extraordinary zoo and the Diamond Museum, both of which are adjacent to Centraal Station. The **Diamond Museum** ① covers the entire history of these pricey rocks, from mining to finishing. **T**: *03-202-4890 or* **W***: diamantmuseum.be, Koningin Astridplein 19-23. Open Thurs.–Tues. 10–5:30. Closed Wed.* €€, *includes audio guide.* Practically next door is the **Zoo Antwerpen** ①, a really old and fairly large zoo in which animals roam more-or-less freely, separated by simulated natural barriers. **T**: *03-202-4540 or* **W***: zooantwerpen.be. Open daily from 10 until 4:45, 5:30, 6, or 7, depending on season.* €€.

Leuven

(Louvain)

It seems appropriate that the oldest university in the Low Countries should be in a town famous for its beer. Leuven—dare it be called the Heidelberg of Belgium? —excels both at education and at having fun. An easy daytrip here will reward you with some outstanding art and architecture, lovely gardens, an unusually picturesque beguinage, and a lively student scene in the old marketplace.

Located on the medieval trade route between Cologne and Bruges, Leuven became an important town in the 12th century, when it was the capital of Brabant and a leading center of cloth weaving. Shifting trade patterns and internal political strife caused a rapid decline during the 14th century, but the town's prosperity was renewed in 1425 by the founding of the university. At first a leading center of liberal thought, with such renowned scholars as Erasmus and Mercator, the school turned to more traditional Catholic values in reaction to the Reformation. Another fundamental change occurred in 1968 when its French-speaking faculty and students moved south to form their own university in Walloon territory. The Flemish-speaking school at Leuven presently has about 26,000 students spread throughout the city and in the immediate surroundings.

GETTING THERE:

Trains depart Brussels' three major stations at half-hour intervals for the 25-minute ride to Leuven *(Louvain)*. Return service operates until late evening.

By Car, Leuven is 26 km (16 miles) east of Brussels via the E-40 highway to exit 22, then the E-314 into town. Park as close to the Grote Markt as possible.

PRACTICALITIES:

Avoid going to Leuven on a Monday, when some of the sights are closed. On Sundays and holidays they are open from 2-5 p.m. only. Good weather will make the outdoor cafés and gardens of the town much more enjoyable.

The local **Tourist Office**, **T**: 016-211-539 or **W**: leuven.be, is by the Town Hall at Grote Markt 9.

FOOD AND DRINK:

Leuven has a good range of restaurants and cafés in all price ranges. Some choices are:

Belle Epoque (Bondgenotenlaan 94, a block west of the station) Exquisite French cuisine, served in an elegant town house or on the terrace. Reserve, **T**: 016-223-389. X: Sun., Mon. €€€

't Zwart Schaap (Boekhandelstraat 1, by the Town Hall) Excellent French cuisine right in the center of things. **T**: 016-232-416. X: Sun., Mon. €€

Y Sing (Parijsstraat 18, 2 blocks southwest of St. Pieterskerk) Chinese and Thai cuisine. **T**: 016-228-052. X: Wed. €

De Blawe Schuit (Vismarkt 16, 3 blocks northwest of St. Pieterskerk) A popular student hangout, with traditional local dishes. **T**: 016-220-570. €

Lukemieke (Vlamingenstraat 55, near Naamestraat between the Beguinage and the Town Hall) A cozy place for vegetarian dishes, indoors or out. **T**: 016-229-705. X: Sat., Sun. €

The many outdoor cafés on the Oude Markt cater to students and tourists alike. Be sure to try the products of the local Artois Brewery, whose many brands include the popular Stella Lager.

SUGGESTED TOUR:

Circled numbers correspond to numbers on the map.

Leave the **Train Station** ① and walk or take a bus a half-mile down Bondgeno-tenlaan to Fochplein, the center of town. In the middle of the square stands the modern "Fonske" Fountain, in which a student attempts to pour knowledge into his head but sometimes only succeeds in wetting the passersby. Behind him is one of the most astonishing structures in Belgium, the unbelievably ornate ***Town Hall** *(Stadhuis)* ②, a miracle of the 15-century Flamboyant Gothic style. Its richly sculpted façade is decorated with turrets, pinnacles, and no fewer than 236 statues. The latter were planned from the start but not actually added until the early 19th century. The local tourist office is here, and guided tours of the elaborate interior are offered. **T**: 016-*211-540. Tours April–Sept, Mon.–Fri, at 11 and 3, on Sat.–Sun. and holidays at 3; Oct.–March, daily at 3. €.*

Just across the Grote Markt square stands ***St. Pieterskerk** (St. Peter's Church) ③, a splendid 15th-century late Gothic structure that has been repaired after severe wartime damage. Its interior has an impressive **rood screen** topped with a wooden Christ, an extravagant **pulpit**, and a **chapel** devoted to "Proud Margaret," the patron saint of servant girls. In its **Treasury** are some truly remarkable art treasures, foremost of which is the magnificent triptych, *The Last Supper;* a 15th-century masterpiece by the local painter Dirk Bouts. **T**: 016-226-906. *Church open Tues.–Fri. 10–5, Sat. 10–4:30, Sun. & holidays 2–5; from mid-March to mid-Oct. it is also open on Mon. 10–5. Treasury open same times, but closed mid-Dec, to mid-Jan. Treasury admission €, includes the Municipal Museum Vander Kelen-Mertens, below.*

From here, it is a short stroll into the **Oude Markt** ④, a large open square lined with old houses and bordered on the south by university buildings. Much of this pedestrian area is filled with delightful outdoor cafés frequented by students, making it a particularly attractive place to sample the local brew.

Now follow the map to the **Botanical Gardens** *(Kruidtuin)* ⑤, an especially lovely spot where even tropical plants flourish. Begun in 1738 for the scientific study of medicinal herbs and other botanicals, the gardens have expanded greatly and now cover a vast variety of plantings. **T**: *016-294-488. Open daily 8–8, closing at 5 in winter. Free.*

From here, the route leads to the **Great Beguinage** *(Groot Begijnhof)* ⑥, an enclosed town-within-a-town founded in the early 13th century. Among its oldest surviving buildings are a 14th-century **church** and several 16th-century houses. Its narrow streets and tiny stream make it a highly picturesque place to explore, perhaps the most inviting of all the beguinages in the Low Countries. Fully restored, it is now used to accommodate university students and faculty. *Open daily. Free. Church open April–Sept., Tues.–Sun. 1:30–4:30.*

Return via Naamsestraat; perhaps stopping at the baroque **St. Michielskerk** ⑦ or the nearby **St. Donatus Park**, where you can see remains of the 12th-century ramparts.

Turn right just before the Town Hall and visit the **Municipal Museum Vander Kelen-Mertens** ⑧, which features paintings of the 15th-and 16th-century Leuven School, Gothic statues, and many other local art treasures. Housed in a 19th-century mansion, its many nooks and crannies are also filled with archaeological finds, furnishings of many ages, and —in the inner courtyard—a wonderful medieval garden. **T**: *016-226-906. Open Tues.–Sat. 10–5, Sun. and holidays 2–5. Closed mid-Dec, to mid-Jan. Combined admission with St. Pieterskerk Treasury, above, is €.* From here, you can take a bus or walk back to the train station.

The "Fonske" Fountain and the Town Hall

LEUVEN 208

Bokrijk

Europe has an ever-increasing number of outdoor folk museums where the rural past is brought back to life, but perhaps none of them surpass Bokrijk in sheer entertainment value. Although it may have certain "cultural" overtones, for the foreign tourist a visit here is just plain fun.

Farm structures, village houses, churches, schools, country inns, wind and water mills, and even urban buildings have been brought here from all over the Flemish provinces of Belgium and reassembled into typical villages as well as a small corner of a city. Dating from the 12th through the late 19th centuries, many of the preserved buildings are furnished with authentic antiques to appear as they would have in times past. The old crafts and farming methods continue to be practiced as a way of keeping ancient traditions alive.

Located in the large Provincial Domain of Bokrijk (an estate once owned by an abbey and purchased by the province of Limburg in 1938 as a nature preserve), the Flemish Open-Air Museum opened in 1958 as one of the largest outdoor folk museums in Europe. An English-language guide booklet with a map is available at the entrance so you can explore the entire area on your own, traveling by foot or riding one of the horse-drawn wagons. Authentic rural inns with outdoor tables, serving real country beer and home-cooked meals make for pleasant stops along the way. The suggested route described here takes you past all of the interesting highlights, which are numbered and described in great detail in the guide booklet.

GETTING THERE:

Trains bound for Genk depart Brussels' three major stations at hourly intervals for the 90-minute ride to Bokrijk. Be sure to get on a car marked for Genk, as the trains split en route. Bokrijk has no station, but the trains stop at a platform close to the museum entrance. Return service runs until mid-evening. Those without a railpass should purchase a "Train + Museum" combination ticket.

By Car, leave Brussels on the A-3/E4O and go east, almost to Leuven, then take the A-2/E-314 northwest to exit 30 and follow signs south to Park Midden Limburg, then to Domein Bokrijk. The total distance is 83 km (52 miles).

PRACTICALITIES:

The open-air museum at Bokrijk operates daily between April and September, with more activities on Sundays and holidays. Good weather is essential for this trip. For further information **T**: 011-265-300 or **W**: limberg.be/bokrijk, clicking on the English logo.

FOOD AND DRINK:

There are several places to eat and drink within the open-air museum, as well as a good restaurant just outside the entrance. They are:

't Koetshuis (Bokrijklaan, outside the entrance) In a mock castle near the open-air museum. French cuisine in an intimate, rustic atmosphere. **T**: 011-265-407. X: Tues. off season. €€

De Kleinaert (in the open-air museum, #3 on the map) Flemish-Burgundian dishes and regional beers are served in this familial tavern in the Haspengouw style. **T**: 011-265-417. €€

't Gulle Zwijn (at the entrance to the open-air museum, #2 on the map) Indoor/outdoor dining and drinking under the sign of the pig, in the former gatehouse. **T**: 011-265-414. € and €€

St. Gummarus Inn (#5 on map) This former tavern from Lier, situated in the Campine Village of the museum, specializes in farmers' dishes, Flemish stew and buckwheat cakes. Indoor and outdoor tables. **T**: 011-265-415. €

In den Dolfijn (#6 on the map) A tavern from West Flanders, serving local specialties, indoors and out. **T**: 011-265-416. €

Bierkelder (#8 on map) A typical old beer cellar from Antwerp. A huge variety of beers are available, but only snack food. **T**: 011-265-418. €

SUGGESTED TOUR:

Circled numbers correspond to numbers on the map.

Leave the **train halt** ① and walk a short distance to the:

*****FLEMISH OPEN-AIR MUSEUM** *(Openluchtmuseum)* ②, Het Domein Bokrijk, B-3600 Genk, **T**: 011-265-300 or **W**: limburg.be/bokrijk. *Open daily, April through September, 10–6. Admission on Sun. and holidays and daily July–Aug. €€€; weekdays in April–June and Sept. €€. Audioguide rental in English €. Book in English €€.*

Begin your visit at the **Welcome Pavilion**, where a 7-minute video in 5 languages will orient you to the layout. From here follow the map to **Haspengouw** ③, a South Limburg village complete with a 17th-century farmstead, a 16th-century granary, a laborer's cottage, a 19th-century school, an 18th-century chapel, and a cozy tavern.

Continue on to a 17th-century country **brewery** ④. Grouped around this is a 17th-century half-timbered house, an especially nice pigsty, a bakehouse with a latrine, and a small chapel. Head towards the octagonal windmill of the 18th

Bokrijk
Open Air Museum

N

500 Yards

PARK

PARK

⑥ Inn

Inn ⑤

⑦

Inn ④

③

② Info. Entrance

⑧ Urban Area

Parking

① Train Halt
TO GENK →

← TO BRUSSELS   Return Train Halt

BOKRIJK 211

A Horse Wagon passes the Dolphin Inn

century, the 12th-century Romanesque church, the archers' mast, and the cave hut.

Turn left at the next windmill and left again at another farmstead. You are now in a village typical of Antwerp Province. Opposite the pillory is the **St. Gummarus Inn** ⑤, an 18th-century structure restored to its condition of 1900. This is a great place for simple meals and especially for the tasty regional and local brews. A souvenir shop is nearby, as is the 18th-century vicarage. Also nearby are more pigstys and outhouses, and a 17th-century farmhouse.

The route now leads past an ancient abbey farmstead, a water mill, and more farms to the **Dolphin Inn** *(In den Dolfijn)* ⑥, a 17th-century meeting place from West Flanders. Restored to its early-20th-century condition, it now offers a good selection of regional dishes and brews, including the very strong black Abbey beer.

Continue on through a rural area typical of **West Flanders** ⑦ and an undeveloped part of the museum to the **Urban Section** ⑧. City buildings from Antwerp are being moved here brick by brick to save them from the wrecker's ball. Dating from as far back as the 15th century, the ones that are now finished house exhibitions as well as a delightful and very popular beer cellar that features a fabulous choice of brews. This is the perfect place to relax before heading back to the train-halt.

Liège

(Luik)

Quaint it's not, but Liège is the very heart and soul of French-speaking Wallonia. Snuggled into a narrow valley of the Meuse River, this large industrial city has its own distinctive way of life, characterized by a fierce sense of independence and a taste for lusty living. Its main attraction for tourists lies in its splendid museums, which cover an unusually broad range of subjects.

Liège was founded in the 8th century as the seat of a bishop and prospered as a center of learning. During the 14th century it was the capital of a principality ruled by prince-bishops and aligned with the Holy Roman Empire. In the 15th century nearly all of Belgium was captured by the dukes of Burgundy, but Liège put up a fierce resistance, falling at last to Charles the Bold, who exacted revenge in 1468 by destroying everything except a few churches. That is why so few medieval structures remain in the town.

Regaining its independence in 1477 and later rebuilding over the ruins, Liège prospered with the development of coal mining, ironworks, and a world-famous armaments industry. The French Revolution brought an end to dominance by the prince-bishops, and since Belgian independence in 1830 the city has been self-governing. The opening of the Albert Canal in 1939 has made it one of the major inland ports of Europe.

GETTING THERE:

Trains leave Brussels' three major stations at half-hour intervals for the ride of slightly over an hour to Liège's Guillemins Station. Return service operates until mid-evening.

By Car, Liège is 96 km (60 miles) east of Brussels via the A-3/E4O highway to exit 32. Park as close to the cathedral as possible.

PRACTICALITIES:

Avoid going to Liège on a Monday, when most of its sights are closed. Some of the smaller museums may be closed on Tuesdays instead.

The city **Tourist Office, T**: 04-221-9221 or **W**: liege.be (click on the British flag), is at Feronstree 92, 2 blocks southwest of the Church of St. Barthélemy.

FOOD AND DRINK:

You can always dine well in Liège. The restaurant choices below are in the area covered by the walking tour.

Au Vieux Liège (Quai de la Goffe 41,4 blocks southeast of the Museum of Walloon Life) Superb cuisine in a 16th-century riverside building. Dress nicely and reserve. **T**: 04-223-7748. X: Wed. eve., Sun. €€€

Chez Max (Place de la République Française 12, by the Royal Theater) An elegant brasserie with traditional French cuisine. **T**: 04-222-0859. X: Sat. lunch. €€ and €€€

As Ouhès (Place du Marché 21, a block east of the Palace of the Prince-Bishops) Seafood and other local dishes. **T**: 04-223-3225. €€

Shanghai (Galeries Cathedrale 104, just north of the cathedral) Chinese cuisine. **T**: 04-222-2263. X: Tues. € and €€

SUGGESTED TOUR:

Circled numbers correspond to numbers on the map.

From the **Guillemins Train Station** ① to the center of town is a pleasant walk of about one mile. It is also possible to get there by taking bus number 1 or 4. However you go, Liège's cathedral is a good place to start your tour:

*****CATHEDRAL OF SAINT PAUL** ②. *Church open daily 8–noon and 2–5. Free. Treasury,* **T**: *04-232-6132 or* **W**: *tresordeliege.be, open Tues.–Sun. 2–5. €.*

Founded in the 10th century, the present Gothic structure dates partly from the 14th century but mainly from the 16th. It became a cathedral in 1801 after the former Cathedral of St. Lambert was destroyed in the French Revolution. Inside, there are several fine 16th-century stained-glass windows in the south transept, along with some interesting sculptures. The real gems, however, are in the *****Treasury** *(Trésor),* accessed through the cloister. These include the marvelous gold reliquary donated by Charles the Bold in a fit of conscience after destroying the city, the majestic 16th-century reliquary of St. Lambert, 11th-century ivories, medieval manuscripts, and paintings.

Now follow the map through a series of pedestrian shopping streets and galleries and pass the imposing **Royal Theater** of 1818. Rue Joffre leads into Place St. Lambert, a large open square built over the site of the former Cathedral of St. Lambert. On the north side of this stands the enormous **Palace of the Prince-Bishops** *(Palais des Princes-Evêques)* ③, now used as the Court of Justice. First built in the 11th century as the seat of government, it was reconstructed in 1533 and given a new façade in 1737. You can usually walk through the entrance to see one of the interior Gothic courtyards, a quite impressive sight.

Just beyond the palace is the lovely Place du Marché, with its famous 17th-century **Perron Fountain** symbolizing the city's communal freedoms. Opposite

Liège

500 Yards

The Baptismal Font in the Church of St. Bartholomew

this stands the 18th-century **Town Hall** *(Hôtel de Ville),* whose entrance lobby is richly decorated. Continue on the nearby:

*MUSEUM OF WALLOON LIFE *(Musée de la Vie Wallonne)* ④, **T**: 04-237-9040. *Open Tues.–Sat. 10–5, Sun. 10–4. Closed major holidays. €. Partially closed for renovation until sometime in 2006.*

This is easily one of the best folk museums in Belgium. Housed in a 17th-century convent, it features period room settings, workshops, a huge collection of everyday objects relating to past life in the region, a puppet theater, and even a rather elaborate guillotine. Be sure to ask at the cloakroom about going down into the reconstructed coal mine in the basement.

The route now threads around to the tiny **Impasse des Ursulines** ⑤, where architectural elements from the past are on display in a 17th-century former convent *(Ancien Béguinage du Saint-Esprit).* If you feel up to it, you can climb the **very steep steps** up the Montagne de Bueren for a panoramic view from the **Citadel** ⑥, following the route taken in 1468 by local citizens in a futile effort to defeat Charles the Bold. Otherwise, you can follow Rue Hors Château to the next destination.

Whichever way you get there, the **Church of St. Bartholomew** *(Eglise St.-Barthélemy)* ⑦ contains one of the greatest art treasures of Belgium. The

*Baptismal Font, cast in bronze in 1118, is a stunning example of the metalworker's art with its sculpted baptismal scenes supported on the backs of ten small oxen in extremely high relief. **T**: *04-223-4998. Open Mon.–Sat. 10–noon and 2–5, Sun. 2–5.* €.

Stroll around to the nearby **Ansembourg Museum** ⑧, housed in an 18th-century mansion noted for its fine interiors. The displays here, in a rich setting, are of the decorative arts, including furniture and tapestries. **T**: *04-221-9402 or* **W***: multimania.com/ansembourg. Open Tues.–Sun. 1–6. Closed major holidays.* €.

One of the more unusual attractions of Liège is the **Museum of Arms** ⑨, just around the corner on Quai de Maestricht. Long a major industry of the city, armaments for both sporting and military uses have been collected from all over the world and displayed here in a mansion that twice housed Napoleon. The exhibitions range from 14th-century firearms to contemporary weaponry. Anyone with an interest in guns should not miss this treat. **T**: *04-221-9416 or* **W***: museesarmes.be. Temporarily closed, should reopen in 2006.*

Almost next door to this is the **Curtius Museum** ⑩, which occupies a fabulous mansion built in 1610. It contains one of Belgium's best collections of medieval decorative arts along with a rich assortment of archaeological artifacts from prehistoric, Gallo-Roman, and Merovingian times. Among its treasures is the famous 10th-century gospel book of Bishop Notger, covered in exquisitely carved ivory. Within the same institution is the **Museum of Glass** with its interesting displays of glass objects from all over the world, dating from Classical to modern times. **T**: *04-221-9404. Temporarily closed, should reopen in 2006.*

Now follow the map past the main tourist office to the Îlot St. Georges ⑪, where you will find the **Museum of Walloon Art**, specializing in the arts of Belgium's southern provinces from the 16th through the 20th centuries. There you will also find the **Salle St.-Georges**, a venue of notable art exhibitions. **T**: *04-221-9231. Open Tues.–Sat. 1–6, Sun. 11–4:30. Closed major holidays.* €.

The route now leads through some old and sometimes very narrow streets back to Place St. Lambert, where you can get a bus back to the station. If you would rather walk there it may be more pleasant to follow along the banks of the river. Liège, by the way, has quite a few other museums and interesting churches scattered all over town, which the tourist office will be happy to tell you about.

Trip 34

Namur

(Namen)

G uarding the confluence of the Meuse and Sambre rivers and acting as the gateway to the Ardennes, Namur has always been a strategic military bastion. Its enormous citadel originally dates from Roman times and has been frequently rebuilt throughout nearly 2,000 years of an often violent history. Today it is a major tourist attraction, reached by minibus or car on a long, winding road. The town itself is unusually pleasant, with several good museums and a wealth of 17th-and 18th-century buildings.

By eliminating the museums, this trip could easily be combined in the same day with one to Dinant, described in the next chapter.

GETTING THERE:

Trains depart Brussels' three major stations at half-hour intervals on weekdays and hourly intervals on weekends for the 54-minute ride to Namur. Return service operates until mid-evening.

By Car, Namur is 64 km (40 miles) southeast of Brussels via the A-4/E-411 highway. Park as close to the station as possible.

PRACTICALITIES:

The most important attraction of Namur, its Citadel, is open daily from June through September, and on weekends and holidays from Easter through May. Some of the museums are closed on Mondays, while others have various closing days. Good weather is essential for this trip.

The local **Tourist Office** *(Office du Tourisme),* **T**: 081-246-449 or **W**: ville.namur.be, is at Square Leopold, just east of the station. There is a handy seasonal branch at the bridge by the rivers' confluence. The bus for the Citadel leaves from there.

FOOD AND DRINK:

Some good restaurant choices in Namur are:

L' Espièglerie (Rue des Tanneries 13, in the Hôtel Les Tanneurs, 2 blocks east of the Convent) An inspired place for gourmet-level French cuisine. **T**: 081-240-024. €€€

Château de Namur (Ave. Ermitage 1, at the Citadel) Good French food prepared by student chefs; with a view. **T**: 081-729-900. €€ and €€€

La Bruxelloise (Ave. de la Gare 2, near the station) A good value, with mussels in season. **T**: 081-220-902. €€

La Petite Fugue (Pl. Chanoine Descamps 5, 2 blocks east of Félicien Rops Museum) Exceptional French-Belgian cuisine. **T**: 081-231-320. €€

Le Grill des Tanneurs (Rue des Tanneries 13, upstairs in the Hôtel Les Tanneurs, 2 blocks east of the Convent) Good French bistro fare, and a bargain compared to the other restaurant in the same hotel. **T**: 081-240-024. € and €€

Brasserie Henry (Pl. St.-Aubain 3, by the Cathedral) Traditional brasserie fare, served indoors or out. **T**: 081-220-204. €

SUGGESTED TOUR:

Circled numbers correspond to numbers on the map.

Leave the **Train Station** *(Gare)* ① and follow Avenue de la Gare to the tourist office, then turn down Rue de Fer to the **Museum of Old NamurArts** *(Musée des Arts Anciens du Namurois)* ②. Housed in an 18th-century mansion, the collections here are predominantly sculptures, paintings, and metalwork of the region, from both the Middle Ages and the Renaissance. **T**: *081-220-065. Open Tues.–Sun. 10–6; closing at 5 in winter. €, higher during special exhibitions.*

Now follow the map to the **Convent of the Sisters of Our Lady** *(École des Soeurs de Notre-Dame)* ③, which houses Namur's greatest art treasures. The collection of early-13th-century gold plate by the master Brother Hugo of Oignies is a superb example of the stylistic lengths to which reliquaries, chalices, crosses, and other items of religious art could be carried. **T**: *087-230-342. Open Tues.–Sat. 10–noon and 2–5, Sun. 2–5. €.*

The route leads across a bridge to the seasonal **Tourist Information Office** at the confluence of the two rivers. From here you can ride a minibus up to the Citdel high above the town, as the cable car is presently out of service. *Fare €.* Or you could walk up the steep hill, or drive. Another option is to take bus #3, marked Citadelle, from the town.

Once at the top ⑤, stroll down Avenue d'Artois and into the woods to the **Museum of the Forest** *(Musée de la Forêt)* ⑥, a charming rustic structure from 1910 in which subjects such as forestry, hunting, and fishing are explored along with samples of the flora and fauna of the Ardennes region.

Continue on past a sports stadium to the entrance of the:

*CITADEL *(Citadelle de Namur-Domaine Fortifié)* ⑦, **T**: 081-226-829. *Open June–early Oct., daily 11–5; early April–May weekends and holidays 11–5. €€€. Admission incudes use of the "tourist train," a guided tour, an audiovisual show, and visits to the dungeons and special exhibitions.*

Namur's great Citadel is a massive complex of fortifications spread over an area of 20 acres. It is believed that a stronghold has stood on this site since at least Roman times, but most of what exists today is from the 17th through the 19th centuries. Parts of it remained in use by the Belgian Army until 1975, and the

Namur

400 Yards

Boulevard du Nord

TO BRUSSELS
N-91

TO DINANT

TO BRUSSELS

Station

Av. du Square Léopold

Bd. Cauchy

Av. de la Gare

info.

Rue Borgnet

Rue Dewez

Bd. E. Mélot

Rue Rogier

Rue Lucien

Rue des

Croisiers

Rue Godefroid

Rue F. Wodon

Av. de Stassart

Rempart de la Vierge

Rue de Bruxelles

Rue des Carmes

Rue de Fer

Rue Pepin

Namêche

Rue du Lombard

Rue J. Grafé

Rue Lelièvre

Rue E. Cuvelier

Rue J. Billiart

SAMBRE

Bd. Frère-Orban

Rue Bruno

Rue Basse Marcelle

Rue du Collège

Rue de la Croix

Rue de l'Ange

Rue des Brasseurs

Rue du Pont

Rue Fumal

Avenue Reine Astrid

Av. Jean 1er

Rue du Bord de l'Eau

Citadel

Route Merveilleuse

Câble Car

Rue Notre Dame

Av. Baron L. Huart

MEUSE

Casino

Av. Baron de Moreau

Av. Bd. Jean Materne

Rue Renée

Stadium

Route Merveilleuse

Rue de Lopoin

Prinz

Av. Marie D'Artois

Bd. de la Meuse

Rue Mottiaux

Rue St-Martin

TO DINANT

N-92

Rue du Paradis

1 2 3 4 5 6 7 8 9 10 11 12

N

whole fortress was opened to the public in 1978. You can visit it on foot or by riding the little "tourist train;" or you can take a guided tour. Either way, be sure to visit the exhibitions in the former barracks *(Caserne).*

Return to town via the mini-bus or on foot. Just across the bridge is the **Archaeological Museum** *(Musée Archéologique)* ⑧, housed in a 16th-century meat hall. The collections here are particularly rich in prehistoric, Gallo-Roman, Merovingian, and Early Christian artifacts from the region. There is also a reproduction of the relief map of Namur created by an engineer of the court of Louis XV of France. **T**: *081-237-637. Open Tues.–Fri. 10–5, weekends 10:40–5. €.*

Stroll ahead to Place d'Armes and turn left near the 14th-century **Belfry** *(Beffroi),* once part of the medieval town walls. The route leads through a delightful part of town to the **Félicien Rops Museum** ⑨ at Rue Fumal 12, where some 600 works by the popular—and rather weird—19th-century artist can be seen. Both a serious painter and an illustrator, Rops (1822–98) dabbled in the occult and was obsessed with erotic and perverse subject matter. **T**: *081-220-110 or* **W***: ciger.be/rops. Open Easter–June and Sept., Tues.–Sun. 10–6; July–Aug., daily 10–6; rest of year Tues.–Sun. 10–5. €.*

Continue on to the **Hôtel de la Croix Museum** *(Musée de Groesbeeck de Croix)* ⑩, an 18th-century mansion with a splendid interior. It contains some marvelous local paintings and other artworks from the 17th and 18th centuries, shown on tours. **T**: *081-237-510. Open Tues.–Sun. 10–noon and 1:30–5. €.*

Close to this is the **Cathedral of St. Aubain** ⑪, an unremarkable neoclassical structure of the 18th century, built on the site of churches dating back to the 3rd century. Just behind it is the **Diocesan Museum** ⑫ with a notable collection of medieval religious art and artifacts, including a reliquary decorated with thorns allegedly taken from Jesus' crown of thorns. **T**: *081-444-285. Reserve in advance. €.* From here walk back through the town to the train station.

Trip 35
Dinant

Dinant's spectacular location at the foot of a cliff overlooking the strategic Meuse River has long made it a prime destination for visitors. Not all of these have been friendly, as its bloody history will attest. Every war that ever raged in this area has left the little town in ruins, but always its lovely setting brought the people back to rebuild once again.

During the 15th century, Charles the Bold sacked Dinant and had 800 of its inhabitants bound back-to-back and tossed into the river. In what is nearly a repeat of that brutal action, the Germans, in 1914, executed 674 of its civilians and then put the town to the torch. Towards the end of World War II it became the target of American artillery fire as the Nazis were driven out of their stronghold in the Citadel.

But all of that is in the past, and hopefully will remain there. Dinant today is an exceptionally beautiful and very popular place with several outstanding attractions. By rushing a bit, a visit here could be combined in the same day with one to Namur, described in the previous chapter.

GETTING THERE:

Trains depart Brussel's three main stations hourly for the 90-minute ride to Dinant, with no weekend service in winter. Additionally, there is frequent year-round service to Namur, with connecting trains to Dinant on weekends and holidays from October through May. Return service operates until mid-evening.

By Car, leave Brussels on the A-4/E-411 highway and follow it to Namur, where you change to the N-91 and N-92 roads to Dinant. The total distance is 93 km (58 miles) southeast of Brussels.

PRACTICALITIES:

Dinant's major attraction, the Citadel, is open every day from April through September. Between October and the end of March it is open daily, except on Fridays and a few holidays, and is open on weekends only in January. The other attractions are generally open daily from April through September or October. Good weather is essential for enjoyment of this trip.

The local **Tourist Office** *(Maison du Tourisme),* **T**: 082-222 870 or **W**: dinant-tourisme.be, is at Quai Cadoux 8, near the station, just before the bridge.

FOOD AND DRINK:

Being a major tourist area, Dinant has an enormous selection of restaurants and cafés. Some choices are:

Le Grill (Rue du Rivage 88, a mile south of the Citadel via Ave. Churchill) Grillades and seasonal cuisine of the highest quality. **T**: 082-226-935. X: Mon. eve., Tues. €€€

Le Jardin de Fiorine (Rue Cousot 3, along the river just southeast of town) A local favorite for fine cuisine. **T**: 082-227-474. X: Wed., Sun. eve. €€

Brasserie Casanova (Ave. Winston Churchill 9, near the bridge) Pizza and other simple Italian dishes. **T**: 082-227-634. €

SUGGESTED TOUR:

Circled numbers correspond to numbers on the map.

Leave the **Train Station** ① and follow the map across a bridge to the foot of the **Citadel Cable Car** *(Téléférique)* ②. Here you can either ride the cable car or hike the 408 steps up on foot. Those with cars can also drive there via Rue St Jacques. Either way, visit the:

CITADEL FORTRESS ③, **T**: 082-223-670 or **W**: citadelledinant.be. *Open April– Sept., daily 10–6; Oct.–March, Sat.–Thurs., weekends only in January. €€.*

The Citadel Fortress offers a fabulous view of the town and the scenic Meuse Valley. A castle has occupied this spot since around 1050, both guarding the town and making it liable to enemy attack. The present massive structure was built by the Dutch in 1821 and has played a combat role in all the wars since. Guided tours through the entire complex are conducted frequently, although you may still want to purchase an illustrated guide booklet in English to make more sense of what you're seeing. Among the sights shown are the carriage of Madame de Maintenon (who stayed here while Louis XIV was attacking Namur), the military prison dungeons, the kitchens and workshops, an arms collection, and a reconstructed trench and destroyed shelter from World War I, which you can climb through.

At the end of the tour you have a choice of going back down to the town by cable car, or following the map across the top of the hill for some good views at the old **Mont-Fat Tower** ④. From there, you can walk down a stepped path to the Prehistoric Caves ⑤ *(Grotte de Mont-Fat, presently closed).*

Continue downhill to the town and stroll around to the **river bank** ⑥, where **boat rides** lasting from 45 minutes to several hours are conducted by a few different companies.

Dinant

300 Yards

View of the Citadel and the Church

Next to the bridge stands the strange-looking **Church of Notre-Dame** ⑦, first built in the early 13th century and many times destroyed, but always rebuilt to the original plan. Its weird bulbous spire is a trademark of the town, and its interior contains some good paintings by a local artist.

If you feel up to it, a 15-minute walk on the other side of the river will bring you to the **Grotto of Dinant "La Merveilleuse"** ⑧. Noted for its beautiful white stalactites and underground waterfalls, these caves are among the most fantastic in this part of Europe. **T**: *082-222-210. Open April–Oct., daily 11–5, remaining open until 6 in July–Aug.; Nov.–March weekends only 1–4. €€. Allow an hour for the tour.*

Another sight within hiking distance (or an easy drive) of the town is the **Abbey of Leffe,** where you can visit the abbey's museum and taste the monk's beer. *Rue du Moulin 18 in nearby Leffe,* **T**: *082-647-583 or* **W***: leffe.be. Open April–June and Sept.–Oct., weekends 1–6; July–Aug., Tues.–Sun. 1–6. €.*

Trip 36

Tournai
(Doornik)

T he five unique towers of Tournai's great cathedral crown an ancient Roman town that gave birth to the French monarchy. It was here that Clovis was born around AD 465, and it was from here that he set out to conquer the many little kingdoms to the south and consolidate them into what is now France. Although the capital was soon moved elsewhere, Tournai retains much of its regal past, despite the many wars it has endured.

Always the survivor, its magnificent 12th-century cathedral is regarded as the finest in Belgium and easily among the most interesting in Europe. The town itself, although badly damaged in past conflicts and brutally bombed during World War II, has been restored along traditional lines and is today an utterly delightful place to visit.

GETTING THERE:

Trains leave Brussels' three major stations hourly for the 65-minute ride to Tournai. Be sure to get on the correct car, as the trains split en route. Return service operates until mid-evening.

By Car, head south from Brussels on the N-6 to Halle, then west on the A-8 to Tournai. The total distance is 85 km (53 miles).

PRACTICALITIES:

Avoid going to Tournai on a Tuesday or Thursday, when much of interest other than the cathedral is closed.

The local **Tourist Office** *(Centre de Tourisme)*, **T**: 069-222-045 or **W**: tournai.be, is opposite the Belfry at Vieux Marché aux Poteries 14.

FOOD AND DRINK:

Tournai has a fine selection of excellent restaurants and cafés, among them being:

Le Pressoir (Vieux Marché aux Poteries 2, by the cathedral entrance) Gourmet level regional cuisine in a 17th-century building. **T**: 069-223-513. X: late Aug. €€€

Charles Quint (Grand' Place 3) A nice restaurant with a view of the

Belfry **T**: 069-221-441. X: Wed. eve., Thurs., Sun. eve. €€€

Le Carillon (64 Grand' Place) An excellent choice right on the main square. **T**: 069-211-848. X: Sat. lunch, Sun. eve., Mon., Aug. €€ and €€€

Le Giverny (Quai du Marché au Poisson 6, 3 blocks northeast of the cathedral) Excellent French cuisine in tasteful surroundings. **T**: 069-224-464. X: Sun. eve., Mon., late July. €€

Chez Pietro (Rue de L'Hôpital Notre-Dame 15, a block northeast of the cathedral) Pizzas and other Italian specialties. **T**: 069-223-562. X: Mon. eve., Tues. €

SUGGESTED TOUR:

Circled numbers correspond to numbers on the map.

Leave the **Train Station** ① and follow the map to the small **Rue Barre St. Brice** ②, where you will find two of the oldest private houses in Europe at numbers 12 and 14. Dating from the 12th century, these Romanesque dwellings are remarkably well preserved. Close to them are some nice Gothic homes from the 13th century. At the south end of the street stands the 12th-century Church of St. Brice, built next to an old cemetery where King Childeric, the father of Clovis, was buried in 481. His tomb was discovered in 1653 and its relics removed to Paris.

Now cross the Schelde River, here called the Escaut, and stroll around to the:

***CATHEDRAL OF NOTRE-DAME** ③. Open April–Oct., daily 9:30–noon and 2–5:30; Nov.–March daily 10–noon and 2–4. Free. Treasury open April–Oct., Mon.–Fri. 10:15–noon and 2–5:15, Sat.–Sun. 2–5:15; Nov.–March, Mon.–Fri. 10:15–11:45 and 2–3:45, Sat.–Sun. 2–3:45. Treasury admission €.*

Built on the site of earlier churches, the present structure combines elements of both the Romanesque and Gothic styles and was consecrated in 1175. Its five towers are highly unusual as they crown the crossing rather than the west front. The best view of the cathedral is from the square facing the north transept.

Step inside to see the arcaded triple nave, whose St. Louis Chapel has superb stained-glass windows and a wonderful *Crucifixion* by Jordaens. Under the crossing stands an elaborate 16th-century Renaissance rood screen, which marks the entry into the graceful Gothic choir. A heavily restored painting of *Souls in Purgatory* by Rubens hangs in a chapel off the south ambulatory. Just beyond this is the **Treasury**, where one of Europe's great collections of medieval religious art is on display. You will discover many other interesting objects as you wander around inside the cathedral.

Exit from the south transept and walk over to the **Belfry** *(Beffroi)* ④. The

TOURNAI 228

The Belfry and the Cathedral Towers

first such structure in Belgium, it was built between the 12th and 14th centuries to celebrate the town's freedom. It's bottom, however, once served as a tiny prison, and the balcony used for public proclamations. You can climb to the top (257 steps) for a great view of the cathedral, and enjoy the multimedia show on the city's history in the base. *Open March–Oct., Tues.– Sun. 10–1 and 2–6:30; Nov.–Feb., Tues.–Sun. 10–noon and 2–5.* €.

Next to this is the triangular **Grand' Place** ⑤, a lively marketplace lined with ancient structures that were rebuilt following World War II destruction. The Cloth Hall on its south side is particularly impressive.

Stroll around to the *****Folklore Museum** ⑥ in the picturesque 17th-century *Maison Tournaisienne*. Life in old Tournai is re-created through a series of authentic room settings, shops, and other displays. This highly evocative and very interesting museum, although quite old-fashioned, should not be missed. **T**: *069-224-069. Open April–Oct., Wed., Fri.–Mon. 9:30–12:30 and 2–5:30; Nov.– March Wed., Fri.–Sun. 10–noon and 2–5. Closed Tues., Thurs., and major holidays.* €.

Three other museums in the immediate vicinity might interest you. The first of these is the **Tapestry Museum** on Place Reine Astrid, celebrating a long-time local industry with wonderful examples dating from medieval times right up to the present. **T**: *069-842-073. Open Wed. and Fri.–Mon. 9:30–12:30 and 2–5:30; Nov.–March, Wed. and Fri.–Mon. 10–noon and 2–5.* €. A second is the **Museum of History and Decorative Arts** on Rue Saint-Martin, renowned for its collection of superb porcelains. **T**: *069-843-795. Open same times as the Tapestry Museum, above.* €. Also nearby, on Rue Roc-Saint-Nicaise, is the home of the **Museum of Weapons** *(Musée d'Armes)* with its large collection of World War II arms used by American, British, and German forces, as well as by the Belgian Resistance. **T**: *069-211-966. Open same times as the Tapestry Museum, above.* €.

Now follow the map to the:

*MUSEUM OF FINE ARTS *(Musée des Beaux-Arts)* ⑦, **T**: *069-222-043. Open April–Oct., Wed. and Fri.–Mon. 9:30–12:30 and 2–5:30; Nov.–March Wed. and Fri.–Mon. 10–noon and 2–5.* €.

This major museum houses in its splendid 1928 structure —designed by Victor Horta—a large and generally excellent collection of works by such renowned artists as Tournai's own Rogier van der Weyden, Bruegel, Rubens, and others. Among the moderns represented are Manet, Seurat, Van Gogh, Monet, and James Ensor.

The route now leads through some quiet old streets to the **Museum of History and Archaeology** ⑧. The collections on display here include local Roman artifacts, medieval sculptures, books, manuscripts, and many other fascinating objects. **T**: *069-221-672. Open same times as the Tapestry Museum, above.* €.

Continue on and go through a small park to the **Pont des Trous** ⑨, a 13th-century fortified bridge that once guarded the river approach to Tournai. River cruises lasting about an hour depart from the landing stage near the bridge—ask the tourist office for current schedules.

Stroll along the river's edge to the next bridge and cross it. From here, you can return to the station via the **Henry VIII** Tower ⑩, built in 1515 after the English king had captured Tournai. The rest of his citadel was demolished by France's Louis XIV, but this massive circular keep remains. A short walk along a tree-shaded avenue brings you back to the station.

Section IV

Daytrips in
LUXEMBOURG

I t may be tiny, but the Grand Duchy of Luxembourg packs a surprising amount of magnificent scenery into its 999 square miles. Medieval castles look down from their hilltop perches over unspoiled forests and idyllic valleys. Both its industries and its only city are located in the south, leaving the rest of the country in a largely undisturbed state of natural beauty. While it has little in the way of major tourist sights, Luxembourg offers the perfect interlude in your European adventures.

The many castles and fortifications dotting the landscape are mute testimony to a violent past. Throughout its long history, Luxembourg was the battleground for countless invading armies. Conquered by Caesar's legions, ruled by Charlemagne, fought over by the Germans, the French, the Spaniards, the Dutch, and just about everyone else who tried to establish hegemony over one of Europe's most strategic crossroads, this minuscule nation has changed its boundaries many times while struggling to retain its identity. Twice in the 20th century it has been the scene of terrible warfare, the most recently during the decisive Battle of the Bulge in 1944–45.

Today the people of Luxembourg still cling to their ancient motto *"Mir woelle bleiwe wat mir sin"*—"We want to remain what we are." And what they are today is something worth noting. With one of Europe's highest standards of living and a *per capita* industrial output that rivals just about any country on Earth, Luxembourgers remain intimately bonded to the land and to the rhythms of nature. They care deeply about their countryside, always maintaining it in a state of pristine beauty.

Luxembourg City is a much more cosmopolitan place than its size would suggest. A major international banking center, it is also the headquarters of the Secretariat of the European Parliament, the European Court of Justice, and the European Investment Bank. For three months of each year, it is the meeting place of the Council of Ministers of the European Union. By basing yourself in one of the city's many hotels or other accommodations, you can easily explore the entire Grand Duchy on comfortable daytrips.

PRACTICALITIES

TRANSPORTATION:

The four one-day adventures in Luxembourg described in this book can all be made either by train, by bus, or by car. Some facts to consider in making a choice are:

BY RAIL AND BUS:

The **Luxembourg National Railways** *(Société Nationale de Chemins de Fer Luxembourgeois,* or CFL) operates a network of both trains and buses, covering more than 870 route-miles. They serve virtually every locality in the Grand Duchy, making it quite easy to get around without a car.

Train service to Brussels and much of Belgium is excellent, and there are good schedules to France and Germany as well. Direct rail connections with Holland are not as good, so you may be better off going to Amsterdam by way of Brussels.

Both trains and buses for destinations throughout Luxembourg depart from the train station in Luxembourg City *(Gare de Luxembourg).* You can get **information and schedules** from the Railtour center in the station's main hall, **T**: 4990-4990 (6 a.m.–10 p.m. daily) or **W**: cfl.lu. Reservations cannot be made for travel within the country but you may want to consider them for long international journeys. There is no food service on domestic trains, so bring your own snacks. First-class cars are identified with the numeral "1" near the door, and with a yellow stripe above the windows. Some trains do not carry first-class cars, but second class is perfectly adequate for the short journeys involved. English is widely spoken, so you will have no trouble with language. The French Rail Traveler's Glossary in Section V will help you decipher any signs or notices.

Railpasses can be a wonderful bargain if you plan on making many trips by train throughout Holland, Belgium, and Luxembourg, and other European countries. The Luxembourg National Railways (CFL) accepts the following passes for both trains and buses (except for local buses within Luxembourg City):

EURAILPASS
EURAIL SAVERPASS
EURAIL FLEXIPASS
EURAIL YOUTHPASS
EURAIL SELECT PASS (validated for Benelux)
BENELUX TOURRAIL PASS

All of these are described in Section II. In addition, Luxembourg offers its own national passes:

NETWORK TICKET—*(Billet réseau),* a one-day pass for all trains and buses within the Grand Duchy, but not to border points. It is worthwhile for both the Vianden and Clervaux daytrips. Travel on trains is in second class. *Buy it at the station for €.*

Grand Duchy
of
Luxembourg

Only places mentioned in text
are shown

16 km

10 Miles

TO
LIEGE

BELGIUM

GERMANY

Clervaux

Vianden

Ettelbruck Diekirch

Berdorf
Echternach

TO
KOBLENZ

TO
BRUSSELS

Luxembourg
City

TO
PARIS

FRANCE

TO PARIS
& BASEL

LUXEMBOURG   233

Remember that all railpasses must be used in accordance with the rules and instructions accompanying them, and that you must always be prepared to show your passport. When having passes validated, be certain that you agree with the dates before allowing the agent to write them in.

Another deal to consider is the **LUXEMBOURG CARD**, sold at tourist offices, train and bus stations, and attractions. Available for periods of 1, 2, or 3 days from Easter through October, it allows unlimited transportation (bus and rail) throughout the Grand Duchy, along with free admission to most major attractions and a 30% discount on some others. *Individual cards cost: 1 day, €€; 2 days, €€€; and 3 days, €€€€. Families of up to 5 persons including up to 3 adults can get a family card for double the price of an individual card.*

City bus #9 operates between Findel Airport and Luxembourg City at frequent intervals and is a real bargain, although they may refuse passengers with luggage during rush hours. Otherwise, there is taxi service.

BY CAR:
Driving in the Grand Duchy is easy, and you should encounter no problems. A valid driver's license from your own country, insurance, and a vehicle registration are all that you need. Except for the few motorways around Luxembourg City, the roads tend to be narrow, and there is not too much traffic to contend with. The speed limit on motorways is 130 kph (81mph), on country roads 90 kph (56 mph), and in built-up areas 50 kph (31 mph). Seat belts must be worn and the horn used for emergency situations only. A parking time-disc is needed for parking in marked "blue zones" in the city and larger villages.

WHEN TO GO:
The best time to visit Luxembourg is between May and mid-October, when the weather is at its best. Many of the attractions are closed during the off-season, as is noted in the town descriptions that follow. June, with its longer days, offers the most sunshine. Luxembourg has a more sheltered climate than either Holland or Belgium—but you should still carry protection from rain or chill.

HOLIDAYS:
Public holidays in Luxembourg are:
New Year's Day
Carnival (late February)
Easter
Easter Monday
Labor Day (May 1st)
Ascension Day (6th Thursday after Easter)
Whit Monday (7th Monday after Easter)
National Day (June 23rd)
Assumption (August 15th)

All Saints' Day (November 1st)
Christmas Day
Boxing Day (December 26th)

LANGUAGE:

The native language, learned from birth, is *Letzebuergesch (or Luxembourgish)—a* weird and unpronounceable mixture of low German and old French. This would present problems for a country that relies on international trade for its living were it not for the fact that everyone learns German and French in school. The government and most institutions function in French, but English is widely spoken by a great many people. You won't have any language problem in Luxembourg.

MONEY:

Price ranges for attractions are shown in *euros* (€), the currency for both Luxembourg and most of Western Europe. These are for full adult admissions; discounts are usually available for seniors, students, and children:

€	Up to 5 euros.
€€	6-10 euros.
€€€	11-20 euros.
€€€€	21 or more euros.

The value of the euro varies daily, but is usually in the range of US $1.20 to US $1.40. Banknotes are issued in values of 5, 10, 20, 50, 100, 200, and 500 euros; and coins in values of 1, 2, 5, 10, 20, and 50 cents as well as 1 and 2 euros. The design of banknotes is the same in all countries, but the coins vary by nationality — however all coins are valid in all Eurozone countries. Currently, besides Luxembourg these include Austria, Belgium, Finland, France, Germany, Greece, Holland, Ireland, Italy, Netherlands, Portugal, and Spain.

It is always advisable to do your money exchange transactions at a commercial bank, where you will get the best rate. Some tourist information offices are handy places to change money when the banks are closed. Other money changers often charge outrageous commissions.

Traveler's Checks are the safest way to protect your money while abroad. They often, however, entail service charges both when you buy them and again when you convert them into euros in Luxembourg.

Automated Teller Machines (ATMs) offer the best exchange rates to be found anywhere, and allow you to take money directly out of your home bank account as you need it. They are usually open 24 hours a day, are conveniently located all over Luxembourg, and yield cash in euros. Check with your issuing bank before leaving home to make sure that your PIN code will work in Luxembourg. Bear in mind that these machines don't always work, so always have a backup plan (or starve).

Credit cards are widely accepted at the more expensive establishments throughout Luxembourg, but less often by budget hotels and restaurants. They may also be used to yield cash advances from ATM machines, provided you have a compatible PIN code. The most commonly accepted cards are **Visa** *(Carte Bleue)* and **MasterCard** *(EuroCard),* with **American Express** a distant third.

TELEPHONES:

Public telephones in Luxembourg use use the convenient Telecard, a pre-paid debit card in which the cost of each call is subtracted until its face value is all used up. These cards are available in €5, €10, and €25 denominations at post offices, train stations, newsstands and other merchants.

Luxembourg does not have area codes. If calling from outside the country, dial the international access code for the country that you're in, then the country code for Luxembourg (352), followed by the number.

You may wish to rent or purchase a **cell phone** while in the Benelux countries, which is certainly a convenience if you're staying for a few weeks or longer. Most American cellular (mobile) phones will not work there unless they are of the tri-band (900/1800/1900 MHz) variety on the GSM system with a compatible SIM card. Even then, you may be billed at very high rates by your American service provider. Check with them first. One source of rentals is **W**: cellularabroad.com. Purchases of prepaid phones can be made at specialty shops in Luxembourg City.

FOOD AND DRINK:

Virtually any kind of cuisine, from the most elegant French to American fast food, can be found in Luxembourg. The local specialties, however, are very well worth trying, as you are not likely to find them elsewhere. Usually hearty and copious, the dishes to look for are: *Jambon d'Ardennes* (smoked ham with a difference), *Quenelles de foie de veau* (calf's liver dumplings), *Treipen* (black pudding and sausages with potatoes), *Jud mat gardebo'nen* (smoked pork with broad beans), and *Cochon de lait en gelée* (suckling pig in aspic). Seafood lovers will appreciate the local trout, pike, and crawfish. Luxembourg pastries are renowned for their richness.

The white Moselle wines, rarely exported, are superb. These are also made in a sparkling version, similar to champagne. Beer from the Grand Duchy is similar to that of Germany, and some popular brand names are Mousel, Diekirch, Funck, and Bofferding. Fruit liqueurs are also produced locally.

Several restaurant choices are suggested for each daytrip destination. Most of these are longtime favorites of experienced travelers and serve regional cuisines unless otherwise noted. Their price range, based on the least expensive meal offered, is indicated by these symbols:

€ — Inexpensive, but may have fancier dishes available.

€€ — Reasonable. These establishments may also feature daily specials.

€€€ — Luxurious and expensive.

X: — Days or periods closed.

Those who take dining very seriously should consult an up-to-date restaurant and hotel guide such as the classic red-cover *Michelin Benelux,* issued annually around the beginning of each year. It is always wise to check the posted menus before entering, paying particular attention to any daily set-meal specials.

A handy **menu translator** and a glossary of dining terms can be found in Section V.

SUGGESTED TOURS:

The do-it-yourself walking tours in the next section are relatively short and easy to follow. Some of them include simple country walks for which suitable shoes are required. On the assumption that most readers will be traveling by train or bus, they always begin at the local station or bus stop. Those going by car can make a simple adjustment. Suggested routes are shown by heavy broken lines on the maps, while the circled numbers refer to attractions or points of reference along the way, with corresponding numbers in the text.

Virtually every locality of tourist interest has its own information office. You may want to check ahead with them if seeing a particular sight is crucially important to you, since it may be closed for one reason or another. These offices are shown on the town maps in this book by the word "info.," and mentioned along with the phone number and website in the text.

*OUTSTANDING ATTRACTIONS:

An * asterisk before any attraction, be it an entire daytrip or just one item in a museum, denotes a special treat that in the author's opinion should not be missed.

ADVANCE PLANNING INFORMATION:

The **Luxembourg National Tourist Office** provides a wealth of information on its website: **W**: ont.lu. An extensive brochure is available as a free download in the pdf format.

They can also be contacted at:

17 Beekman Place, **New York**, NY 10022, U.S.A.
T: 212-935-8888, FAX 212-935-5896, **W**: visitluxembourg.com

122 Regent Street, **London**, W1R 5FE, England, U.K.
T: 020-7434-2800, FAX 020-7734-1205, **W**: luxembourg.co.uk

Trip 37

Luxembourg City

Other European towns built walls and castles to defend themselves during the turbulent Middle Ages, but Luxembourg City went a step further and made the whole place into one massive fortress, literally the "Gibraltar of the North." Dramatically sited on a high plateau overlooking deep ravines, the city is a natural stronghold if ever there was one. Most of its fortifications were dismantled in the late 19th century, but enough of them remain to make this a very intriguing place to explore. The Old City itself is exceptionally pleasant, with a fine cathedral, a palace, some excellent museums, and a delightful main square lined with outdoor cafés.

Although a settlement of sorts has existed on this spot since at least the 4th century, the present city traces its origins to a castle built in 963 by Count Sigefroi, around which a town developed. By the 15th century, this covered roughly the same area as today's city. Changing hands many times between the Burgundians, the French, the Spaniards, the Austrians, and the Germans, it was always a pawn on the chessboard of European power struggles. The Grand Duchy was freed from foreign domination in 1867 in return for a proclamation of neutrality and the partial dismantling of its fortresses.

As a transportation hub and with its wide choice of accommodations, Luxembourg City is the obvious base for daytrips throughout the entire country.

GETTING THERE:

Trains connect Luxembourg City with Belgium, France, Germany, and beyond. Service to Brussels operates at about hourly intervals and the ride takes less than 3 hours. There is limited direct service to Amsterdam. Paris is three-and-a-half hours away by express, and Koblenz, in Germany, only two hours. **T**: *4990-4990 or* **W***: cfl.lu.*

By Car, Luxembourg City is 218 km (136 miles) southeast of Brussels, 389 km (243 miles) southeast of Amsterdam, and 373 km (233) miles northeast of Paris. Most of these distances are over superb modern highways.

By Air, Luxembourg's Findel Airport has convenient flights to many of Europe's major cities via Luxair, British Airways, KLM, Sabena, and other European carriers. **T**: *2456-4242 or* **W***: luxair.lu.*

PRACTICALITIES:

The best time to visit Luxembourg City is from March through October, when the Bock Casemates are open. Note that the major museums are closed on Mondays, and that the palace is open from mid-July through August only. Good weather is essential for this largely outdoor trip.

The **City Tourist Office**, **T**: 222-809 or **W**: lcto.lu, is at Place d'Armes in the center of the Old Town. For the rest of the country, you should contact the **National Tourist Office** in the train station, **T**: 4282-8220 or **W**: ont.lu

FOOD AND DRINK:

The city is blessed with a huge variety of good restaurants in all price ranges. Some choices on or near the suggested walking route are:

Speltz (8 Rue Chimay, a block south of Place d'Armes) Traditional cuisine in an old town house. **T**: 474-950. X: Sat. lunch, Sun., holidays. €€ and €€€

Breedewee (9 Rue Large, near the City History Museum) French cuisine, served in summer on a terrace with a great view. **T**: 222-696. X: Sun. €€

Roma (5 Rue Louvigny, a block south of Place d'Armes) A wide range of Italian dishes, indoors or out. **T**: 223-692. X: Sun. eve., Mon. €€

Bacchus (32 Rue Marché aux Herbes, near the Ducal Palace) A stylish pizzeria with other Italian favorites. **T**: 471-397. X: Mon. € and €€

Mousel's Cantine (46 Montée de Clausen, a few blocks beyond the Bock Casemates) Copious servings of local dishes, right in the brewery. **T**: 470-198. X: Sun. € and €€

Café Céladon (1 Rue du Nord, 2 blocks northwest of the Art Museum) Exotic food of Thailand. **T**: 474-934. X: Sat. lunch, Sun. € and €€

Café Chiggeri (15 Rue du Nord, 2 blocks northwest of the Art Museum) Light French cuisine, with salad and vegetarian options. **T**: 228-236. € and €€

SUGGESTED TOUR:

Circled numbers correspond to numbers on the map.

Those staying at one of the many hotels near the **Train Station** *(Gare)* ① should follow Avenue de la Liberté to the Pont Adolphe Bridge and cross it to the real starting point of this walk, the **Place de la Constitution** ②. The views across the Pétrusse Valley from here are quite spectacular, although it is difficult to understand how such a minuscule stream could have cut a gorge as deep as this.

Next to a kiosk near the center of the square is the entrance to the **Pétrusse Casemates**, a part of the old fortifications that can be seen on half-hour guided tours conducted at posted times in summer. While not quite as exciting as the Bock Casemates that you will come to later on, these do offer a fascinating plunge into a subterranean world of tunnels where cannons peer out of loopholes, as you climb down through levels built by the Spaniards, the French, and the Austrians during the 17th and 18th centuries. Some 15 miles of underground passages still honeycomb the Old City, and were used as bomb shelters during World War II.

Luxembourg City

500 Yards

N

Boulevard Grand-Duchesse Charlotte

Boulevard Joseph II

Avenue Marie-Thérèse

Bd. Dr. C. Marx

Rue Wilson

Rue des Etats-Unis

Rue A. Fischer

Rue A. Fischer

Rue de Strasbourg

Rue du Fort Wedell

Rue Glesener

Rue d'Epernay

Rue Jos.

Junck

Place de la Gare

Station

Info.
Air Terminal

TO BRUSSELS

Rue de Bonnevoie

Rue des Gaulois

Rue des Trèvres

Rue A. Fischer

Rue Michel Welter

Rue Michel Rodange

Rue d'Anvers

R. Duchscher

Avenue de la Liberté

R. J. Origer

R. d. Fort Elisabeth

Avenue de la Gare

Rue du Fort Neipperg

Rue du Fort Wallis

Rue du Laboratoire

Rue Goethe

Bd. de la Pétrusse

Rue Ste-Zithe

Rue Dicks

Avenue de la Liberté

Bd. de la Pétrusse

PÉTRUSSE

Pont Adolphe

Passerelle

Bd. d'Avranches

Rue St-Ulric

① ⑪ ⑫

LUXEMBOURG CITY   240

LUXEMBOURG CITY   241

The tour descends all the way down to the river level and comes back up via a different route, returning you to the same place. **T**: *222-809. Open Easter, Whitsun, and daily during the summer school vacation, 11–4. €.*

Close to the square is the **Cathedral of Notre-Dame** ③, begun as a Jesuit church in 1613 when the Gothic style was still in vogue this far north. An extension, through which you enter, was added in the 1930s. The somewhat austere interior is in keeping with the needs of the Jesuit order, while the modern crypt contains the mortal remains of Count John the Blind, killed in the Battle of Crécy in 1346. There are also the tombs of the Grand Ducal royal family. *Open Mon.–Sat. 10–noon and 2–5:30, Sun. 2–5:30.*

Leave the cathedral by way of its Renaissance front portal and stroll around to Place Guillaume, where a colorful **market** is held on Wednesday and Saturday mornings. The statue in its center is of William II, King of the Netherlands and Grand Duke of Luxembourg in the mid-19th century.

Just a block away stands the **Grand Ducal Palace** ④, originally the Town Hall and then the official city residence of the Grand Duke, Luxembourg's head of state. Most of the present structure dates from 1573 and has a fine Renaissance façade, although additions were made in the 19th century. Its lavish interior may be visited on guided tours from mid-July through August. Arrangements for this must be made through the nearby City Tourist Office in Place d'Armes, preferably a day or so in advance. **T**: *222-809. Tours Mon.–Sat. €€.*

Continue on past the adjacent Chamber of Deputies and through some narrow old streets in the most ancient part of town, perhaps making a little sidetrip to the:

*MUSEUM OF THE HISTORY OF THE CITY OF LUXEMBOURG *(Musée d'Histoire de la Ville de Luxembourg)* ⑤, 14 Rue du St.-Esprit, **T**: 4796-4500 or **W**: musee-hist.lu. Open *Tues.–Sun. 10–6, remaining open on Thurs. until 8. €.*

Although installed in four historic houses, this fascinating museum is thoroughly modern in both concept and execution. A glass elevator takes you down through a thousand years of the city's history as it descends towards the valley below. There are interactive audiovisual shows and, of course, models of the city as it was in various centuries.

Continue on to the Rocher du Bock, a rocky promontory that juts out into a loop of the Alzette River. This is where Sigefroi built his castle in 963. The entire rock is honeycombed with the city's most fascinating fortifications, entered by steps to the right:

*BOCK CASEMATES ⑥, **T**: 222-809. Open *March–Oct, daily 10–5. €.*

Begin your visit to Luxembourg City's major attraction at its **Archaeological Crypt**, where an audiovisual show introduces you to the story of the fortifications. After that, you can explore as many of the tunnels and gun placements

Inside the Bock Casemates

as you feel up to, following the printed diagram and explanatory notes in English that are given to you at the entrance. Try to make it all the way to the end (section "C"), which is the most intriguing part, even though doing this entails some steep subterranean climbs. The loopholes through which the cannons were fired were greatly enlarged when the fortress was dismantled, and they now provide excellent views across both sides of the valley.

The top of the rock, where a fortress once stood, now carries a road. To one side of this are ruins of the original 10th-century castle, and on the other side is the **Dent Creuse** ("Hollow Tooth") ⑦, a broken bit of a 17th-century defensive tower. Return to town via Rue Sigefroi. **St. Michael's Church** ⑧ was first built as the castle chapel in 987, but has been restored several times since then. Its present 17th-century porch was a gift from Louis XIV. Open *Easter–Oct., daily 10–5; rest of year, Sat.–Sun. 10–5. Closed during services.*

Just across the old **Fish Market** *(Marche aux Poissons)* is the:

*NATIONAL MUSEUM OF HISTORY AND ART *(Musée National d'Histoire et d'Art* ⑨, **T**: 479-330-1 or **W**: mnha.lu. Open *Tues.–Sun. 10–5. €.*

Luxembourg's largest museum contains a strange (and engaging) mixture of just about everything, including archaeological finds, historical artifacts, Renaissance art, scientific oddities, and folkloric knick-knacks. Be sure to see the model of the Bock Castle as it appeared in its heyday, as well as the reconstructed room interiors from different eras. There is a great deal of art, both contemporary and ancient, some of which is priceless. Across the street, reached by footbridge, is an annex covering the country's industrial past.

You can now head directly for Place d'Armes ⑬, a charming square lined with inviting outdoor cafés, or continue with an exploration of the lower town, down in the valley. The latter choice involves a fairly long walk with a stiff climb at its end, but takes you through some interesting neighborhoods that few tourists see.

If you decide to push forward, follow Rue Wiltheim through the old town gates to the Trois Tours, a major 11th-century fortification with a good view across the Alzette. Continue downhill via the Montée de Pfaffenthal and cross the river on the fortified **Tours Vauban footbridge** ⑩. Just above this, the modern Pont Grande-Duchesse Charlotte spans the entire valley in one giant leap.

Return along Rue Vauban and go under the Bock fortifications, then turn left and follow the map across another footbridge and through the lower town to the **Chapel of St. Quinn** ⑪. Hewn out of the living rock, this is the oldest sanctuary in town and may originally date from pagan times. Now re-cross the very narrow Petrusse stream and go under the 19th-century Viaduct. A strenuous climb returns you to the upper town and the ruins of the **Holy Ghost Citadel** ⑫.

From here, the Chemin de la Corniche path offers stunning panoramic views as it takes you back to the Bock Casemates ⑤. It is now only a short walk through the Old Town to the **Place d'Armes** ⑬, where you can sit down at a delightful outdoor café for some very welcome refreshments. Those heading back to the station may prefer to follow the route across the Viaduct, as shown on the map.

The Grand Ducal Palace

Vianden

Towering high above a romantic village, the fairytale castle of Vian-den casts its spell on the narrow, cobbled streets below. This is, quite simply, the most picturesque little town in the Grand Duchy, and the most enticing destination for a daytrip from Luxembourg City. In addition to its restored medieval castle, it offers a visit to the exile home of Victor Hugo, an excellent folklore museum, magnificent scenery, and a delightful atmosphere that attracts visitors from all over Europe.

The story of Vianden is the story of its castle. A small fort has existed on this hill since Roman times, and a castle was built over it in the 9th century. This was greatly enlarged during the 11th, 12th, and 15th centuries and became an ancestral home of the House of Orange-Nassau, the dynasty that supplies both the kings and queens of the Netherlands as well as the grand dukes of Luxembourg.

Although you should really devote an entire day to enjoying Vianden, it is possible to combine a daytrip there with one to either Clervaux or Echternach, described in the next two chapters. Doing this is much more practical by car, even though there is direct bus service between Vianden and Echternach. To reach Clervaux involves a bus to Ettelbruck and then a train.

GETTING THERE:

Trains depart the Luxembourg City Station several times in the morning for the half-hour ride to **Ettelbruck**, where you change to a connecting bus for Vianden. The bus ride takes about 30 minutes and railpasses are accepted. Return service operates until early evening—be sure to check times, so you don't get stranded.

By Car, head north from Luxembourg City on the N-7 road to Diekirch, then follow local roads to Vianden. The total distance is 43 km (27 miles).

PRACTICALITIES:

Vianden may be visited on any fine day from April through October. The local **Tourist Office** *(Syndicat d'lnitiative)*, **T**: 834-257-1 or **W**: tourist-info-vianden.lu, is at 1a Rue du Vieux Marché, just across the bridge.

FOOD AND DRINK:

Le Châtelain (126 Grand Rue, in the Hôtel Oranienburg just below the castle) A popular restaurant with French cuisine and an outdoor terrace. **T**: 834-153. €€ and €€€

Auberge du Château (74 Grand Rue, near the folklore museum) Good-value meals at an attractive inn. **T**: 834-574. €€

Heintz (55 Grand Rue, near the parish church) A small hotel with good food in an ancient building. **T**: 834-155. € and €€

Aal Veinen (114 Grand Rue, below the castle) Hearty, simple cooking in a rustic house from 1683. **T**: 834-368. € and €€

Auberge de l'Our (35 Grand Rue, by the river, near the Victor Hugo House) Local specialties, with a view. **T**: 834-675. €

SUGGESTED TOUR:

Circled numbers correspond to numbers on the map.

Leave the **Bus Station** *(Gare Routière)* ① and stroll down Rue de la Gare to the **Victor Hugo House** ②. The great French writer loved Vianden and stayed there several times, including a period of political exile in 1871. Reconstructed after World War II damage, the house is now a small museum containing some of the author's belongings, and documents relating to his visits. **T**: *2687-4088 or* **W**: *victor-hugo.lu. Open Tues.–Sun. 11–5. €.*

Just before the bridge there is a bust of Victor Hugo. In the middle of the span you'll see a statue of St. Nepomuk, the patron saint of bridges. Continue across the Our River and head up Grand Rue to the **Parish Church of the Trinitarians** ③, a Gothic structure with a double nave dating from 1248. It is one of the oldest religious buildings in Luxembourg and is noted for its fine rococo altar. A short visit here is definitely worthwhile, as are a few moments spent in the 14th-century cloisters behind it. *Open daily 9–6.*

The route now leads uphill and climbs steeply to one of the great architectural treasures of the region, the:

*CASTLE OF VIANDEN *(Château de Vianden)* ④, **T**: 834-108 or **W**: castlevianden.lu. *Open Jan.–Feb. daily 10–4; March, daily 10–5; Apr–Sept, daily 10–6; Oct., daily 10–5; Nov.–Dec., daily 10–4. Closed New Year's Day, Nov. 2, Christmas. €.*

Until a few decades ago, Vianden's great castle lay in a state of semi-ruin, but a major restoration project has revived its former medieval splendor. The roof is back on, and many of the rooms are again furnished with period pieces. A printed diagram in English will be given to you at the entrance.

Return to the village and follow the very charming Vieille Rue until it joins Grand Rue. Across the street is the **Museum of Rustic Arts and Puppets** *(Musée de la Poupée et d'Art Rustique)* ⑤, where local crafts, antiques, household items,

Vianden

Route de Diekirch

Vieille Rue

Grand Rue

Montée du Château

Castle

④

Museum

⑤

Church

③

⑥

Town Walls

Grand Rue

Rue du Vieux Marché

Rue Victor Hugo

Rue du Sanatorium

Chairlift

⑦

Dam

⑧

②

OUR

Rue Théodore Bassing

Rue de la Gare

Kalchesbach

①

Bus Station

Route de la Frontière

N

300 Yards

The Castle of Vianden

toys, and puppets are displayed in a charming old house. **T**: *834-591. Open Easter–Oct, daily 11–5. Closed on Mon. in the off-season. €.*

You could easily return to the river by strolling down Grand Rue, but a more interesting (if slightly rugged) way to get there is by following the remnants of the ancient **Town Walls** ⑥. Now re-cross the bridge and turn left on Rue Victor Hugo, which brings you to the **Chairlift** *(Télésiège)* ⑦. From here, you can take an enjoyable ride across the river and up to the top of a hill overlooking the valley, town, and castle. There's also an outdoor café for refreshment while taking in the lovely **view*. **T**: 534-323. *Operates Easter to mid-Oct, daily 10 to 5 or 6. Closes in bad weather. €.*

Ambitious walkers may want to continue on to the **Dam** *(Barrage)* ⑧. This forms the lower reservoir of a vast pumped-storage hydroelectric complex. During the night, when demand for power is low, surplus electricity is used to pump water from here to a higher reservoir. During peak-use periods this is released, turning generators on its way down. If you have a car, you might want to drive about three miles beyond the dam to the underground gallery, which may be visited. **T**: *449-021. Open daily 10–5. Free. Ask at the tourist office for details concerning guided tours.*

Walk across the top of the dam and follow the trail past the 17th-century Church of St. Rochus. From the bottom of the hill, Rue du Vieux Marché brings you back to town, where you can stop for some refreshment before heading out to the bus station.

Clervaux

Deep in the hilly Ardennes forest, in what nearly amounts to a wilderness area, lies the medieval village of Clervaux. Now a popular resort, it is still dominated by its 12th-century castle and by its Benedictine Abbey. There are several interesting things to see, including the Battle of the Bulge Museum, but mostly this is a place to get away from civilization for a few hours and go for a walk in the woods. Maps and suggested trail routes are available from the tourist office, or perhaps you would prefer to stick to the simple walk outlined here and spend more time in the restaurants and outdoor cafés. Either way, you're sure to enjoy a carefree visit to Clervaux.

GETTING THERE:

Trains depart the Luxembourg City Station several times in the morning for the lovely hour-long scenic ride to Clervaux. Return service operates until mid-evening.

By Car, head north from Luxembourg City on the N-7 road to Marnach, then take the N-18 west into Clervaux. The total distance is 62 km (39 miles).

PRACTICALITIES:

The castle at Clervaux is open daily in July-August, and from Tuesdays to Sundays the rest of the year, but closed in January and February. Some parts of it are open only on Sundays and holidays from mid-September to December and March to May. Good weather is essential for this trip.

The local **Tourist Office** *(Syndicat d'lnitiative),* **T**: 920-072 or **W**: tourisme-clervaux.lu, is in the castle complex.

FOOD AND DRINK:

Being a popular resort, Clervaux has a good number of restaurants and cafés, many of which are in small hotels. A few choices are:

Hôtel du Commerce (2 Rue de Marnach, a block southwest of the castle) Quality cuisine in comfortable surroundings. **T**: 929-181. X: Tues. lunch, Wed. lunch. €€ and €€€

Restaurant Splendid (9A Grand Rue, beneath the castle) Seafood and other dishes at reasonable prices. **T**: 921-044. €€

Hôtel-Restaurant Koener (14 Grand Rue, beneath the castle) Traditional cuisine with a bit of atmosphere. **T**: 921-002. X: Feb. €€

Vieux Château (4 Rue du Château, by the castle) A rustic tavern with a wide choice of dishes, served indoors or out. **T**: 920-012. €€

SUGGESTED TOUR:

Circled numbers correspond to numbers on the map.

Leave the **Train Station** *(Gare)* ① and follow the map past several small resort hotels to the **pedestrian zone** ②. This very pleasant area is filled with shops, restaurants, and outdoor cafés—a fine place to return to after seeing the castle. While here, you might want to visit the small **Toy Museum** *(Musée du Jouet),* where those wonderful toys from bygone times are on display. The collection includes model trains, doll and their houses, steam engines, ships, toy automobiles, magic lanterns, rocking horses, and much more. *9 Grand Rue.* **T**: *920-228. Open Easter–Dec., Wed.–Mon. 10-12 and 2–6; Jan.–Easter, Sun. and holidays, 10–12 and 2–5. €.*

Steps lead from the market square to the **Castle** *(Château)* ③. Parts of this date from the 12th century, while other sections were added during the 15th and 17th centuries. The presence near its entrance of an American army tank and an artillery piece remind you that the castle played a significant role during World War II and was severely damaged in December, 1944. Now restored, the castle houses three interesting exhibitions as well as the local tourist office. You might want to stop in here to ask about walks that can be taken in the surrounding forest.

The main attraction here is a renowned photographic exhibition that traveled to museums around the world during the 1950s. Assembled by the famous photographer Edward Steichen, a native of Luxembourg who made his career in America, the ***Family of Man** show consists of several hundred poignant photos on the human condition by photographers all over the globe. Although the black-and-white images may seem a bit dated today, their power to stir the emotions remains intact. **T**: *929-657. Open March–Dec., Tues.–Sun. 10–6., also on Mon. in high season. €.*

A separate entrance in the castle's courtyard brings you into the ***Battle of the Bulge Museum**. Correctly known as the Battle of the Ardennes Forest, this was the final major conflict of World War II in Europe, and raged around Clervaux and in neighboring parts of Belgium during December of 1944 and January of 1945. The museum displays weapons, uniforms, personal effects, and other reminders of the war from both the American, British, and German forces. **T**: *921-048-1. Open March–June and mid-Sept–Dec., Sun. and holidays 1–5; July–mid-Sept., daily 11–6. Closed Jan.–Feb. €.*

The third museum in the castle is an **Exhibition of Models of Luxembourg Castles** *(Musée des Maquettes),* several of which include the surrounding villages and immediate countryside. **T**: *929-686. Same times and admission as the Battle*

Outside the Castle of Clervaux

of the Bulge Museum, above.

From here, you may want to take one of the walks suggested by the tourist office or continue on to the Abbey and return to the station. To do this, just follow the map to the **Parish Church** ④, built in 1910 in the Rhenish Romanesque style to harmonize with the castle. Steps opposite this lead up to a woodland trail marked "Abbaye," also identified as path "C." Follow it around to the **Benedictine Abbey of St. Maurice** ⑤, a Neo-Romanesque structure high above the village. The present abbey was constructed in 1910 after the monks moved here from France. You can visit their exhibition of contemporary monastic life, which is located in the crypt. Open *daily 9–7.*

At the foot of the abbey is the **Monument to the Peasants' War** ⑥, honoring the local farmers who lost their lives fighting the French Revolutionary Army in the late 18th century. Trails lead directly from here to Rue de la Gare, returning you to the train station. This path, however, is a little bit rough and not too well marked, although certainly passable. Otherwise, you can return to town the way you came, and perhaps stop at one of the inviting outdoor cafés before walking back to the station.

Echternach

People who love walking in the woods will really enjoy this daytrip, which combines a marvelous medieval town on the German border with the most spectacular sylvan splendor in the Grand Duchy. Echternach is the center of a region known as the "Little Switzerland of Luxembourg," a name obviously coined by Dutch tourists who have never seen a real mountain. Although not very high, the hills around here are indeed rugged and permeated with fantastic rock formations. The deep, narrow ravine of the Gorge du Loup is perhaps the most famous of these and can be reached on foot from the town in considerably less than an hour.

Originally a Roman camp, Echternach developed around an abbey founded here in 698 by the Anglo-Saxon missionary St. Willibrord. Until the French Revolution it was ruled by the local abbots, but has since been secularized. Following wholesale destruction in World War II, it was rebuilt along the old lines and is today a favorite destination for visitors from Germany, which lies just across the town bridge.

GETTING THERE:

Buses depart from the front of the Luxembourg City Train Station (to the left as you leave it) about hourly for the hour-long ride to Echternach. These are operated by the railroad (CFL) and accept railpasses. Return buses run until early evening.

By Car, Echternach is 35 km (22 miles) northeast of Luxembourg City via the E-27 road. A detour through Berdorf will take you into the most spectacular scenery.

PRACTICALITIES:

Echternach may be visited at any time in good weather, preferably between May and October. Those intending to hike in the Gorge du Loup should wear suitable shoes.

The local **Tourist Office, T**: 720-230 or **W**: echternach-tourist.lu, is next to the entrance of the Basilica.

FOOD AND DRINK:

This popular resort has a wide selection of restaurants and cafés, among them being:

Du Commerce (16 Place du Marché) Good-value French and Luxembourg cuisine, indoors or out, near the Old Town Hall. **T**: 720-301. X: mid-Nov. to Feb. € and €€

Hostellerie de la Basilique (7 Place du Marché) Indoor or outdoor dining around the Old Town Hall. **T**: 729-483. € and €€

SUGGESTED TOUR:

Circled numbers correspond to numbers on the map.

Leave the **Bus Station** *(Gare Routière)* ① and follow the main shopping street, Rue de la Gare, to Place du Marché, the old marketplace and the center of the town's activities. On its north side stands the **Old Town Hall** *(Hôtel de Ville,* locally called *Denzelt)* ②, a fabulous arcaded structure from the early 15th century.

Continue on to the:

BASILICA OF ST. WILLIBRORD ③, **T**: 727-472 or **W**: willibrord.

lu/uk/abbey. *Open daily 8:30 a.m. to 7:30 p.m. Museum open April–Oct, daily 10–noon and* 2–5; 10–6 *in July–Aug. Museum admission €.*

The Basilica of St. Willibrord is a part of the former abbey founded in 698 by the Anglo-Saxon missionary who first brought Christianity to this part of Europe. The present basilica originally dates from the 11th century, but was altered in the 13th century, very badly damaged during World War II, and reconstructed in 1952. Still a place of pilgrimage, it is regarded as the most important religious structure in Luxembourg. Its 9th-century ***Crypt**, a part of a former church on the site, has survived more or less intact and still contains the sarcophagus of St. Willibrord, which you can see.

The adjoining abbey, also rebuilt after World War II destruction, is now a state school. It does, however, have a small **Abbey Museum** with some fine illuminated manuscripts and items pertaining to the monastic life along with related artifacts from ancient times. Be sure to stop into the **Tourist Information Office** just outside the basilica, where you can obtain maps for a **walk** in the nearby Gorge du Loup or other woodland trails.

Just across the street is the 18th-century **Orangerie** ④, a formal garden of great beauty, which can be seen through the ornate gate. Now continue around to the Municipal Park with its splendid **Pavilion** ⑤ in a pure Louis XV style. A lovely walk along the Sure River—which is the national boundary—leads to a bridge built on Roman foundations. The far side of this is in Germany.

Heading back towards the marketplace, you'll arrive at the **Museum of Prehistory** (Musée de Préhistoire) ⑥, which you might want to visit. **T**: 720-296 or **W**: prehistoire.lu/en/. Open *April–mid-Nov., Tues.–Sun. 10–noon and 2–5, open 10–5 during July–Aug. €.* Close to it stands the **Parish Church of St. Peter and St. Paul** ⑦, reputed to be the oldest Christian sanctuary in the country. First built in the 7th century on the remains of a Roman fortress, it has been reconstructed many

Echternach

200 Yards

N

Promenade B-1

Route de Diekirch

TO BERDORF

Rue Ermesinde

Rue Maximilien

1

Bus Station

TO LUXEMBOURG CITY E-27

Rue André Duchscher

Rue Neuve

Rue de la Gare

Rue de Luxembourg

Rue des Merciers

Place du Marché

2

Rue des Chemin de Fer

4

R. du Curé

3

Info.

7

6

SURE

GERMANY

Rue de la Montagne Hooyelek

Rue des Tanneurs

Rue du Pont

5

Rue de la Sure

8

The Old Town Hall

times since but still retains traces of the original structure.

The most popular woodland hike in this region is to the ***Gorge du Loup** *(Wolfschlucht)* ⑧, off the map. The trail to this leaves from near the bus station ①and is identified as *Promenade B-1.* You can reach its most rugged and spectacular part in about a half-hour or so, but remember to allow enough time to get back to the bus station before the last departure for Luxembourg City.

Section V
APPENDIX
MENU TRANSLATOR

Dutch/Flemish (D), French (F), and Luxembourg (L) terms into English:

Aardappel (D) potato
Aardappelpuree (D) mashed potatoes
Aardappelsoep (D) potato soup
Aardbei (D) strawberry
Abricot (F) apricot
Abrikoos (D) apricot
Agneau (F) lamb
Aiglefin (F) haddock
Ail (F) garlic
Aîoli (F) garlic mayonnaise
Alsacienne (F) in the style of Alsace, often with sauerkraut, sausages and ham
Amande (F) almond
Amandelbroodje (D) almond-filled roll
Ananas (F)(D) pineapple
Anchois (F) anchovies
Andijvie (D) endive, chicory
Andouillette (F) chitterling sausage
Aneth (F) dill
Anguille (F) eel
Anijs (D) aniseed
Anis (F) aniseed
Ansjovis (D) anchovy
Appel (D) apple
Appelmoes (D) apple sauce
Appeltaart (D) applepie
Arachides (F) peanuts
Artichaut (F) artichoke
Artisjok (D) artichoke
Asperges (F)(D) asparagus
Assiette (F) assorted mixture of cold hors d'œuvre
Aubergine (F)(D) eggplant
Augurk (D) gherkin, pickle
Avocat (F) avocado
Azijn (D) vinegar
Baars (D) perch
Babi pangang (D) roast suckling pig, Indonesian style
Baguette (F) long loaf of bread
Bami goreng (D) Indonesian dish of noodles, vegetables, pork and shrimp
Banaan (D) banana

Banane (F) banana
Bar (F) sea bass
Barbue (F) brill
Basilic (F) basil
Basilicum (D) basil
Baudroie (F) anglerfish
Béarnaise (F) sauce with egg yolks, tarragon, shallots, butter, and white wine
Béchamel (F) white sauce
Beenham (D) country ham
Beignet (F) fritter
Belegd broodje (D) mixed sandwiches
Bercy (F) sauce with white wine, shallots and herbs
Betterave (F) beet
Beurre (F) butter
Bief (D) beef
Biefstuk (D) beefsteak
Bieslook (D) chive
Bifteck, biftek (F) beefsteak
Bisque (F) shellfish soup, chowder
Bitterball (D) small meatball
Blanquette (F) fish stew with egg-and-cream sauce
Bloedworst (D) blood sausage
Bloemkool (D) cauliflower
Boerenkool met worst (D) mashed potatoes, kale and sausage
Boerenomelet (D) omelette with bacon and veggies
Boeuf (F) beef
Boeuf à la mode (F) beef braised in red wine, with vegetables
Boeuf Bourguignon (F) beef stew in red wine, with vegetables
Bombe (F) fancy ice cream dish
Bonensoep (D) bean soup
Boon (D) bean
Bordelaise (F) in the style of Bordeaux, with red wine, shallots, beef marrow, and mushrooms
Borststuk (D) breast, brisket
Bosbes (D) blueberry, bilberry
Boter (D) butter
Boudin (F) blood sausage
Boudin blanc (F) white sausage of veal, pork or chicken
Bouillabaisse (F) fish-and-seafood stew
Bouquet (F) shrimp
Bourguignonne (F) in the style of Burgundy, with red wine, onions and bacon
Bourride (F) fish-and-shellfish soup with aioli
Braadhaantje (D) spring chicken
Braadworst (D) fried sausage
Braam (D) blackberry
Brioche (F) soft, yeasty roll
Brochette (F) skewered meat or fish
Brood (D) bread
Broodje (D) roll
Bruine bonen met spek (D) kidney beans with bacon
Brussels lof (D) endive, chicory
Caille (F) quail
Canard (F) duck

Caneton (F) duckling
Capucijners met spek (D) beans with bacon
Carbonnade flamande (F) beef braised in beer
Carotte (F) carrot
Carpe (F) carp
Carré d'agneau (F) rack of lamb
Cassis (F) blackcurrant
Cassoulet (F) casserole of white beans with pork, goose, duck and sausage
Céleri (F) celery
Cèpes (F) wild flat mushrooms
Cerises (F) cherries
Cervelles (F) brains
Champignons (F)(D) mushrooms
Chantilly (F) sweet whipped cream
Chapon (F) capon
Charcuterie (F) cold cuts, pâtés, cured meats, and terrines
Chasseur (F) hunter style
Châteaubriand (F) thick fillet of beef
Chèvre (F) goat or goat cheese
Chicorée (F) curly endive
Chocolade (D) chocolate
Chou (F) cabbage
Chou de Bruxelles (F) brussels sprouts
Choucroute (F) sauerkraut
Choucroute garnie (F) sauerkraut with pork, sausage, or other meats
Choufleur (F) cauliflower
Ciboulettes (F) chives
Citroen (D) lemon
Citron (F) lemon
Citron vert (F) lime
Civet de lièvre (F) jugged hare
Clémentine (F) tangerine
Cochon (F) pig
Cochon de lait en gelée (F)(L) suckling pig in aspic
Concombre (F) cucumber
Confit (F) preserved
Confit de canard (F) duck preserved in its own fat
Confiture (F) preserves, jam
Consommé (F) clear broth
Contre-filet (F) sirloin steak
Coq (F) cock, hen or chicken
Coq au vin (F) stewed chicken in red wine with mushrooms, onions and bacon
Coquillage (F) shellfish
Coquille St.-Jacques (F) sea scallop
Cordon bleu (D) veal scallop with ham and cheese
Cornichon (F) small pickle
Côte (F) chop or rib
Côtelette (F) cutlet
Coupe de fruits (F) fruit cup
Courgette (F) zucchini
Crabe (F) crab
Crème (F) cream
Crème caramel (F) custard

Crêpes (F) thin pancakes
Cresson (F) watercress
Crevette (F) shrimp
Croissant (F) flaky crescent-shaped roll
Croque-monsieur (F) grilled ham-and-cheese sandwich
Croquetten (D) croquettes of meat, cheese or prawns
Croquettes aux crevettes (F) shrimp deep fried in cakes
Cru (F) raw
Crudités (F) raw vegetable salad
Crustacés (F) shellfish
Cuit (F) cooked
Dadel (D) date
Daube (F) meat stew in wine stock
Daurade (F) sea bream
Dijonnaise (F) in the style of Dijon, with mustard
Dille (D) dill
Dinde, dindon, dindonneau (F) turkey
Doperwt (D) green pea
Druif (D) grape
Duif (D) pigeon
Duitse biefstuk (D) chopped steak
Échalote (F) shallot
Écrevisses (F) crayfish
Edammer kaas (D) mild yellow cheese
Eend (D) duck
Ei (D) egg
Émincé (F) thin slice
Endive (F) endive
Entrecôte (F) rib steak
Épices (F) spices
Épinards (F) spinach
Erwt (D) pea
Erwtensoep (D) pea soup
Escalope (F) thin slice
Escargots (F) snails
Estragon (F) tarragon
Faisan (F) pheasant
Farci (F) stuffed
Farine (F) flour
Faux-filet (F) sirloin steak
Fazant (D) pheasant
Fenouil (F) fennel
Flageolets (F) small green kidney beans
Flan (F) custard tart
Foie (F) liver
Foie gras (F) goose liver
Fondue (F) melted cheese dish
Forel (D) trout
Forestière (F) with mushrooms
Four (F) oven
Frais, fraîche (F) fresh, chilled
Fraises (F) strawberries
Framboises (F) raspberries

Framboos (D) raspberries
Frappé (F) surrounded by crushed ice
Fricassée (F) stewed or sautéed, braised in wine with cream
Frikadel (D) meatball
Frit (F) fried
Frites (F)(D) french fries
Friture (F) small fried fish
Fromage (F) cheese
Fruits de mer (F) seafood
Fumé (F) smoked
Gado-Gado (D) Indonesian veggies, eggs, rice and peanut sauce
Galantine (F) cold meat, fish or vegetables in jelly
Galette (F) pancake with stuffing
Gambas (F) large prawns
Gans (D) goose
Garbure (F) thick soup
Garnaal (D) shrimp, prawn
Garni (F) garnished
Gâteau (F) cake
Gaufres (F) Belgian waffles
Gebak (D) cake or pastry
Gebonden soep (D) cream soup
Gebraden (D) roasted
Gehakt (D) minced or chopped
Gekookt (D) boiled
Gelée (F) aspic
Gember met slagroom (D) fresh ginger with whipped cream
Gepocheerd ei (D) poached egg
Gerookt (D) smoked
Gerookte paling (D) smoked eel
Gestoofd (D) braised
Gevuld (D) stuffed
Gibelotte (F) rabbit stewed in wine
Gibier (F) game
Gigot d'agneau (F) leg of lamb
Glace (F) ice cream
Glacée (F) iced or glazed
Goudakaas (D) mild cheese from Gouda
Graisse (F) fat
Gratin (F) crisp topping of cheese and bread crumbs
Grenouilles (F) frogs (legs)
Griet (D) brill
Grillade (F) grilled meat
Grillée (F) grilled
Groenten (D) vegetables
Groentensoep (D) vegetable soup
Gromperenkichelchen (L) potato cakes with apple sauce
Groseille (F) red currant
Haas (D) hare
Haché, hachis (F) minced, hashed
Hachee (D) minced meat hash
Hardgekookte eieren (D) hard-boiled eggs
Hareng (D) herring

Haricots (F) beans
Haricots verts (F) green beans
Haring (D) herring
Hazepeper (D) jugged hare
Heilbot (D) halibut
Heldere soep (D) clear soup, consommé
Hersenen (D) brains
Hollandse biefstuk (D) porterhouse or T-bone steak
Hollandse nieuwe (D) fresh herring
Homard (F) lobster
Honing (D) honey
Hoofdgerechten (D) main course
Huile (F) oil
Huîtres (F) oysters
Hutspot (D) mashed potatoes and carrots
Hutspot met klapstuk (D) boiled beef with potatoes, carrots and onions
Huzarensla (D) salad of cold cuts, potatoes, hard-boiled egg and pickles
Ijs (D) ice or ice cream
Jachtschotel (D) meat, onions and potatoes in a casserole
Jambon (F) ham
Jambon d'Ardennes (F)(L) smoked ham
Jardinière (F) garnished with fresh vegetables
Jonge kaas (D) fresh cheese
Jud mat gardebo'nen (L) smoked pork with broad beans
Julienne (F) fresh sliced vegetables
Jus (F) juice
Jus (D) gravy
Kaas (D) cheese
Kalfslapje (D) veal cutlet
Kalfsrollade (D) roast veal
Kalfsvlees (D) veal
Kalkoen (D) turkey
Kapucijners met spek (D) peas with bacon, onions, potatoes and salad
Karbonade (D) chop or cutlet
Karper (D) carp
Kastanje (D) chestnut
Kerrie (D) curry
Kersen (D) cherries
Kibbeling (D) deep-fried cod
Kip (D) chicken
Kippenborst (D) chicken breast
Kippebout (D) chicken leg
Kippensoep (D) chicken soup
Knakworst (D) small knockwurst, frankfurter
Knoflook (D) garlic
Komkommer (D) cucumber
Konijn (D) rabbit
Koninginnesoep (D) cream of chicken soup
Kool (D) cabbage
Koolschotel met gehakt (D) meatballs and cabbage casserole
Kotelet (D) cutlet or chop
Koudvlees (D) meat cold cuts
Krab (D) crab

Krabbetjes (D) spare ribs
Kroket, Kroketten (D) croquette(s)
Kwark (D) fresh white cheese
Lait (F) milk
Laitue (F) lettuce
Lamproie (F) lamprey eel
Lamsbout (D) leg of lamb
Lamsvlees (D) lamb
Lanfoest (D) spiny lobster
Langouste (F) spiny lobster
Langue (F) tongue
Lapereau (F) young rabbit
Lapin (F) rabbit
Lard (F) bacon
Légumes (F) vegetables
Lendestuk (D) sirloin
Lentilles (F) lentils
Lever (D) liver
Linze (D) lentil
Loup (F) sea bass
Macédoine (F) diced mixed fruit or vegetables
Magret de canard (F) duck steak or breast
Maïs (F) sweet corn
Makreel (D) mackerel
Mandarijntje (D) tangerine
Mandarine (F) tangerine
Maquereau (F) mackerel
Marrons (F) chestnuts
Matelote (F) freshwater fish stew
Meloen (D) melon
Menthe (F) mint
Miel (F) honey
Mirabelle (F) yellow plum
Mornay (F) cheese sauce
Morue (F) salt cod
Mossel (D) mussel
Mosterd (D) mustard
Moules (F) mussels
Moutarde (F) mustard
Mouton (F) mutton
Myrtille (F) blueberry
Nasi goreng (D) Indonesian dish of rice, meat, chicken, shrimp, onions, vegetables and fried egg
Navet (F) turnip
Nieuwe Haring (D) fresh herring
Nier (D) kidney
Noisette (F) hazelnut, or round piece of boneless meat
Noix (F) nuts, walnuts
Noot (D) nut
Nouilles (F) noodles
Oester (D) oyster
Oeufs, œufs (F) eggs
Oie (F) goose

Oignons (F) onions
Olie (D) oil
Olijf (D) olive
Oseille (F) sorrel
Oude kaas (D) ripe, strong cheese
Oursins (F) sea urchins
Paddestoel (D) mushroom
Paillard (F) slice of veal or chicken breast
Pain (F) bread
Paling (D) eel
Palombe (F) pigeon
Palourdes (F) clams
Pamplemousse (F) grapefruit
Panaché (F) mixture of foods
Pannekoek (D) pancake
Papillote (F) cooked in parchment or foil
Parfum (F) flavor
Parmentier (F) dish with potatoes
Pastèque (F) watermelon
Patates frites (D) french fries
Pâté (F) cold minced meat or fish spread
Pâtes (F) pasta
Pâtisserie (F) pastry
Pêche (F) peach
Peer (D) pear
Peper (D) pepper
Perche (F) perch
Perdix (F) partridge
Peren (D) pears
Persil (F) parsley
Perzik (D) peach
Petis-pois (F) little green peas
Pied de porc (F) pig's foot
Pigeonneau (F) squab
Pignons (F) pine nuts
Piments (F) pimentos
Pinda (D) peanut
Pintade (F) guinea fowl
Pipérade (F) omelette with peppers, onions, tomatoes and ham
Piquante (F) spicy
Pisang goring (D) fried banana
Pistache (F) pistachio
Pistou (F) purée of basil, garlic and olive oil
Plateau de fromages (F) cheese board
Poché (F) poached
Poffertje (D) dessert fritter
Poire (F) pear
Poireau (F) leek
Pois (F) peas
Poisson (F) fish
Poivre (F) pepper
Poivron (F) sweet bell pepper
Pomme (F) apple

Pommes de terre (F) potatoes
Pommes frites (F) french fries
Pompelmoes (D) grapefruit
Porc (F) pork
Porcelet (F) young suckling pig
Potage (F) soup
Pot-au-feu (F) boiled beef-and-vegetable stew
Potée (F) boiled pork and vegetables
Poularde (F) capon
Poulet (F) chicken
Poulpe (F) octopus
Praire (F) clam
Profiterole (F) cream puff filled with chocolate
Provençale (F) in the style of Provence, with garlic, tomatoes and olive oil
Pruimen (D) plums
Prune (F) plum
Pruneau (F) prune
Quenelles (F) dumplings of fish or poultry
Quenelles de foie de veau (F)(L) calf's liver dumplings
Quiche (F) open pie with egg and cream plus filling
Raclette (F) melted cheese dish
Radijs (D) radish
Radis (F) radish
Ragoût (F) stew
Raie (F) skate
Raisins (F) grapes
Ratatouille (F) vegetable casserole
Rémoulade (F) sauce of mayonnaise, capers, mustard, anchovies and herbs
Ribstuk (D) rib of beef
Rijst (D) rice
Rijsttafel (D) an Indonesian feast of meat, fowl, vegetables, rice, fruits, nuts and spices
Rillettes (F) potted meat
Ris de veau (F) veal sweet breads
Riz (F) rice
Rode biet (D) red beet
Rode kool (D) red cabbage
Roerei (D) scrambled eggs
Roggebrood (D) rye bread
Rognons (F) kidneys
Rognons de veau à la Liègeoise (F) roast veal kidneys
Rolmops (D) Bismark herring
Rolpens (D) chopped beef, apples and red cabbage
Rosbief (D) roast beef
Rosbif (F) roast beef
Rôti (F) roast
Roti Kip (D) Surinamese curried chicken with veggies and pancake
Rouget (F) red mullet
Roulade (F) meat or fish, rolled and stuffed
Rundvlees (D) beef
Safran (F) saffron
Salade composée (F) mixed salad
Salade Niçoise (F) salad with tuna, olives, tomatoes, potatoes and beans
Salade vert (F) green salad

APPENDIX   265

Salé (F) salted
Sateh (D) Indonesian barbequed meat on skewers, with peanut sauce
Saucijzebroodje (D) sausage roll
Saucisses (F) fresh sausages
Saucisson (F) dried sausage
Sauge (F) sage
Saumon (F) salmon
Saus (D) sauce
Sauté (F) browned in fat
Sauvage (F) wild
Scarole (F) escarole
Schaaldier (D) shellfish
Schnitzel (D) cutlet
Sel (F) salt
Selderij (D) celery
Shoarma (D) pita stuffed with sliced lamb, gyro
Sinaasappel (D) orange
Sjaslik (D) skewered meats with tomatoes, onions and bacon
Sla (D) lettuce
Slaboon (D) green bean
Slagroom (D) whipped cream
Soep (D) soup
Sorbet (F)(D) sherbet
Soupe (F) soup
Spek (D) bacon
Spiegelei (D) fried egg
Spinazie (D) spinach
Stammpot (D) mashed potatoes with vegetables and meat
Stampot (D) cabbage with sausage
Steak au poivre (F) steak with crushed peppercorns
Steak haché (F) chopped steak
Steak tartare (F) minced raw beef
Stokbrood (D) french bread
Sucre (F) sugar
Suiker (D) sugar
Suprême de volaille (F) filet of chicken breast in cream sauce
Tarte (F) pie
Terrine (F) cold baked minced meat or fish
Tête de veau (F) calf's head
Thon (F) tuna
Thym (F) thyme
Tjap tjoy (D) chop suey
Tomaat (D) tomato
Tomate (F) tomato
Tomatensoep (D) tomato soup
Toost (D) toast
Tosti (D) grilled ham and cheese sandwich
Tournedos (F)(D) center cut beef fillet
Tranche (F) slice
Treipen (L) black pudding and sausage with potatoes
Truffes (F) truffles
Truite (F) trout
Ui (D) onion

Uiensoep (D) onion soup
Uitsmijter (D) ham or roast beef sandwich with fried eggs
Vapeur (F) steamed
Varkenvlees (D) pork
Veau (F) veal
Venaison (F) venison
Vers (D) fresh
Viande (D) meat
Vichyssoise (F) cold potato-and-leek soup
Vinaigre (F) vinegar
Vinaigrette (F) oil-and-vinegar dressing
Vis (D) fish
Vlaamse frites (D) Flemish-style french fries
Vlaamse karbonade (D) braised beef and onions
Vlees (D) meat
Volaille (F) poultry
Vol-au-vent (F) puff pastry case with stuffing
Voorgerechten (D) appetizers
Vrucht (D) fruit
Vruchtensalade (D) fruit salad
Waterzooi (D) stew of chicken or fish, and vegetables
Wild (D) game
Witlof (D) endive, chicory
Witlof op zijn Brussels (D) chicory rolled in sliced ham, with cheese sauce
Worst (D) sausage
Wortel (D) carrot
Yaourt (F) yogurt
Zachtgekoot ei (D) soft-boiled egg
Zalm (D) salmon
Zeekreeft (D) lobster
Zeevis (D) ocean fish
Zout (D) salt
Zuurkool (D) sauerkraut
Zwezerik (D) sweetbread

A GLOSSARY OF DINING TERMS

English into Dutch/Flemish (D) and French (F) terms:

Meal (D) maaltijd, (F) repas
Breakfast (D) ontbijt, (F) petit déjeuner
Lunch (D) middageten, (F) déjeuner
Dinner (D) warme maaltijd, (F) diner

Headwaiter (D)(F) maître d'hôtel
Waiter (D) ober, (F) monsieur
Waitress (D) serveerster, (F) mademoiselle, madame
The menu, please (D) de spijskaart, alstublieft, (F) la carte, s'il vous plait
Set meal menu (D)(F) menu à prix-fixe
Ordering items individually (D)(F) à la carte

Today's special (D) dagschotel, (F) plat du jour
Sampling of dishes or wines (F) dégustation
The wine list (D) de wijnkaart, (F) la carte des vins
Another serving of ..., please (F) encore un ..., s'il vous plait
The check, please (D) de rekening, alstublieft, (F) l'addition, s'il vous plait

Drink included in price (D) drank inclusief, (F) boisson comprise
Cover charge (F) couvert
Tip included (D) bediening inbegrepen, (F) service compris, s.c., prix net
Tip not included (D) bedizening exclusief, (F) service non compris, s.n.c.
Gratuity (D) fooi, (F) pourboire

Plate (D) schotel, (F) assiette
Knife (D) mes, (F) couteau
Fork (D) vork, (F) fourchette
Spoon (D) lepel, (F) cuillère
Glass (D) glas, (F) verre
Cup (D) kopje, (F) tasse
Napkin (D) servet, (F) serviette

Drink (D) drank, (F) boisson
Pre-dinner drink (D)(F) aperitif
After-dinner drink (F) digestif
White wine (D) wittewijn, (F) vin blanc
Red wine (D) rodewijn, (F) vin rouge
Rosé wine (D) roséwijn, (F) vin rosé
Half-bottle (D) half-fles, (F) demi-bouteille
Beer (D) bier, (F) bière
Draft beer (D) bier van het vat, (F) bière à la pression
Mineral water (D) mineraalwater, (F) eau minérale
Carbonated (F) gazeuse
Still (F) non-gazeuse
Tap water (D) kraanwater, (F) eau fraîche, une carafe d'eau

Hot (D) warm, (F) chaud
Cold (D) koud, (F) froid
Very rare (D) rauw, (F) bleu
Rare (D) ongaar, (F) saignant
Medium (D) net gaar, (F) à point
Well done (D) gaar, (F) bien cuit
Sweet (D) zoet, (F) doux
Dry (D) droog, (F) sec

Bread (D) brood, (F) pain
Butter (D) boter, (F) beurre
Salt (D) zout, (F) sel
Pepper (D) peper, (F) poivre
Mustard (D) mosterd, (F) moutarde
Oil (D) olie, (F) huile
Vinegar (D) azijn, (F) vinaigre

Coffee (D) koffie, (F) café
Small black coffee (D) espresso, (F) café express

Coffee with cream (D) koffie met room, (F) café crème
Breakfast coffee with milk (D) koffie verkeerd, (F) café au lait
Tea (D) thee, (F) thé
Lemon (D) citroen, (F) citron
Chocolate (D) chocolade, (F) chocolat
Milk (D) melk, (F) lait
Sugar (D) suiker, (F) sucre
Orange or tomato juice (D) sinaasappelsap / tomatensap, (F) jus d'orange / de tomate

A DUTCH / FLEMISH
RAIL TRAVELER'S GLOSSARY

For use in Holland and northern Belgium

Aankomst arrival
Aansluiting connection
Alleen Werkdagen weekdays only
Alleen Zon en Feestdagen Sundays and holidays only
Bagagedepot left-luggage office
Bagagekluizen baggage locker
Bespreking reservation
Binnenland inland
Boot boat, ferry
Buitenland foreign
Conducteur conductor, ticket collector
Dagretour one-day return excursion
Dagtocht daytrip
Damen women
Dienst service
Dienst voor Toerisme local tourist information office (Belgium)
Doorgaande Trein through train to destination
Douane customs
Eerste Hulp first aid
Eerste Klas first class
Enkele to go one way
Feestdagen public holidays
Fietsen te Huur bicycle rental (in station)
Geen no, forbidden
Geen Doorgang no entrance
Geldig valid
Gesloten closed
Gevaarlijk danger
Gevonden Voorwerpen lost-and-found
Heren men
Hoofdlijn main line
Ingang entrance
Inlichtingen information
Instappen get on (the train)
Kaartje ticket
Kruier porter

Ligplaats couchette, inexpensive sleeping car with bunks
Luchthaven airport
Metro subway, underground
Naar to
Niet not
Niet Instappen don't board this train
Niet Roken no smoking
NMBS Belgian National Railways, also called SNCB
NS Netherlands Railways
Overstappen change of train
Overstapverbinding change to connecting train
Perron platform
Prijzen price
Reis journey
Reisbureau travel agency
Reizen to travel
Reiziger traveler
Retour return (round-trip ticket)
Roker smoking car
Slaapwagen sleeping car
Spoor track
Spoorbaan railroad
Spoorboekje timetable book
Spoorkaartjes train tickets
Spoorweg railroad
Stilte! Werkcoupe do not disturb, quiet compartment
Stoomtrein steam train
Strippenkaarten multiple ride public transportation ticket
Terugbetaling refund
Toegang entrance
Toeslag supplementary fare, surcharge
Trein train
Tweede Klas second class
Uitgang exit
Van from
Verboden forbidden
Verboden te Roken no smoking
Verloren Voorwerpen lost-and-found
Vertraging delay
Vertrek departure
VVV local tourist information office (Holland)
Wachtkamer, Wachtzaal waiting room
Werkdag workday
Wisselkantoor money exchange
Zitplaats seat
Zon en Feestdagen Sundays and holidays

A DUTCH / FLEMISH DRIVER'S GLOSSARY

For use in Holland and northern Belgium

Afdaling steep hill
Afgesloten Rijweg no through road
Allen voor Voetgangers pedestrians only
Alle Richtingen all directions
ANWB Royal Dutch Touring Club
Autoweg motorway
Band tire
Benzine gasoline (petrol)
Benzinestation gas (petrol) station
Bromfietsen mopeds
Bushalte bus stop
Centrum to the center of town
Doorgand Verkeer through traffic
Douane customs
Eenrichtingsverkeer one-way traffic
Eigen Weg private road
Fietsen bicycle
Fietsers Oversteken cycle crossing
Fietspad bicycle path
Filevorming get into lane
Geen no
Geopend open
Gesloten closed
Gestremd forbidden
Gevaar danger
Gevaarlijke Bocht! Dangerous curves ahead
Gladde Weg slippery road
Halte tram stop
Ingang entrance
Inhaalverbod no passing
Langzaam Rijden drive slowly
Let Op! attention!
Links left
Lucht air
Naar Links to the left
Naar Rechts to the right
Niet Brommen! No mopeds!
Olie oil
Omleiding detour
Onbewaakte Overweg unattended railway crossing
Parkeerplaats parking place
Parkeren Verboden no parking
Pas Op! attention!
Politie police
Rechts right
Rechts Houden keep to the right

Rem brakes
Rijbewijs driver's license
Rijksweg national road
Rijwielpad bicycle path
Slecht Wegdek rough surface
Slop-Doodlooende Weg dead-end road (cul-de-sac)
Smalle Brug narrow bridge
Snelheid Verminderen reduce speed
Spoorweg Kruising railway crossing
Steenslag gravel road
Stoplichten traffic lights
Straat met Eerichtingsverkeer one-way street
Tegenliggers two-way traffic
Toegang access to
Tol toll
Tweesprong fork in road
Tussen between
Uitgang exit
Uitrit Vrachtwagens truck exit
Verboden Toegang no entry
Verkeerslichten traffic lights
Voetgangers pedestrians only
Voetpad footpath
Weg Omlegging detour
Werk in Uitveoring road construction work
Zachte Berm soft shoulders

A FRENCH RAIL TRAVELER'S GLOSSARY

For use in French-speaking Belgium and Luxembourg

Abonnement season ticket or pass
Aller to go one way
Aller et Retour round trip
À Partir from (date) on
Arrêt stop, halt
Arrivée arrival
Autobus, Autocar bus (coach)
Autorail railcar
Avec Supplément with surcharge
Banlieue suburban (commuter trains)
Billet ticket
Billet Simple ordinary one-way ticket
Bureau de Change currency exchange
Cadencé regularly repeating interval, such as hourly
CFL Luxembourg National Railways
Changement change (of trains)
Chariot luggage cart (trolley)
Composition des Trains train makeup
Composteur ticket validating machine
Compostez votre Billet validate your ticket

Consigne checkroom, left luggage
Consigne Automatique luggage locker
Contrôleur ticket collector
Correspondence connection
Couchette inexpensive sleeping car with bunks
Couloir aisle (seat)
Dames women
Défense de Fumer no smoking
Demi-Tarif half fare
Départ departure
Deuxième Classe second class
Douane customs
Emporter to take out, as in items from a snack bar
Enregistrement to send baggage ahead
Entrée entrance
Entrée Interdite do not enter
Étranger foreign, foreigner, stranger
Facultatif optional, on request (train or bus stop)
Fenêtre window (seat)
Fêtes holidays
Fumeurs smoking
Gare station
Gare Routière bus station
Grandes Lignes main lines
Grève strike of workers
Guichet ticket window
Hommes men
Horaire timetable
Jusqu'au until (date)
Libre free, available
Libre Service self service
Ligne line
Location de Voitures car rental (hire)
Métro subway, underground
Messieurs men
Monter to board (the train)
Objets Trouvés lost-and-found
Occupé occupied
Place seat
Plein Tarif full fare
Post-PTT post office, telephone service
Pré-Métro underground trams/streetcars
Première Classe first class
Prochain next (departure)
Quai platform
Quotidien daily
Remboursement refund
Renseignements information
Réseau network, system
Réservation reservation
Retardé delay
Salle d'Attente waiting room
Sauf except

Sortie exit
Sortie de Secours emergency exit
SNCB Belgian National Railways
Tarif fare
Tous les Jours every day
Vers to
Voie track
Voiture car (of train or otherwise)
Voiture Directe through car to indicated destination
Voyage trip, travel
Voyager to travel
Voyageur traveler, passenger
Wagon railroad car
Wagon-Lit sleeping car
Wagon-Restaurant dining car

A FRENCH DRIVER'S GLOSSARY

For use in French-speaking Belgium and Luxembourg

Accotement non Stabilisé soft shoulder
Allumez vos Phares turn on headlights
Arrêt Interdit no stopping
Attention caution
Au Pas slow
Autoroute high-speed limited-access highway
Autres Directions other directions
Carte Grise car registration papers
Carte Routière road map
Céder le Passage yield
Centre Ville to the center of town
Chaussée Déformée bad road surface
Chantier road construction
Chute de Pierres falling rocks
Circulation Interdite no throughfare
Descente Dangereuse steep hill
Déviation detour (diversion)
Douane customs
Eau water
École school
Entrée Interdite no entrance
Essence gasoline (petrol)
Fin d'Interdiction end of restriction
Fin de Limitation de Vitesse end of speed restriction
Gravillons gravel road surface
Halte stop
Hauteur Limitée low clearance
Huile oil
Impasse dead-end road (cul-de-sac)
Interdiction de Doubler no passing
Interdiction de Stationner no parking

Limitation de Vitesse speed restriction
Location de Voitures car rental (hire)
Nids de Poule pot holes
Passage à Niveau grade crossing
Passage Interdit entry forbidden, no thoroughfare
Passage Protégé right-of-way at intersection ahead
Pente Dangereuse steep incline
Permis de Conduire driver's license
Piétons pedestrians
Piste Reservée aux Transports Publics lane reserved for public transport
Pneus tires
Poids Lourds truck (lorry) route
Priorité à Droite vehicles coming from the right have the right-of-way
Priorité à Gauche vehicles coming from the left have the right-of-way
Ralentir reduce speed
Rappel previous sign still applies
Réservé aux Piétons pedestrians only
Réservée aux Transports Publics (lane) reserved for public transport
Route Barrée road closed
Route Étroite narrow road
Route Glissante slippery road
Sauf (Seulement) Riverains (private road) for residents only
Sens Interdit wrong direction
Sens Unique one-way street
Serrez à Droite keep to the right
Serrez à Gauche keep to the left
Sortie exit
Sortie de Camions truck crossing
Stationnement Autorisé parking allowed
Stationnement Interdit no parking
Tenez vos Distances keep your distance
Toutes Directions all directions
Travaux road work
Verglas slippery road
Virages curves ahead
Voie de Dégagement private entrance
Voie Unique single-lane traffic
Voiture car, vehicle
Voiture à Louer rental car
Zone Bleue time-indicator disc required for parking
Zone Rouge tow-away zone

OTHER VOCABULARY
DAYS OF THE WEEK
In DUTCH / FLEMISH

Maandag Monday
Dinsdag Tuesday
Woensdag Wednesday
Donderdag Thursday
Vrijdag Friday

Zaterdag Saturday
Zondag Sunday
Vandaag today
Morgen tomorrow

SEASONS in DUTCH / FLEMISH

Seizoen season
Voorjaar Spring
Zomer Summer
Herfst Autumn
Winter Winter

DAYS OF THE WEEK
In FRENCH

Lundi Monday
Mardi Tuesday
Mercredi Wednesday
Jeudi Thursday
Vendredi Friday
Samedi Saturday
Dimanche Sunday
Aujourd'hui today
Demain tomorrow

SEASONS in FRENCH

Saison season
Printemps Spring
Été Summer
Automne Autumn
Hiver Winter

QUICK CONVERSIONS

1 mile = 1.6 km
1 km = 0.6 miles
1 U.S. gallon = 3.78 litres
1 litre = 0.26 U.S. gallons

Index

Special interest attractions are also listed under their category headings. Countries are identified as: (H) Holland, (B) Belgium, and (L) Luxembourg.

INDEX 281

IJsselmeer, The (H) 39, 51, 54, 58

Keukenhof Gardens (H) 50
Kinderdijk (H) 104
Kortrijk (B) 188–192

LANGUAGE:
        Belgium 155
        Holland 19
        Luxembourg 235
Leeuwarden (H) 128–131
Leiden (H) 74–78
Leuven (B) 205–208
Liège (B) 213–217
Ljouwert — see Leeuwarden
Louvain — see Leuven
Luik — see Liège
Luxembourg 231–256
Luxembourg City (L) 231, 238–244
Luxembourg National Railways 232–234
Luxembourg National Tourist Office 237

Maastricht (H) 141–147
Madurodam, Scheveningen (H) 89
Malines — see Mechelen
MARITIME INTEREST:
        Marine Biological Museum, Scheveningen (H) 88
        Maritime & Beachcombers Museum, Texel (H) 73
        Maritime Museum Prins Hendrik, Rotterdam (H) 97
        Mercator sailing ship, Oostende (B) 187
        National Maritime Museum, Antwerp (B) 202
        Netherlands Maritime Museum, Amsterdam (H) 37
Marken (H) 39, 42–43
MARKETS:
        Alkmaar (H) 66
        Amsterdam (H) 35
        Antwerp (B) 199
        Delft (H) 93
        Edam (H) 44
        Ghent (B) 171
        Gouda (H) 117–119
        Haarlem (H) 46
        Leiden (H) 76
        Luxembourg City (L) 242
        Maastricht (H) 142–143
        Mechelen (B) 194
Mechelen (B) 193–196
Medemblik (H) 51, 54
Middelburg (H) 105–109
MONEY:
        Belgium 155–156
        Holland 19

INDEX 284

ABOUT THE AUTHOR:

EARL STEINBICKER is a born tourist who believes that travel should be a joy, not an endurance test. For over 35 years he has been refining his carefree style of daytripping while working in New York, London, Paris, and other cities; first as head of a firm specializing in promotional photography and later as a professional writer. Whether by public transportation or private car, he has thoroughly probed the most delightful aspects of countries around the world — while always returning to the comforts of city life at night. A strong desire to share these experiences has led him to develop the "Daytrips" series of guides, which he continues to expand and revise. Recently, he has been assisting other authors in developing additional "Daytrips" books, further expanding the series. He presently lives in the Philadelphia suburbs.

SIXTH EDITION

Daytrips
FRANCE

48 *one day adventures by rail, bus or car*
includes Paris walking tours

EARL STEINBICKER

• OTHER EUROPEAN TITLES •

LONDON
By Earl Steinbicker. This long-time favorite guide explores the metropolis on 10 one-day walking tours, then describes 45 daytrips to destinations throughout southern England — all by either rail or car. 7th edition, 352 pages, 61 maps, 32 B&W photos, glossaries and a menu translator. ISBN: 0-8038-2056-9.

SCOTLAND & WALES
By Judith Frances Duddle. From Neo-Classical cities and historic towns to the beautiful, untouched countryside and tranquil villages, both Scotland and Wales offer something for everyone. The book includes 37 one-day adventures throughout both lands. 206 pages, 43 maps, 24 B&W photos, appendix, index. ISBN: 0-8038-2055-0.

EXTRAORDINARY PLACES ... CLOSE TO LONDON
By Elizabeth Wallace. 30 Exceptional destinations in Southeast England, offering a personal and unique view into the life and history of the counties around London. Recommended sights, hotels, inns, and pubs. 250 pages, map, 14 B&W photos, index. ISBN: 0-8038-2031.3.

IRELAND
By Patricia Tunison Preston. Covers the entire Emerald Isle with 55 one-day self-guided tours both within and from the major tourist areas, plus sections on shopping. Expanded 2nd edition, 400 pages, 57 maps. ISBN: 0-8038-2003-8.

FRANCE
By Earl Steinbicker. Describes 48 daytrips—including 5 walking tours of Paris, 24 excursions from the city, 5 in Provence, and 14 along the Riviera. 6th edition, 332 pages, 60 maps, photos, glossaries and a menu translator. ISBN: 0-8038-2061-5.

ITALY
By Earl Steinbicker. Features 40 one-day adventures in and around Rome, Florence, Milan, Venice, and Naples. 5th edition, 314 pages, 45 maps, 40 B&W photos, glossaries and a menu translator. ISBN: 0-8038-2058-5.

GERMANY
By Earl Steinbicker. 60 of Germany's most enticing destinations can be savored on daytrips from Munich, Frankfurt, Hamburg, and Berlin. Walking tours of the big cities are

included. 6th edition, 352 pages, 68 maps, 36 B&W photos, glossaries and a menu translator. ISBN: 0-8038-2033-X.

SPAIN & PORTUGAL

By Norman P.T. Renouf. 50 one-day adventures by rail, bus, or car — including many walking tours, as well as side trips to Gibraltar and Morocco. All the major tourist sights are covered, plus several excursions to little-known, off-the-beaten-track destinations. Revised 2nd edition, 382 pages, 51 maps. ISBN: 0-8038-2012-7.

SWITZERLAND

By Norman P.T. Renouf. 45 one-day adventures in and from convenient bases including Zurich and Geneva, with forays into nearby Germany, Austria and Italy. 320 pages, 38 maps. ISBN: 0-8038-9417-7.

• AMERICAN TITLES •

NEW YORK

By Earl Steinbicker. Completely rewritten and sporting many new maps for its eighth edition, Daytrips New York now features 10 walking tours of the Big Apple itself. Beyond that, the book describes some 40 one-day adventures in nearby New York State, Connecticut, New Jersey, and Pennsylvania. 338 pages, 68 maps, and 27 B&W photos. ISBN: 0-8038-2021-6.

WASHINGTON, D.C.

By Earl Steinbicker. 50 one-day adventures in the Nation's Capital, and to nearby Virginia, Maryland, Delaware, and Pennsylvania. Both walking and driving tours are featured. 368 pages, 60 maps. Revised 2nd edition. ISBN: 0-8038-9429-5.

PENNSYLVANIA DUTCH COUNTRY & PHILADELPHIA

By Earl Steinbicker. Completely covers the City of Brotherly Love, then goes on to probe southeastern Pennsylvania, southern New Jersey, and Delaware before moving west to Lancaster, the "Dutch" country, and Gettysburg. There are 50 daytrips in all. 288 pages, 54 maps. ISBN: 0-8038-9394-9.

SAN FRANCISCO & NORTHERN CALIFORNIA

By David Cheever. 50 enjoyable one-day adventures from the sea to the mountains; from north of the wine country to south of Monterey. Includes 16 self-guided discovery tours of San Francisco itself. 336 pages, 64 maps. ISBN: 0-8038-9441-4.

NEW ENGLAND

By Earl Steinbicker. Discover the 50 most delightful excursions within a day's drive of Boston or Central New England, from Maine to Connecticut. Includes Boston walking tours. Revised 2nd edition, 320 pages, 60 maps. ISBN: 0-8038-2008-9.

• PACIFIC TITLES •

HAWAII

By David Cheever. Thoroughly explores all the major islands — by car, by bus, on foot, and by bicycle, boat, and air. Includes many offbeat discoveries you won't find elsewhere, plus all the big attractions in detail. 2nd edition, 288 pages, 55 maps. ISBN: 0-8038-2019-4.

EASTERN AUSTRALIA

By James Postell. Discover the 60 most exciting excursions from Sydney, Melbourne, Brisbane, Rockhampton, the Outback, and Cairns. Enjoy encounters with Australia that tourists usually miss. 400 pages, 48 maps, 24 B&W photos, appendix, glossary, index. ISBN: 0-8038-2501-8.

HASTINGS HOUSE/DAYTRIPS
Book Publishers

P.O. Box 908, Winter Park, FL 32790-0908
Phone orders toll-free 1-800-206-7822
Internet: www.daytripsbooks.com
E-mail: Hastings_Daytrips@earthlink.net

Made in the USA
Lexington, KY
27 February 2012